The Upper Half of the Motorcycle

On the Unity of Rider and Machine

The Upper Half of the Motorcycle

On the Unity of Rider and Machine

Bernt Spiegel

English translation by Meredith Hassall

Whitehorse Press
Center Conway, New Hampshire

Whitehorse Press books are also available at discounts in bulk quantity for sales and promotional use. For details about special sales or for a catalog of motorcycling books, videos, and gear write to the publisher:

Whitehorse Press
107 East Conway Road
Center Conway, New Hampshire 03813
Phone: 603-356-6556 or 800-531-1133
E-mail: CustomerService@WhitehorsePress.com
Internet: www.WhitehorsePress.com

ISBN-10 1-884313-75-2
ISBN-13 978-1-884313-75-2

5   4   3   2   1

Printed in China

For Helmut W. Bönsch
1907–1996
With honor, friendship, and gratitude.

Contents

Foreword

by Ken Condon

Motorcycling has been a part of my life for more than 30 years. I was first introduced to motorcycles as a child in the 1960s, was licensed in the 1970s, started road racing in the 1980s, became a motorcycle safety instructor in the 1990s, and was first published as an author of motorcycle skills articles and books in the 2000s.

Like most riders of my generation, I learned to ride with a few helpful tips from friends, followed by simple trial and error. I relied on my innate sense of balance and traction, derived from the simple acts of walking, running, and bicycle riding, to make my first forays into motorized two-wheeled travel. The concept of taking a riding course or reading a book on motorcycle skills was foreign, because safety courses did not exist (at least not in any meaningful form) and the only motorcycle-skills publications one was likely to find were thin pamphlets explaining the absolute basics.

As we all eventually come to realize, motorcycling involves a lot more than just balance, turning, and stopping; it also demands a sophisticated understanding of how a motorcycle fits into the situation that surrounds it. It requires the wisdom to anticipate the actions of other motorists, the consciousness to predict possible hazards in order to avoid them, and the self-awareness to monitor and control our circumstances moment-by-moment.

Motorcycle training has come a long way since I first began to ride. In addition to (or instead of) advice from friends, we now have rider training courses for riders at all levels: MSF *RiderCourses,* Lee Parks' *Total Control Clinics,* and the *Stayin' Safe* training courses, to name a few. We also have comprehensive books to help us learn to ride more skillfully; prominent examples are the MSF's *Motorcycling Excellence,* David Hough's *Proficient Motorcycling,* and my own recently published work, *Riding in the Zone.* Rather than relying simply on seat time to refine our skills, we now have track venues such as Keith Code's *California Superbike School,* Reg Pridmore's *CLASS* school, and *Tony's Track Days,* to let us practice in a secure setting with watchful guidance from expert rid-

ers and teachers. And we even have high quality videos to teach and demonstrate various riding skills.

We are fortunate to have a wide variety of books, videos, courses, and track schools to choose from. Most focus on riding techniques and strategies for surviving on the street, while a few focus on track and high performance riding skills—more than is useful for the average rider. Some attempt to enlighten technically minded motorcyclists about how motorcycles work. Most rely on anecdotal evidence to support best practices.

Bernt Spiegel comes to the subject of motorcycle riding from his unique perspective as a behavioral psychologist, having built his career in product design and advertising, working to optimize product and ad campaigns based upon how those activities relate to workings of the human mind.

The Upper Half of the Motorcycle: On the Unity of Rider and Machine starts right at the heart of the subject by first exploring how the brain works: how it was shaped by evolution, how many of our physical actions are controlled by "built-in programs," how we perceive our world (our "mesocosm"), how we use foresight, and how we learn. The second section describes the interaction between our built-in programs and our conscious actions, and explores man's use of tools to extend his capabilities. (A motorcycle is one such "tool.") The third section deals with "integration" of man and tool—in particular, riders and motorcycles, and how useful it is when horse and rider, or man and motorcycle, begin to perform as an integrated unit, rather than a means of conveyance and a bundle of cargo. The fourth section focuses on developing the techniques for self-training for higher performance, and the fifth section offers many suggestions for practical training.

In contrast to other rider training books, videos, and courses, this book elevates our understanding of the complex relationships between rider and motorcycle to a new level. It helps us appreciate not just *what* we do when riding, but *why* we do it. By understanding the interactions between our conscious actions and our built-in programs (some inherited and some acquired as we learn new physical skill), we are able to see in a new light why in some situations we can (and must) trust our automatic responses and not allow our conscious thoughts to interfere.

It would be enough if *The Upper Half of the Motorcycle* explored only the physiology and psychology of motorcycling, but Spiegel also shines his verbal light onto motorcycling dynamics and physics in a way that laypeople can easily comprehend.

If all of this sounds like heavy, tedious reading, fear not; it is anything but. He illustrates every point with interesting, often humorous, examples, and applies lessons from many forms of human activity—music, personal sports, motorsports—to keep the discussions lively.

After reading this book, you will begin to see motorcycling from a fresh new perspective. For the first time, a book digs beneath the surface of this wonderful world of motorcycling, and shows us relationships with our beloved machines we didn't even know existed. Bernt Spiegel has given us the foundation of understanding that will enable us to take rider training to a new, higher level. For those of us who seek mastery of this wonderful sport, we have received an important gift.

Ken Condon is the author of the *Proficient Motorcycling* and *Street Strategies* columns for *Motorcycle Consumer News* and author of *Riding in the Zone: Advanced Techniques for Skillful Motorcycling*. He is also a veteran MSF instructor and is the chief instructor for Tony's Track Days.

Preface

This book is not about motorcycles per se. Rather, it is about motorcycle riding and the motorcycle rider as a thinking, acting, reacting human being with the unique ability to create, use, and adapt tools, instruments, equipment, and machines in an integrative way as extensions, or components, of himself. In other words, motorcycle riding—that is, the proper way for the rider to interact and become *integrated* with the motorcycle—is the central theme of the book.

As a particularly highly developed machine, the motorcycle is an object of wonder because its use, even by virtuoso riders, comes close to the limits of human capabilities (physical, mental, and instinctive). There is no one who, under extreme pressure, would be able to ride a motorcycle completely error-free for more than an hour or two. Therein lies a key to the fascination of motorcycling for its enthusiasts.

This book reveals and examines not only the challenges that motorcycle riders face in riding well or superbly, but also *why* this is so challenging. To distill anything to its essential elements, one must start at the beginning. In the case of motorcycling, this happens to be human evolution, specifically *what* has made man unique in his capacity for using and adapting tools, instruments, equipment, and machines, which is where Part 1 begins.

Discussing human evolution in a book on motorcycling may seem very odd indeed. In addition, there are many concepts and theories discussed in the first part of the book that the average reader may also find unusual as inclusions in a book about motorcycling, but they are important in understanding the essence of motorcycling in all its complexities and as the enthralling activity it is for riders. Furthermore, the book not only discusses historical figures who may be obscure to some readers—figures such as Heinrich von Kleist and Thomas Mann, Herbert von Karajan and Arthur Rubinstein, Charlie Chaplin and Karl V—but also schools of fish and flocks of birds; chimpanzees and bears; eagles and spiders; all kinds of sports and musical instruments (the cello, the piano, the oboe); the knife and fork; marionettes; language and language arts activities; and a variety of unusual tools and implements. I trust that these topics will intrigue, not intimidate, readers as well as inform them.

In summary, this book methodically examines the most basic elements that constitute the activity of motorcycling in order to deepen riders' understanding of its complexities and the requirements for achieving riding proficiency, or even superb riding skills, and reaching specific riding goals. Ultimately, it is hoped that this book fans the flames of riders' enjoyment of, and fascination with, motorcycling.

Bernt Spiegel

Acknowledgments

A book such as this, with its interdisciplinary approach, could not have been produced by a single person. Three men from Porsche's development center at Weißach, were remarkable sources of expert, sometimes arcane, knowledge about motorcycles. For advice on technical matters, I am indebted to Helmuth Bott, who died far too early. In his days as manager of development at Porsche, and especially in the far too brief period afterward, Helmuth was a great friend of the motorcycle and motorcycling. I am also grateful to Wolfheim Gorrisen, whose mind is full of lucid "functions" and "curves" and who, depending on the question at hand, could always engage his fine mental "gears" to provide an answer, as well as to Wolfgang Schnepf, who always had an answer for even the most obscure question, even if it was an uphill struggle to arrive at the answer.

Time and again, Arnold Wagner, head of Peraves in Winterthur and the father of the Ecomobile, was an especially important participant in discussions, as was his eternal adversary, Alois Weidele, head of development at Daimler-Benz. When Weidele was still working at the Institute for Vehicle Technology in Darmstadt, he not only clarified a few things about automotive engineering but, much more important, he gave me insight into the entirely different yet fascinating way an engineer thinks.

My sincere thanks goes to Dr. Präckel, an engineering PhD from the Institute for Vehicle Technology, who spent considerable time and effort reviewing the entire manuscript for factual errors and unsupported conceptual formulations. There was a constant struggle between us regarding the precise expressions that he, as an engineer, advised and those I thought crucial so that the information in the book was accessible and understandable to the non-engineer. Our struggle never ceased but always remained interesting, and I appreciate his willingness to continue contributing to the project. Similarly, it is important to note that in spite of my other technical advisors' competence, for the sake of readability I sometimes followed their recommendations only partially or came up with compromises. Therefore, I take sole responsibility for all assumptions and conceptual formulations in the book.

One of the most valuable contributions during my journey toward completion of the book was the support I received from my diverse and multifaceted motorcycling "clan." It was a constant source of advice, encouragement, and active assistance on a broad range of questions and sticking points. In spite of the great patience and indulgence the clan extended to me over a long period of time, all mention of names has been strictly forbidden by them.

To H. W. Bönsch I owe the highest degree of gratitude, which goes far beyond expressions of thanks for advice and assistance. Without Bönsch, this book project would never have come to a successful conclusion. When I met him in the early 1960s at BMW, I was already well acquainted with him through his many publications. He belonged to the close-knit circle of the legendary Paul G. Hahnemann, and he showed much more concern for the continued existence of BMW's struggling motorcycle division than his position as director required. I visited him often when I was at the BMW factory, and our rapport and mutual inspiration were tremendous. Bönsch not only was excellent at explaining even the most complicated topics (and did so with passion) but also an extraordinarily attentive listener—a combination that one encounters only rarely.

In the first hundred years of the motorcycle's existence, there has hardly been a person who has known more about motorcycles than Bönsch—or perhaps better stated, there has never been a person who understood motorcycles better than he does. Simply knowing everything there is to know is a long way from actual understanding. For him, the motorcycle was much more than a complicated, lifeless, technical object. "Here's where it comes alive," he used to say when performing model calculations about a motorcycle that, building speed, reached the point at which it could balance on its own. And he meant this—literally. He would speak very softly, almost in a whisper; it was like a vow and not meant for all ears. "This is no longer just a simple stimulus-response apparatus," he declared to me early on. What he meant was that a number of control circuits develop between rider and machine, which take effect immediately through both, simultaneously. There is no doubt that he was right. The fascinating construction of steel, alloys, and rubber that is the motorcycle truly does come alive: at the same moment, the machine becomes part of the rider and the rider becomes part of it.

In later years, my relationship with Bönsch was not always without tension, and this book was the reason. It wasn't because of any disputes about facts; such differences could never have created a serious strain between us and could always be resolved. Rather it was because of how slow I was. He wrote angry and ultimately bitter letters, was abrupt with me on the telephone, and said many times that he would no longer be involved with the project. However, these ultimately proved to be supportive, "friendly" gestures. I tried to convince him that there was still much that had to be researched and clarified, but he did not agree, saying that there was already enough material worthy of being communicated in book form and that further exploration could be done later. Unfortunately, Bönsch did not live to see the final completion of the manuscript; thus, it is especially fitting that I dedicate this book to him.

Bernt Spiegel
Autumn 1998

Publisher's Note

This publication, in English, of the bestselling German book *Die obere Hälfte des Motorrads: Uber die Einheit von Fahrer und Maschine* by Bernt Spiegel is one of the most ambitious and satisfying projects Whitehorse Press has ever undertaken. It brings to English-language readers the insights and innovative thinking of Spiegel's brilliant mind, his professional knowledge as a psychologist specializing in the man-machine interface, his expertise as a highly accomplished motorcyclist, and his passion for motorcycling.

In 2006, Whitehorse was approached by Meredith Hassall to consider translating this unique work. An avid motorcyclist and associate editor of *OTL* (the magazine of the BMW Riders Association), Meredith had spent time in Germany and, while there, learned of the German edition's remarkable popularity. As we discussed the project with Meredith, it became clear that Spiegel's book embodies an utterly new and unique way of understanding the fine points of motorcycle riding and training. We were hooked! The project got underway formally when Meredith agreed to translate the book from German herself. She soon delivered a manuscript in English that was both faithful to the German original and true to the universal language of motorcycling.

The author's foreword for the third edition of the German publication attests to its enthusiastic reception by readers:

> [The] author and publisher were entirely surprised by the success of the book, which, after three printings by Heinrich Vogel Verlag (1998 and 1999) and two larger printings from Motorbuch Verlag (1999 and 2000), needed a third edition. The continued success of the book shows that the engaged motorcyclist approaches his challenging hobby with a thirst for knowledge and a demand for perfection. Numerous letters from readers have also confirmed this.

In producing this English edition, we have taken some liberties to re-format, reorganize, and edit the German edition to make the information more readily understandable in translation. In particular, the German edition's numerous "Comments and Digressions" at the back of the book were integrated into the text or inserted as sidebars near their relevant main topic to be more immediately accessible for quicker comprehension and fuller understanding of the book's core concepts. In some places, we also rearranged the order in which certain terms and concepts are introduced so that they are defined before their subsequent usage. Perhaps the most important change in the English edition is substitution of alternate terminology for Spiegel's "self person" and "deep person," which we felt would not be understood intuitively by English readers. For these terms we have substituted "conscious self" and "subconscious self," respectively, as we believe these more accurately convey Spiegel's intended meaning.

As with most complex projects, completion of this translation required the collaboration of several people. Lisa Dionne and Siegfried Wevering read the initial translation and made many invaluable suggestions for reorganizing the text and making it more accessible. Special appreciation goes to the talented Kathy O'Brien Adjemian, who edited the manuscript with great care to help the language flow smoothly and made many other refinements that have enhanced the readability of the book. Molly Dore, who applied her flair for design in creating a new layout and adding graphics to enhance the printed pages, also deserves our high praise and appreciation.

Finally, we gratefully acknowledge the valuable encouragement and assistance provided by Bernt Spiegel and Matthias Reisemann, his colleague at the Spiegel Institut, who remained patient and constant in their support of this English translation, undertaken to bring the knowledge, profound insights, and unique concepts in the German publication to more riders worldwide. We are confident that the book will not only greatly expand your knowledge of motorcyling and improve your riding skills but will also fascinate you.

Dan Kennedy,
Publisher

PART 1

It's a miracle that motorcycling works at all!

BEGINNINGS

Man did not arrive until the last minute

The year was long, the desert endless. Water, wind, heavy clouds, lifeless stone, and nothing but grey.

In September, a low-level undersea animal world must have arisen. At the beginning of October, the earliest fish began to appear. At the end of October, the first plants crept out of the water along the coasts and began slowly, very slowly, to take over the continents that had been dormant up until then. Toward the end of November, the very earliest mammals appeared. A week later, at the beginning of December, the first bird arrived.

The reader will no doubt recognize this story as a descriptive model of the sort frequently used in biology to represent the story of higher life forms on Earth by compressing its unimaginable age into one single calendar year. But there's more.

At just about the end of the year, the picture becomes more turbulent. The higher mammals begin to evolve—right around Christmas—and become notably widespread.

Man, however, still hasn't arrived. He appears, shaggy and naked, mind you, on New Year's Eve, the last day of the year, and even then not until evening. He has until midnight, or about a million and a half years, to develop into his modern form. About two hours before midnight comes the death of Homo Heidelbergensis. All that we commonly refer to as "world history," which includes at least 6000 years, begins on December 31st at 11:58.30—when everyone is standing and filling glasses to toast the end of the old year and ring in the new.

But what is the point of including this story? It is certainly not to say, "And motorcycles did not appear in large numbers until the very last second," although that would be true. The purpose is to illustrate as vividly as possible that man did not arrive on Earth until very, very late. His arrival was so late because, at previous points in evolutionary history, there simply was not enough extant brain matter. Most lacking was the cerebrum (more precisely, the cerebral cortex, or neocortex), the capabilities of which set humans apart. The powerful cerebrum developed in the last few million years, remarkably quickly on the time scale of evolutionary history.

Our cerebrum, an "aftermarket accessory"

We will see that the cerebrum is a very important part of the human brain, one upon which the motorcycle rider (and the golf player, the musician, and the artist) relies heavily. We will also see, however, that man is equipped with a tremendous number of basic, "built-in" functions, some highly perfected, that do not have much at all to do with the cerebrum. Further, we will see that failure or disaster is the outcome if we let the cerebrum get involved with these built-in functions.

In addition, we will learn that the cerebrum is something of an "aftermarket accessory" that has opened up vast new possibilities for man but cannot replace older parts of the brain. Thus, man continually finds himself faced with his greatest challenge: balancing the cooperation between his cerebral functions and his built-in functions. This is the fundamental goal of any kind of training endeavor. In fact, it underlies the process of managing oneself, and therefore of managing all human activities, including riding a motorcycle.

SYSTEMS AND SUBSYSTEMS

Man: a limiting subsystem with weaknesses

Whatever the details of how the human is equipped, one thing is certain: he is not, by nature, prepared to ride a motorcycle. (The range of other activities for which humans, by nature, are not prepared is overwhelming.) To properly prepare to ride, we should start early on to think in terms of "systems," and thus to view street traffic as a system. In this book, the "man-machine" subsystem is of central interest; this subsystem functions within the system street traffic.

The more we think about systems, the more obvious it will become that man, who is himself actually a sub-sub-system within the man-machine subsystem, is a limiting element with weaknesses. Some critics declare flatly that many people (other than themselves, of course) are simply too dumb to ride a motorcycle or to drive a car, and they even list examples that do, in fact, show dumb behavior. These examples are usually so striking that we are inclined to agree with the critics, and we can probably identify examples of our own behavior to support their claim if we are honest with ourselves.

Is humankind really too dumb?

> "Because man is not smart enough for this life,"
> (Bertolt Brecht, The Threepenny Opera).

Instead of studying definitions of intelligence and stupidity, let's look at a few examples:

A hungry puppy, for whom we have placed a treat at the end of an overhanging plank, falls for our sneaky trick (Figure 1). He has only his goal, that nice sausage, in mind, and walks to the end of the plank with the assumption—or rather, the expectation—that he is on solid ground. (More precisely, he doesn't assume anything, but rather doesn't pick up any clues to an outcome other than what he expects.)

This is certainly dumb behavior: potential dangers that can be predicted (by us, but not by the dog) are apparently not even recognized.

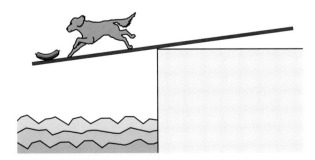

Figure 1

Figure 2

A motorcycle rider, riding on a narrow and familiar road with minimal traffic, flies around a blind curve and crashes head-on into a logging truck. He has fallen victim to a trick of statistics, although I would have a hard time calling it a sneaky one (Figure 2). The rider has only his immediate goal in mind and takes the corner under the assumption that, as he has become accustomed, everything will turn out exactly as expected. (More accurately, like the dog, he doesn't pick up any clues that run counter to what he expects.)

This, indeed, is also dumb behavior: potential dangers that could have been predicted are apparently not even recognized. However, the differences between the two examples are considerable. The poor dog had no chance at all to gain any insight into the situation: he is, in fact, too dumb. At best, if he encounters a situation that appears similar to him in the future, he will be leery. The motorcyclist, on the other hand, should have had the insight to anticipate risk in his situation. He has probably done so often enough in similar situations but, disastrously, not this time. So is he really so dumb after all, or perhaps only too distracted, too inattentive, or too reckless? Or is it something else?

In both examples, rational evaluation was lacking and there was no **hypothesis construction**[1] about what could happen. In the dog's case, the necessary cognitive capabilities were lacking, and in the motorcyclist's, these capabilities were just not used. And why not? The answer to this question will occupy us for some time in the following pages of this book.

---

1   The use of **boldface** indicates that there is an explanation of the concept in the glossary. Glossary terms are not boldfaced everywhere they appear, but normally at their first occurrence and at places where they are central to the discussion.

Our "built-in" speed

In order to recognize the insufficiencies of a human being, we don't have to concern ourselves with such complicated questions as whether his intelligence is adequate. To grasp his vulnerabilities within a system, we can begin with far simpler facts.

The speed associated with locomotion that is "built into" man, based on his senses and motor function (that is, his ability to carry out the necessary coordinated motions), is about 5 to 6 meters per second (about 20 km/h): this is the speed at which he can run at a fairly rapid pace, even in somewhat rough terrain. If, at this speed, he glances to the side to look at something, he'll need at least 0.8 seconds for this turn of the head and the glance; during this time, he will have covered about four meters along his path. Of course, he had this short stretch in view before he looked aside, and nothing significant will have changed in those four meters during the 0.8 seconds.

On a motorcycle, however, during this same glance to the side, which takes the same 0.8 seconds, the rider could easily have covered 20, 30, or even 50 meters. If it's something especially interesting, and the rider carelessly thinks he can get away with a longer look (maybe 2.3 seconds), he could cover 60, 90, or 150 meters. (A 2.3-second glance such as this is not as rare as one might believe; it has frequently been measured in real-life behavior studies.) However long the rider might look away in any given instance and at whatever speed this occurs, one thing is certain: in this "blink of an eye," he builds up a "blind zone" of considerable length in front of him. It's as if he were riding with wide-open throttle into an opaque bank of fog that he voluntarily put there.

So why does he do this? The answer is simple: because, just as in the case of a runner who unwittingly covers four meters during a sideways glance, the rider has convinced himself that he can afford a glance, the path is clear, and no dangers are lurking. However, if during this time (which is really very short), while riding through this stretch (which is actually rather long), an incident were to occur that required hard braking, an enormous amount of time would be added to the reaction time. Additional time, however, means additional distance. Reaction time, activation time, response time, and the time it takes for full braking pressure to build after the brakes have been activated must be added to the braking distance itself, and all of these together make up the stopping distance. All of this is delayed because of a "brief" glance to the side, during which the rider is doing absolutely nothing to compensate for the situation. The sum of all these parts easily produces a distance that is much longer than either the usual following distance or the distance available within his line of sight. During these 0.8 or 2.3 seconds, a child could suddenly leap out from behind an obstruction and into the road.

When two people do the same thing

But there's something trickier than a glance to the side, with its skewed relationship to one's own speed: riding in a line of vehicles. This is tricky because the danger is not readily evident; the rider can only be aware of the *potential* danger. However, it is well known that human behavior can't always be adequately influenced by knowledge alone.

Let's say that a short line of cars is being driven along at 100 km/h. Since this speed is perceived as harmless, the drivers are maintaining too short a following distance—let's say an average of 15 meters. Although this may not seem all that alarming, we all know that the completely clueless tend to follow much more closely. If Car 1 suddenly has to stop, and if we figure an average deceleration rate of 7.5 m/s² for all vehicles in the line, as well as an optimistic 0.7 seconds for reaction time and activation time, then Car 2 would need an additional 5 meters of braking distance, Car 3 would need 10 meters more, Car 4 would need 15, etc. If for a moment we don't consider the deformation of the vehicles that would occur in such a crash, it would mean that even though Car 2 needed only an extra car-length, it still hits Car 1 at a decent 35 km/h. Car 3 would crash at 44 km/h, and Car 4 would crash at 54 km/h—and a crash at even this speed can have a fatal outcome! And just a few cars behind, the driver won't even get the chance to move his foot from the gas to the brake before crashing at full speed (that is, at 100 km/h) into the pile-up.

In this example, the most pertinent point is not so much the mechanics of the accident but rather the fact that the danger is not evident and the participants do not experience anything threatening. It is rare for a driver in a line of cars to have the slightest notion that, for the same mistake, his punishment will be much harsher at the back of the line than in the second position.

In observations of drivers and riders, "design flaws" in human reasoning are readily apparent. Certainly an engineer forced to use a human subsystem as a regulator in designing a reasonably fast-moving man-machine system would regard this required component with a furrowed brow because of its insufficiencies. The flaws in human reasoning don't manifest themselves as performance limits of the sort that, once exceeded, immediate failure is inevitable. Actually, it is more complex: at the first instances of flawed reasoning, nothing may happen at all, but the risk of a mistake, and with it the risk of an accident, increases dramatically as poor reasoning persists. Whether an accident actually occurs depends mostly on the circumstances.

FORESIGHT

Not enough imagination

As I have already alluded, in the mental realm there are other considerable problems for motorcycle riders. For example, while riding, the ability to foresee the consequences of an error that might lead to an accident is very limited, especially as one's speed increases. Foreseeing or imagining the consequences does not mean knowing what *will* happen or what *could* happen. Instead, it means imagining what it would be like to truly experience and live through the consequences. Since man and his immediate ancestors have been moving around upright, on two legs, for the past four million years, he has had a pretty good idea of what would happen if he were to run into a tree while jogging and a pretty realistic idea of the kind of pain he would suffer if this were to happen. But how an analogous event on a motorcycle might affect him is a distant and abstract thought. Of course, we've all read accident reports and seen ghastly pictures, but the physical chain of events, even though we are afraid of it, is at best something we grasp only intellectually. We do not have an immediate, sensate experience of these events which could lead to our destruction, because typical vehicular speeds are beyond the experiences of our original habitat, or mesocosm—that is, the environment in which man lived during the early stages of human evolution.

What he doesn't know can't frighten him

At earlier stages of human evolution, the experience of threat was of great biological significance, but this significance has eroded away over time. In today's world, whether or not one actually experiences a threat depends partly on whether a similarly dangerous situation was present at the time of man's early existence or originated more recently. Most often, the dangers modern

Figure 3. Two major errors, which usually occur simultaneously: the motorcyclist not only follows too closely but is also right in the center and thereby gives up, from the outset, his last chance of escape in the event of sudden braking by the car driver.

Maintaining a safe following distance

For the motorcyclist, crashing into a braking car poses especially high risk. Even when the excess speed is minimal—and 15 km/h is enough—the rider will be thrown over his bike (usually with horrific consequences for his legs because the handlebars are in the way). The rider collides with the rear end of the car, and at the same moment the motorcycle bounces backward a little, as if to make room for the rider, who falls neatly through this gap between the car and the motorcycle and lands on the road. In the next moment, the gap closes itself again: the still-moving motorcycle, which was slowed only by its initial impact, crashes once again (usually already half on its side) into the car, which has since come to a stop, and then pushes the rider under the rear end of the car.

In spite of this danger, one constantly sees clueless riders—including quite accomplished ones—who not only carelessly follow a car far too closely but also tend to position themselves precisely in the middle of the lane (see Figure 3), and thus in a position in which, if the car were to suddenly slow, the chances of being able to ride past it are the worst. The possibilities for swerving around a suddenly appearing obstacle are significantly reduced and are often vastly overestimated, just as most riders misjudge what constitutes a safe following distance and follow too closely.

There is a riding exercise to cure this: have an instructor ride at a constant speed—preferably in a car—in front of the rider but one lane over. The rider's task is to maintain the following distance that allows him to bring the motorcycle safely to a stop in the event that the vehicle ahead suddenly stops. If the instructor brakes to a standstill without warning, the rider is almost always surprised and, in most instances, ends up beside the car ahead or even beyond it. Once he has experienced this for himself, he will see how he's been putting himself at great risk. ∎

The concept of the mesocosm plays an important role in evolutionary epistemology, which is a rather recent development in philosophy. The theory describes the human's mesocosm as that particular segment of the world to which he spontaneously orients himself; or more precisely, "that section of the world which he recognizes without artificial assistance, and that he can process by means of reconstruction and identification" (Vollmer 1985, 1986).

Figure 4. Man leaves the mesocosm. Originally: "Man breaks through the arches of the heavens and sees the mechanics of the luminaries and the weather." (Wood engraving from the end of the nineteenth century, using the techniques of the Middle Ages; based on an idea of the French astronomer Camille Flammarion.)

The mesocosm is related not only to "spontaneous orientation" but also to "spontaneous coping." That is, not just *cognition* (which is probably of foremost interest in evolutionary epistemology) but also *action,* to at least the same extent. The latter is our topic, although for our purposes the term "cognitive" could easily be too restrictive, as if rationality and intent always had to be present (Spiegel 1967, 1989).

In all areas, the human mesocosm covers only the mid-ranges of dimensions that are meaningful (that is, important for survival) for us in our developmental history, and nothing more. Thus, in terms of the speed of one's own locomotion, the human mesocosm reaches only as far as the speed of a fast runner (a sprinter might even be beyond the limit!); in terms of acceleration, it reaches about as far as the acceleration of gravity; in terms of weight, it extends from fractions of a gram to about a thousand

pounds; in terms of temperature, it extends from freezing to far beyond body temperature (at least for water; in the air, the range starts a little lower); in terms of time, it spans less than a tenth of a second to many many years. Some dimensions that play important roles for other creatures do not even exist in the human mesocosm. Some dimensions, such as distance, cover enormous ranges: for humans, thanks to their amazing fine-motor skills, the mesocosm starts at tenths of millimeters and extends for miles and miles.

The limits of these ranges are not strict cutoffs—at the edges of the mesocosm the extreme ends of the perceivable ranges in individual dimensions gradually fade away just as their biological significance gradually declines. The more time we spend at the cores of these dimensions (areas that are most prevalent for us), the more familiar everything becomes for us; the further afield we go into the edges of these dimensions (that is, into areas that humans have been less exposed to in the course of their developmental history), the less certain we are about things. We don't have as much intuition for making judgments in these realms, and we need to put that much more effort into additional learning. Through learning, an individual can extend his own limits of recognition beyond these edges. Regardless of the dimension, a complete departure from the mesocosm is, in principle, without limit if conducted in our minds. It is also possible to a certain extent physically, but it always goes hand in hand with a loss of concreteness (and the loss of the experience of evidence). For example, there are certain topics in theoretical physics that cannot be clearly imagined or concretely represented, but can nonetheless be thought about and explained.

Described another way (perhaps more realistically): it is not the departure from the mesocosm that is bound to the loss of concreteness, but rather the opposite. The world as a whole is abstract and incomprehensible, but in our miniscule habitat, our mesocosm, we have created for ourselves a degree of concrete clarity that we can comprehend, and it's only in this small area that "common sense" can help us.

This is what is special about a human being: he can step outside of his inherited mesocosm. In fact, he constantly strives to stretch its edges, even if he has to take enormous risks to do so. ∎

man faces are of the most recent possible origin. Concepts like braking-distance deficits that add up imperceptibly, for example, did not exist in our ancestral environment (mesocosm).

For example, one definitely experiences some threat or danger when he has climbed a tall tree. Even when the perch is solid and there's plenty to hang on to, a person who looks down experiences a fear of falling, which is accompanied commonly by dizziness and increased muscular tension. By contrast, this feeling is completely absent when one looks out the window of an airplane (unless the person has a phobic fear of flying) or when one looks down at the ground while suspended in the harness of a hang glider. (F.K., a colleague who is a masterful and fearless hang glider, has a fit just standing on an ordinary stepladder when he doesn't have anything to hold onto.)

In the same way, looking out from the basket of a hot-air balloon usually does not elicit an experience of threat, even for first-timers. This phenomenon has long been a topic of puzzled debate. In the entire history of human evolution prior to air travel, a human being had never found himself high above the ground without some visible connection between what he was standing on and the ground, whether sitting high in trees or on rocky outcroppings. This kind of physical connection had always been present.

In support of this explanation, one will notice that the first-timer in a hot-air balloon becomes notably more uncomfortable when the tow-line (a fairly long rope used in landing the balloon) is hanging out of the basket. Indeed, the fact that the line is hanging out does not lead to the slightest change in the objective risk, and the elements of the person's visual perception are changed only minimally. However, the individual's conceptual frame of reference has changed crucially: it has become like man's experiences, or lack thereof, in early stages of human evolution—the rope's hanging out elicits the sensation of an absent connection with the ground.

Clueless but full of hope

In a similar fashion, an approximate calculation reveals just how naive we are about the destructive powers that arise at speeds beyond those we can achieve naturally. Although the formula is commonly used, its result is almost always a surprise. I'm talking about the formula for kinetic energy; or more concretely, impact; or still more concretely, the destructive powers in a crash.

Ominously, the speed in the famous formula for kinetic energy $(m \times v^2) / 2$ is squared. A person weighing 72 kg, running at 20 km/h, will have about 1000 Newton-meters of kinetic energy that will be "destroyed" in a crash—or more precisely, it will be converted into form-altering energy. Depending on the rate of deceleration, position, the distribution of the impact points, etc., this impact is survivable. But if the same person mounts a fast motorcycle—now a bit heavier wearing his gear—with which he can easily reach speeds beyond 200 km/h, the result is an incomparably higher level of kinetic energy. What would you estimate? Ten times? (Even that would be catastrophic in a hard crash.) Twenty times? (The consequences are unimaginable.) But, at 180 km/h, the kinetic energy of the rider is *100 times* that of the runner. With a modern liter bike, it could easily exceed 200 times that of the runner .

In this calculation, I increased the rider's weight by a modest 8 kg because of his gear, but I have not taken the mass of the motorcycle into account. Those numbers would become astronomical. But as it relates to us, that really doesn't matter anymore. In both versions, these unimaginable forces are well beyond what we would be able to process into a concrete conception of what the crash would be like—in contrast to a "crash" on foot. This gaping hole in our ability to imagine this experience is adequate proof that man was not meant to move along at speeds well beyond those experienced in his mesocosm.

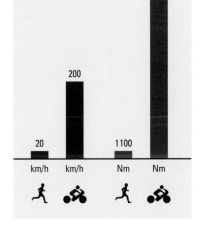

Figure 5. A motorcyclist can easily reach 10 times the speed of a fast cross-country runner (blue), but his kinetic energy (red) will exceed 100 times that of the runner!

From a young engineer's report about his participation in a crash test

. . . The car moved almost soundlessly toward a concrete wall, and it seemed to all of us that it was surprisingly slow. We were wearing sunglasses, because everything was bathed in blindingly bright light (needed for the high-speed cameras that would record the event at 500 to 1000 pictures per second).

Right before the impact, which this time was apparently only going to be one of the milder ones, we heard the cameras start. But then things changed: an unimaginable, deafening, and shrill crash made us all recoil, and the entire floor seemed to shake. Parts flew all over the place, a piece of glass was shattered on the wall, trim pieces whirled around . . .

Then, gradually, there was silence. Only a loose hubcap, or whatever it might have been, clattered on the floor. The silence was almost unnatural; we were speechless. The vehicle was completely destroyed and stood, somewhat compressed, slightly in front of the wall.

Even though we were all familiar with pictures of crashes, none of us had expected such a hellish spectacle. Anyone who has experienced something like what we witnessed will never again drive without his seatbelt fastened!

Knowledge and action

Even if a rider is familiar with the above formula for kinetic energy, it's only a rational knowledge, and it is in no way certain that over time he would be able to internalize this knowledge and mentally train himself to deal with high-speed situations (see p. 121).

The sidebar above shows that even a young automotive engineer, who certainly *knows* in detail what kinetic energy is all about, isn't truly impressed by it until he actually experiences it. This impression is made not only via the cerebrum; direct experience clearly affects a person at a deeper, non-rational level. At this point, there is a real opportunity for a change in behavior. (Incidentally, this occurs in the same way in a person without any theoretical knowledge who witnesses the same event.) The altered behavior might last only for a short time (the way it always does in the first few miles after witnessing an accident on the highway), or it might remain in effect for a long period of time. In any case, the behavior-changing experience leaves a person somewhat intimidated, if not

outright frightened. Still, one should not hastily conclude from this that the ordinary transfer of knowledge in driver or rider education is ineffective and that we should provide instead a hearty dose of intimidation, fear, and views of the worst possible situations. Intimidated riders are bad riders, and frightened riders are even worse. We'll soon see why.

ADAPTATION

Man is a master of adaptation

The remarks above, admittedly, reveal skepticism about just how well suited man is to riding motorcycles, but it turns out that man isn't actually so unsuited after all. Rather, we have shown that man really isn't "built" to ride motorcycles. However, he has certain capabilities that are unique in nature and unheard of in other animals. In spite of his insufficiencies, man generally copes remarkably well with the motorcycle, a rather difficult piece of equipment, in spite of the lamentable accidents described above. Although accidents and their prevention deserve our utmost attention, we should not forget that accident statistics are the result of a negative selection from an unimaginably large number of individual actions by all participants in traffic. The flow of street traffic is nothing other than the totality of these innumerable individual actions and their interaction. The actions that lead to accidents are, in the language of statistics, entirely rare occurrences.

So, although man has extraordinary capabilities that give him the ability to handle an implement as complicated as a motorcycle, anyone who believes that his success is based on rationality and reason will be sorely disappointed. It's true that man's most dominant asset, which he can thank for his special position among species, is his cerebrum. In the last few million years, it has developed more and more into an unsurpassed, tried-and-true tool for survival.

In spite of this, man's intellectual powers are of only secondary interest here (we'll discuss the role of rationality more closely in the last part of the book). There is yet another characteristic that sets man apart: his remarkable plasticity—his supreme ability to adapt to his surroundings. At this point, a digression is necessary, to clarify that this superb capacity for adaptation is an imperative condition for the use of tools.

There is no higher animal that is more plastic, formable, or adaptable to its surroundings than man. This is evident, for example, even with respect to climate, in which man can endure not only the most varied kinds of stresses, but also stresses over amazingly wide geographical ranges. We could pack up our families, head north, and settle down 300 km north of the Arctic Circle; we would certainly curse the intense cold and the long polar night, but we'd survive just fine. The same group could pack up and move instead to an oasis in the Sahara and likewise survive. Our pets and livestock, although domesticated, would have problems. We could certainly take some of them with us to the north of Finland, and others to the Sahara, but there's hardly a single animal other than man that would be able to tolerate both.

Adaptability to climate is hardly the only example: man's plasticity is a general characteristic. His unbelievable ability to adapt to his environment is closely related to the fact that he is not specialized. Man is, in the words of Konrad Lorenz, a "specialist at being unspecialized." With the help of an enormous brain, he has specialized in not being specialized.

In a world full of specialists, not being specialized could, however, become a threat to a species' continued existence if that lack of specialization is not combined with a considerable ability to adapt to surroundings. And the longer this non-specialization lasts over the course of development, the more this ability must increase. It's not just a remarkable ability to think and an equally remarkable imagination that make man unique; it's also his enormous ability and aptitude for adaptation.

On the "center line"

To explore this idea further, we might imagine the entirety of all living things and their development in the form of a mighty tree with many branches, as depicted in a very simplified form in Figure 6. All the way at the bottom of the picture are a few minimally organized life forms. Over the course of evolution, with much branching out, an extraordinary variety of species has developed, with increasingly organized creatures. Each branch is the result of an **adaptation** to particular environmental circumstances, that is, the result of a "specialization." Most species have long since died out or been replaced by further developed types. They are found on the inside of this picture, while those that exist today are found at the edges. There are species of all sorts: those that can fly, some that can swim, others that are very good climbers, etc. But even those that can fly are differentiated among themselves: some eat nuts that they have to crack; others use their beaks to pull food from tree

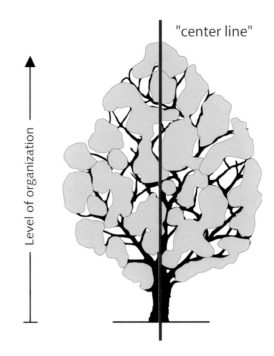

Figure 6. Mankind has moved ever closer to the "center line" in the process of his increasing de-specialization and has thereby become the "flexible universalist."

bark; still others pluck their prey from the waters—in each case, with a different, specialized tool in the form of an appropriately shaped beak. These highly specialized species are dependent on very specific environmental conditions however, and if these conditions change—drastically enough and quickly enough—it would spell doom for the affected species.

Man is the great exception: he stands on the evolutionary center line ("center line theory"). In the course of human evolution, man has become less and less specialized, his only "goal" the formation of the most powerful brain possible. As a highly adaptable non-specialist, he can live in a much broader range of conditions than other species.

The first liberated creatures

In fact, there is no other living thing that can withstand a greater variety of stresses, that can be placed in more different kinds of conditions, and which has such wide tolerance for many different aspects of his environment. A human can do almost everything, but, in a sense, he can't do anything well. He can walk, he can run, he can swim, he can dive, he can climb—the list of his many talents would be quite long—but for each of these there's another expert species, a specialist, that can't do much

➤ Man, the chameleon

Hans Hass does not accept Lorenz's notion of man as a "specialist at being unspecialized." According to Hass, "It's completely the opposite: the human is a specialist in multi-faceted specialization. He is a being who, thanks to his artificial organs, can transform himself like a chameleon to adapt to every situation and task. He alters his environment and surrounding conditions almost at will, and is thus at home in almost any realm: on land, at sea, under water, in the air, and even in space."

Lorenz uses our physical build and the inventory of behaviors as a starting point, while Hass sees human functions in their entirety and emphasizes in particular the functions that aren't possible without the help of artificial "organs" (see p. 88) but truly do lead to an astounding degree of specialization. This is similar to the differentiation between the born specialist and one who has specialized through learning (see p. 27), which could help a little to settle the controversy.

In any case, it's the lack of specialization that gives humans the enormous plasticity necessary for such a multifaceted use of tools. It's only *because* the human being is not specialized that he can create for himself the most diverse types of artificial "organs" and then adapt himself sufficiently to their use. The decisive factor is the enormous versatility of human beings (something also emphasized by Hass) that does not allow any specialization, but instead requires only a single adaptation: *the specific adaptation to versatility.* Lorenz believes that the brain, with its immense size, represents a very tangible, morphological, special adaptation.   ■

more than one of these but does this one thing much better than man. At this point, discussion of programs for managing and mastering actions is in order.

Can't do without them: programs that control actions

Throughout this book, I'll be referring to programs that manage actions, or action programs. Because this concept is so central to the way species, including humans, respond to their environment, it requires some explanation and clarification.

Even in everyday usage—for example, at events or performances—a **program** is more than just a table of contents. It specifies a course of events and is, at the very least, a set of directions about the sequence to be followed under some more or less complex set of conditions. A program is always a matter of some kind of "if-then" relationship. In the simplest case—in a program of purely linear sequence—the program "instructions" are relatively simple, such as: "If Program Item Number n has been completed, then Program Item Number $n+1$ should start." Such purely linear programs are very inflexible as they run their course, but they are adequate for the control of a music box; an orchestrion (an automatic organ that is controlled by means of a tape with holes, seen at some street festivals); machine tools; or a weaving machine, even if it is programmed to produce a very complicated pattern. For these simple programs, no adaptation to changing circumstances is required.

A garden spider who spins a web for the first time in its life does it perfectly the first time. The spider didn't have to *learn* how but instead makes use of a fully complete inborn program that cannot be refined, made easier through learning, or developed further. Nevertheless, such inborn programs, even though inalterable, are actually much more flexible than the control programs that operate a music box or a machine tool. Unlike a programmed weaving machine, a spider never spins the same web but rather adapts each web to the concrete external conditions in which it finds itself. It certainly tries to avoid significant variations in the size of the mesh, but in the selection of anchoring points for the web, it makes decisions based entirely on its environment. The spider follows the chance of the breeze when it throws out the first thread. If there's a branch in a reasonably appropriate direction that catches the thread, the spider initially uses it, even if it might not ultimately need such a long retaining thread.

There is a distinction to be made between the rigidity (or the flexibility and adaptability) of a *program* and the rigidity (or the flexibility and adaptability) of a *system* that is controlled by a program. The machines described above have fixed programs, but usually the programs can be swapped for others, giving the machines some flexibility as systems. In contrast, the spider's program is much more flexible: there are particular details of it that can be adapted to surroundings while the program is being applied. Adaptable programs have been called "open" programs by Konrad Lorenz (1984a, p. 284) and Ernst Mayr, since these programs are open to being oriented to their given environment. However, inborn programs must not be misunderstood as "independent of environment." Still, the spider's program cannot be changed, modified, or swapped with some other program.

Mixed programs

Inborn behavior cannot always be as sharply differentiated from acquired behaviors as the terminology would have us believe. Not so much because inborn behaviors also have to be "acquired" by means of adaptations over the course of developmental history, but rather because most of these programsö, more frequently than one assumes at first glance, are of mixed forms—that is, they are mixed **programs.**

Certainly in a relatively low-order animal, there are programs that do run mechanically, but even the garden spider undertakes very individualized adaptations to the environment when spinning his web, matching it to the particular surroundings in which he finds himself. By the time we get to the vertebrates, not only are the concrete external conditions of a given situation taken into account when using an inborn program, but the basic underlying program will be continually, adaptively improved. That is, *learning* comes into play. Actually, it is often no more than a framework for a capability that is genetically transmitted; further expansion and the filling in of details occur individually and thus are *acquired,* as with the flight of birds.

Mixed programs are readily evident in thousands of examples from the animal world. Man uses genetically transmitted program stubs like bricks and incorporates them here and there into his acquired action programs. In the animal world, basic inborn programs are more common; individual inborn program segments are combined with acquired programs that are, in turn, refinements and improvements on the basic programs. Birds, for example, starting at a certain point in their lives, have a genetically transmitted program available for flying which is unimaginably complicated, but nevertheless a long way from perfect. Especially among the large birds of prey, it is easy to see how much more clumsy the younger birds are compared to their parents with much more flight time. A young, but nearly full-grown white tailed eagle will still need to master such refined skills as over-stroking to the stalling point when landing, or correcting for crosswinds when taking off and landing. Even the **process certainty,** will require effort involving the further acquisition of partial programs or program refinements.

Even what seems to be a culturally defined and highly complex phenomenon such as human language (a prime example of acquired capability) is actually a collaboration of inborn and acquired programs. The basic scaffolding for language is genetically transmitted; further construction and embellishment toward the actual language spoken—the learning of which is completely dictated by the environment—is a matter of learning. However, without this general scaffolding, language acquisition would be just as impossible as it would be without the environment in which the language is spoken.

Even a human being cannot arbitrarily learn things that go against existing **dispositions,** at least not without great difficulty. A disposition is an inherited but not yet actualized preparation or general readiness for certain capabilities. By contrast, learning is especially easy for the human when he has the help of these special **learning dispositions,** which are dominant in language acquisition in early childhood. There's a lot that a human must first learn, but according to Zimmer (1979), "this is the big difference from milieu theory, he doesn't learn everything with equal enjoyment, equal success, and equal speed, and there's a lot that he never learns"—this entirely corresponds to the inherited part of the relevant programs.

This small insight into the different mixed-form programs is useful for an understanding of the subsequent discussions of the action programs that are required for riding a two-wheeler. ∎

Such action programs are really quite practical, provided everything works properly. The living thing that is performing the activity needs to have no insight into the program, and an unbelievable amount of information can be packed into a program, which can then be immediately converted into action, even if the action lasts for hours. There is no better way to more completely "unburden" a living thing, but only, as stated above, provided everything works properly—that is, as long as the external world in which the living thing finds itself and the program with which it is equipped fit together. After all, the programs were "designed" over the course of the species' development and specialization to work in that environment. However, if the environment changes faster than the programs can be adapted, the threat to that species' survival will increase until it becomes extinct. The pace of such genetic adaptive change is extremely slow: innumerable generations are needed before a change becomes evident. If there are rapid changes in the environment, adaptation will always be several steps behind. This is the disadvantage of otherwise successful and reliable inborn programs that are transmitted through the genes.

The further down we go in the animal kingdom hierarchy, the more we will encounter "closed" programs and the more strictly these programs will dominate the animal's behavior. However, the more highly organized a creature, the more programs that creature will have that can be adjusted to the particulars of its environment. An individual can undertake some degree of customization, and among the more highly organized beings, additional learning is more likely to occur. This learning will lead to better coping if a situation repeats itself. At these higher levels of adaptability, we see the transition to a new type of program that is no longer acquired in genetic material but instead is acquired individually by individuals.

Man is largely free of inflexible action programs, and, in this respect, is much more open to different things than the narrowly programmed specialists, but in exchange for this freedom, most everything that man is capable of doing must first be painstakingly learned. However, man is remarkably good at learning and can even defy biological sense to learn the most complicated sets of movements, such as in dance and performance art. Man can even learn to do things that men before him have only imagined, such as hang-gliding. "To learn" here does not mean, as one might assume, to memorize or retain something in our consciousness and in our minds. Instead, it means the creation of a new personal action program.

Although man is largely free of domination by behavior-managing programs, with their strict behavior specifications, he does not arrive in the world with a completely empty and neutral warehouse that, through learning, he can fill up as he pleases. Freedom from predisposed action has great advantages but also has disadvantages. In all of life, liberation from any kind of force has its price. The advantages and disadvantages are readily evident: for example, man is not born with an ability to swim (a "swim-program") that can protect him from drowning. Many animals (even those that don't swim voluntarily) do have an inborn swimming ability. Man must make an effort to learn how to swim. But in return for that effort, man has far greater freedom compared to the animal that can only swim according to its own (inherited) swim-program. Man can swim breaststroke, freestyle, maybe eventually butterfly, and he can swim on his back. Or he can just skip the swimming entirely because he doesn't like the water.

It becomes clear that in contrast to other living creatures, man must first learn to do many things (if not most things), but also in contrast to other creatures, man can learn an amazing number and variety of things. There are hardly two people in the world who have exactly the same repertoire of abilities and possible actions; in other words, who have exactly the same "library" of programs. This is highly distinct from the animals of a particular species, with their limited number of inborn programs. Each of the individuals within a species have the same small library that is passed on through the generations without modification.

The great opportunity: acquired programs

We have discussed inborn programs, and now, with "learnable" programs, there is a new type of behavior programming to consider: management by "acquired programs" (compare the so-called *hereditary* **coordination** with the so-called *acquired* coordination). It is only with the help of these acquired programs that man achieves his unique degree of adaptability (see p. 26). Once he has acquired and solidified his programs, they function in the same way and just as well as genetically transmitted action programs. They reduce the burdens on the individual for carrying out actions that are often quite complicated and detailed. The coordination of complex actions via a "program" is far better than it would be if the action were carried out by conscious control and direction of the individual components of that action. Perhaps the most obvious commonality between the two types of programs is that once a learned program has been acquired, has sunk in sufficiently, and is sufficiently **automated,** it is very nearly as undeletable as an inborn program (see Lorenz, 1985, p. 138f). Once a person has learned to swim or ride a bicycle, he never loses that ability. For example, take a woman who was a skilled bicyclist as a schoolgirl, but then has no opportunity to ride for several decades. When finally, as a spry retiree, she takes it up again to ride with her grandchildren, she might approach it with a bit of trepidation because, in fact, she doesn't "know" whether she can still ride at all. Nevertheless, she'll realize within just a few yards that she's doing just fine. It's true that such programs are better if "looked after," if they are to endure without loss of refinement—and in this regard, the grandmother's initial uncertainty wasn't entirely misplaced—but she retained her fundamental ability intact.

In short, once one has acquired a program in this way, carrying out a learned activity can be left up to its program, just as if it were an inborn program resulting from the evolutionary adaptation process of a species. In order to acquire such programs, he doesn't have to *know* much of anything. Only the fewest people actually "know" how to ride a bicycle, but once someone has learned to ride, he will never "un-learn" it. The same is true for swimming. A person who has learned to swim and wants to kill himself by jumping into deep water (with a plan simply not to swim), will find that it is not quite that simple. His swim-program, although it has "only" been acquired, will be initiated, whether he wants it to or not.

The most miraculous thing is that acquired programs have the tendency to optimize themselves. Thus, whether one learns by **imitating** or by conscious acquisition, a person trying to learn only needs to concentrate on relatively few basic aspects of the procedure or activity. The rest takes care of itself through continued repetition, without particular effort beyond that. If it weren't for this **self-optimization** of programs, the learning of some things, such as playing the violin or skiing, would simply not be possible.

Specialists at birth or with practice

We can therefore contrast the "born" specialist with the "learned" specialist. The born specialist is one-dimensional and unchangeable but doesn't have to learn anything, at least not from the ground up. Depending on the level of organization of the species, the individual might, at most, have to practice the skill a little (as, for example, when a fledgling takes his first few flights). More precisely, pre-existing or easily completed shorter procedures must be pulled together into functional units, which are the complete programs that then just have to be fine-tuned and polished. This also applies to certain activities among human beings, such as when a toddler begins to walk.

The learned specialist, by contrast, can do almost nothing at first, but proves himself to be remarkably capable of adopting this program or that one, or both, and several others, and new ones, like bike riding or swimming. The more routinely he practices an activity, the more the proficiency of its execution will increase and the more like an inborn program it will become. However, a learned program never achieves the rigidity and

🏍 Use it or lose it

A certain deficiency in "program maintenance" occurs in most motorcyclists after even a short break from riding during the winter months. As with all seasonal sports, the loss of proficiency—beyond the subjective impression of the rider himself—is greater for a less-experienced rider than for one with more experience, and greater for younger riders than for older ones. This is obviously connected to the degree of **automation** of the programs and the extent to which they have "sunk in."

A statement such as, "I had to practice a bit before my reflexes were back up to snuff," is a good reflection of the situation. Even if it is not strictly a matter of reflexes, it is nonetheless true that action programs gradually disintegrate from disuse.

Pianist Arthur Rubinstein has been credited with the following expression: "If I don't practice for a day, only I notice it. If I don't practice for three days, my wife notices it. If I don't practice for a month, the audience notices it." ∎

inescapability of an inborn program. Instead, the person who has adopted a learned program can change it and develop it further (although not always easily), or adapt it so that it fits a new situation better. It can also be further shaped according to one's "personal style."

ACTION PROGRAMS FOR MOTORCYCLING

Defamiliarization: a trick for understanding complexity

As we now turn to the special adaptation and programming that a rider needs to bring to the motorcycle, the requirements won't actually be all that clear to us, because everything about that familiar motorcycle already works by itself as a matter of course. We are so well adapted to the things that we always have around us that we don't see how they "actually" are anymore, and thus we don't even notice fundamental traits—for example, how unbelievably complicated it is to handle a motorcycle properly.

But there's a trick to understanding it: we can take this familiar thing, and without changing it in the least, put it in an entirely new environment to make it seem completely "foreign," so it appears to us to be something new and previously unknown.

As a thought experiment, let's imagine that we are part of a large company and are a member of a committee that has to make decisions about new products. Up to now, only cars have been available in the world. Neither bicycles nor motorcycles exist. Then an inventor appears and shows us drawings and models of a strange single-track vehicle that appears to be nothing more than a four-cylinder motor with two wheels attached to it.

- Displacement: economy car
- Engine output: mid-level car
- Speed: sportscar
- Acceleration: race car
- Weight: about 500 pounds

Or in other words, a modern liter-bike. We would probably dismiss this inventor rather quickly, and in our report about the meeting explaining our refusal to take on this product, we would write, half astounded and half amused by this person's lack of judgment, something like the following:

> . . . what's most bewildering is the extraordinarily large number of controls which the rider has to activate with hands and feet, some of which he has to use simultaneously. And during the ride, according to the inventor, he also has to keep a constant hold on a so-called handlebar with both hands. We counted a total of more than a dozen different functions. Even if one does not consider the controls that are only used occasionally, such as the start button, horn, headlight flasher, turn signals, high beam, etc., and aside from the two handgrips (which even on a straight road—and especially at slow speeds—still have to be controlled constantly because of balancing requirements), there are still five other controls that have to be frequently, if not constantly managed. So, for example, the left foot, which is responsible for gear selection, has something like a series-switch with seven positions (six gears plus neutral) to manage.
>
> It might be possible to learn all this on a vehicle in which the operator did not additionally have to pay attention to balancing. But the committee's main objection is related to the fundamental and system-dependent static instability inherent in the single-track nature of the two-wheeler. Our discussion of the physical relationships centered on the forces that would act on, and result from, the system. These forces were examined closely, with particular attention given by the committee members who are involved with research and development. Our study revealed that the gyroscopic forces that are produced by rotating bodies (angular momentum and precession), forces that research and development deal with constantly, could have fundamentally advantageous effects—if in a very complicated way—such that at higher speeds it was theoretically possible to keep such a vehicle stable. Even at lower speeds, such as would occur in heavy traffic, it could be possible, from a physics standpoint, to keep the vehicle in balance for a long stretch, without using the legs, by stringing together a series of very slight curves. But even riding in this way in a straight line would require almost artistic capabilities and a long and potentially risky training period. Finally, riding through a curve would place immeasurable demands upon the rider, because for any given curve radius, there is only one correct lean angle for each cornering speed, and this angle must be achieved precisely each time.

The development committee arrived at a unanimous rejection, and in the meantime, the marketing department, working independently, found no evidence of the slightest demand for such a vehicle.

I am certain that the decision could not have been otherwise. But even if we assume that the technicians had come to a positive decision, the marketing people in the company would never have changed their minds. Their arguments would have convinced everyone. They would have had to do nothing more than compare the objective utility of this vehicle with that of an economy car in approximately the same price range. The special fascination of riding a motorcycle, which might have tipped the scales in its favor, would not have been considered, because at that time, not a single person would have known about that special fascination. Today, of course, we are familiar with it, but we still don't really know just what the basis of this feeling is—everyone describes it differently. We'll return to this topic later.

This thought experiment is appealing because we indeed would have come to a similar decision as the committee. Of course, we already know that riding a motorcycle actually, somehow, works out. We completed our incredible adaptation to riding a motorcycle, the full extent of which is gradually becoming clear to us, long ago. It was a success because we acquired certain behavior programs without much effort. Once a course of action is controlled by a program, it no longer requires *conscious involvement*, as it is termed by traffic psychologists (see **conscious attention** in the glossary), and we experience it as an automatic action. Everything happens without difficulty, and it is only after this kind of thought experiment that we begin to realize just how complicated a motorcycle and its handling can be. In particular, the problems of balancing and of getting the correct lean angle in curves, which caused the committee so much consternation, are something that we, as motorcyclists, do without a second thought, and we do so easily and even playfully.

We can't exactly say that we have forgotten about this complexity over time. The fact is, we never really realized the complexity in the first place. Most motorcycle riders have only incomplete ideas about the physics of riding—and they really don't need more precise knowledge about motorcycle physics in order to handle this tool competently in everyday riding.

➤ Why nothing feels right when changing motorcycles

It's not just a matter of random deviations among the individual models; there are also some very different general development goals (or philosophies) behind each. Very large manufacturers with development teams that work relatively independently of each other can embrace goals that may even be mutually opposing. This can become dangerous when, for example, the differences affect the responsiveness of the front brake. For precisely this reason, the amounts of force needed to achieve a certain amount of deceleration can, in fact, be very different: one developer envisions a motorcycle that can be controlled with the barest minimum of force; another developer wants to build the safest possible motorcycle, with which even a panicky rider, doesn't immediately overbrake the front wheel. ∎

The experienced motorcyclist is as unaware of the innumerable specialized programs he has developed as the grandmother is of her still-functional bicycle-riding program. Without exception, these are *acquired* programs whose acquisition was, at some point, conscious, although the person may not have been consciously aware of all the smallest details. As an example, for the procedure "starting the motorcycle," learning to use the controls necessary to do so was certainly required during the acquisition of the program, but they did not become true programs until they no longer needed **conscious attention** and could run their course automatically.

Sometimes, however, one becomes distinctly aware of the existence of such programs, such as when they suddenly don't quite fit the situation any more and must be improved; that is, when some degree of correction is necessary. For example, the front brake has been adjusted and the point of actuation is now much earlier than it had been; or the friction zone of the clutch has changed; or pulling the clutch lever suddenly requires more or less effort.

It is surprising how quickly our adaptation of programs occurs. It is almost entirely complete when we are no longer aware of the change. It is also astounding how quickly a corrected program can be "re-corrected" when one swaps motorcycles.

We notice the phenomenon most acutely and find it most bothersome when, riding an unfamiliar motorcycle, suddenly "nothing feels right at all." Usually it is not just a new model, but a completely different category of bike. At first we feel highly uncomfortable but can tell that those programs are quickly adapting anew. Whether that motorcycle or that type of motorcycle will work for us in the future depends on how quickly and how completely this process of *program redevelopment* occurs.

When a program no longer fits precisely (that is, when the whole thing no longer feels familiar), then it becomes acutely clear that an action program is not just a series of motor commands that are followed in sequence, but rather that *continuous feedback* is occurring during the entire course of the action. The refinement of control, the precise corrections, and the most accurate possible alignment between the actual outcome and the desired outcome of each individual phase of the action are all dependent on feedback. A simple example is braking to a planned stop. It is not just a matter of a motor command to initiate braking; there is a *constant adjustment* of braking pressure, making constant corrections to bring the expected and received feedback into the closest possible alignment. Thus, aside from the "output" of a program, there is a simultaneous "input"—that is, along with the "motor" output of a program there is "sensory" input flowing in the opposite direction. These two aspects are closely intertwined, and this is why these types of action programs are described as "sensory-motor" programs. For this reason also, mastery of the sensory component—a sufficiently precise expectation, reception, and proper interpretation of feedback—requires as much training as mastery of the motor component. Practically speaking, practicing total high-speed braking while standing still at home in the garage might have some benefit, but it is still a very long way from being sufficient. It is just as important to practice the proper way to respond to large amounts of feedback as it is to practice the physical actions themselves. In general, the quality of an acquired action program is highly dependent upon the sophistication of the associated *sensory* feedback.

I mentioned above that man was largely free of the shackles of inborn programs. I used the modifier "largely" to point out that there are indeed a few of these inborn programs still at work, particularly in the behavior of infants. In the behavior of adults, they are certainly evident in many ways, although they are usually operating under a layer of acquired programs. Endlessly long programs that dictate an activity step by step over a considerable period of time—with steps and activities that are mandatory—are simply not present any more in humans, but individuals have certain **dispositions** that can make specific activities or behaviors easier. The recognition of inherent dispositions is important in understanding that man does not arrive in the world as a blank page (the so-called *tabula rasa* image). More important for our purposes are, however, the actual action programs that are inborn but really still exist only as short "program stubs" and are included as building blocks in other much more complex acquired programs.

A splendid example of a critical program stub in action is maintaining one's balance, which is required when dealing with **lean angles,** riding a single-track vehicle slowly enough that it does not have enough speed to achieve **stability,** or exploring the limits of the tires' stickiness, which is closely related to the lean angle.

Given man's special ability to balance, which he makes use of in many different activities, it's clear that he benefits from having a rather extreme length-to-width ratio in his physical dimensions, which does not occur naturally in any other creature. We don't notice this at all, since it's so familiar to us. But it was because of compelling circumstances in our evolutionary history that man now has an unbelievably slender, narrow, and tall physical build, even when compared to his closest relatives in

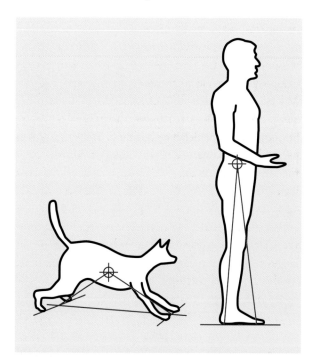

Figure 7. The four-legged beast has a large footprint and a low center of gravity, while the human has a very small footprint and a very high center of gravity.

🏍 Balancing act

Of all mammals, only chimpanzees and certain bears—both of which are somewhat adept, albeit only occasional, "bipeds"—can be taught, with professional training, to ride a bicycle, but they'll never progress in their skills beyond a rudimentary level. Their skills are not much better with other tricks that require balance. Man is far superior in this regard because he is required to balance literally every step of the way. Even when he's standing around, not doing anything, he is at the very least maintaining his balance by continuously making tiny postural adjustments.

Aside from mammals, advanced capabilities for maintaining balance can otherwise be found only in birds, which are equipped with a strikingly large cerebellum, the part of the brain responsible for spatial coordination. Except for humans, birds are the only animals that can keep their balance on the challenging slack wire, a loose version of the tightrope. Birds do this naturally; humans require lengthy training. However, birds can only do this perpendicular to the wire, in the same way that they sit perpendicularly on a branch or power line. Here, the human being is superior, because he can also do this lengthwise—but only once he has acquired programs for slack-wire walking.

The unicycle is particularly difficult to manage, because it additionally needs constant control and correction for balance around the transverse axis (fore and aft). There's hardly anyone who has managed to learn to ride a unicycle starting at a relatively advanced adult age—this fact offers insight into the extreme limit of acquirable **coordination.** ∎

the animal world. In addition, he has a center of mass that seems almost dangerously high compared to the minimal size of his footprint (Figure 7; Spiegel, 1988).

Thus, one could safely make the following statement: man is, as our earlier discussions have shown, not "built" to ride motorcycles, but at least he is "pre-adapted" for riding a two-wheeler. That is, he has been adapted in advance (by evolutionary changes) to his original habitat—most notably, starting to walk upright on two legs—and this **pre-adaptation** comes in very handy when he gets on a two-wheeler. Over the course of his evolution, man has had to develop intricate, genetically transmitted behavior programs which have made possible an ever more perfected two-legged existence, and which prepare him well for riding a motorcycle. The programs that give him the ability to balance appear as smaller components or building blocks integrated into the program for motorcycle riding. If man had not, over the past millions of years, already been dealing with the biomechanical challenges of an extremely high center of mass, combined with a very small footprint, neither bicycles nor motorcycles would exist in their current form.

Similar explanations apply to lean angle and tire stickiness. Owing to millions of years of experience walking on various surfaces, the available **static friction** (stiction) under his feet spontaneously leaps into his conscious attention and becomes clearly and directly evident. Problems arise only with certain surface conditions that don't occur in nature (for example, wet tiles or slick bathtubs) or that occur only rarely (such as ice).

Man can take the ancient building blocks of behavior affecting sensory and motor activities and incorporate them into the programs that he is acquiring today. In this way, once he has attained perfect command of a high-level program (such as riding a motorcycle), the motorcyclist can extend the so-called **evidence experience** all the way into the contact patch of the tires.

With regard to lean angle, there is another useful pre-adaptation, or ancient program stub, that can be used as a building block. As a fast runner, man is already fully able to handle lean angle *but only to about 20 degrees*. It is exactly the same lean angle that arises *everywhere* from fast locomotion, where relatively natural conditions exist with respect to stiction (that is, no knobbies, spikes, fixed track surfaces, etc. (see Figures 8–11). As soon as a person has more or less learned to ride a two-wheeler, he will immediately make use of the "naturally" available 20 degrees of lean angle, but he will not go beyond those 20 degrees. This has applied for millions of years to all fast runners—horses, dogs, ostriches. Beyond 20 degrees, on a natural surface, the danger of losing traction increases quickly.

In order to exceed the 20 degrees, particular technical conditions are not the only requirement. Another key requirement is a long period of continuous practice. This is the time that is needed to build up a new behavior-

Figures 8 through 11. The lean angle is part of our inherited repertoire—but only to about 20 degrees. Larger lean angles are only rarely encountered, because on natural surfaces the danger of losing traction increases quickly beyond 20 degrees.

controlling program that allows the pre-set limits (based on our genetic heritage) to be *exceeded*.

As programs with inborn and acquired parts gradually blend together, and as programs that are acquired in their entirety mature, **self-optimization** begins to occur. In many cases, a program improves simply through repetition and practice, without any external intervention. It gains fluidity; it becomes more efficient; the sensory-motor effort decreases; and it becomes more stable, less easily upset or disturbed. The action sequence requires less and less *conscious* attention, and the person practicing the action can begin to concentrate on specific details and refinements. Self-optimization leads to a constant increase in the degree of "automation" of the action. For activities related to the use of a device or tool, this leads to an ever higher level of **integration** between the user and the device.

However, during the maturation of a program, there are dead ends and "dry spells" in the process of self-optimization during which the "success dividends" stop paying, when, despite improvements, the person encounters a barrier that simply cannot be overcome. As an example of the classic dead end, often observed at the advent of a new technique, consider a gifted young high jumper of whom great things were expected, who was in the hands of the wrong trainer when the "Fosbury Flop" was emerging. He neglected to change over to the new technique at the right time because he was afraid that adopting a totally new method would diminish his performance for a time. He still made great progress with his special roll-style, until the potential of his method was exhausted; thereafter he stagnated at a level below that of the top high jumpers, among whom the new style came to be universally preferred.

A dry spell occurs when a technique improvement is the aim and success dividends don't occur for a long time, or even turn negative. If the person practicing "sticks to his guns," the dry spell ends with a sudden breakthrough. In both situations—dead ends and dry spells—an important role of the teacher, coach, or instructor is to encourage the practitioner to persist, self-optimization of programs notwithstanding.

In any case, whether programs are inborn or acquired, there are many complex human actions that could not be accomplished without "automating" the course of action.

SOME HISTORY

How it all began: Drais & Co.

Now is a good time to get a clear idea of the history of two-wheeled vehicles. The Grand Duke of Baden, Forest Superintendant Karl Freiherr Drais von Sauerbronn (1785–1851), had a much less lofty goal in mind when he created his steerable single-track vehicle, the ancestral father of the bicycle and the motorcycle. As the name *Laufmaschine,* "running machine," expresses, he was seeking relief in walking and running, and no more than that. The legs of the user were conceived as outriggers, so that he wouldn't tip over, and he was to move himself forward by alternating pushes with his legs. Even this was an extraordinary feat of inventiveness. Drais had cleverly broken with an ancient idea that had run firmly aground. Not only had he given up on a four-wheeler (to minimize rolling resistance), but—even better—he took the two remaining wheels, which had shared the same axis (running beside each other for more than 5000 years), and put them *in-line* with each other.

Not to diminish Drais' achievement, but his "real" invention didn't occur until the machine was ridden. Man's capacity to adapt in response to particular (as yet hidden) technical possibilities proved to be so great that within a very short time, riders could get substantially more out of the design than the designer had ever expected from it. In some ways, more was "delivered" than had been "ordered." Not even in his dreams had Drais ever thought of it originally, but in practice, the rider soon figured out that he could balance without constantly having to support himself from the sides. If he pushed off with enough power, or when he went downhill and the vehicle picked up speed, he could pull both legs in and maintain his balance with the help of steering if he was adept enough.

The Draisian running machine, or *Laufrad* (running bike)—or "Draisine," as it was called later—did not have to wait for the invention of pedals to become a *bicycle,* although the pedals were an enormous advance. The running bike actually became a *riding* bike much earlier: that is, when the user—if only for a short stretch—stopped running and instead balanced and rode! Until this occurred, it didn't make much sense to think about pedals anyway.

The Physics of Riding 1:
How the running bike became a riding bike

To understand what actually happened when the running bike became a riding bike and just how people spontaneously learned to balance, we can't go much further without discussing physics. I will try, without formulas and numbers, to make this as clear as possible without misrepresenting or omitting anything substantial. After a general summary of the physics involved, you will be better able to appreciate all the input a human has to regulate—without even knowing it!

To begin, let's first take this example of balancing and describe it from several different aspects.

When I described the Draisine, the running bike, I referred to riders maintaining their balance with the help of steering. In other words, the riders of Drais' invention learned that by using minimal movements around the *vertical* axis—by steering—they could influence the movements of the vehicle around its *longitudinal* axis. In other words, he learned that through small changes in

direction he could gain control of the lean angle. To understand this, we don't need to consider centrifugal, centripetal, or gyroscopic forces; a rider did nothing more than steer his vehicle back and forth under his body, with small deflections to the right or left of his actual path, in the same way that bicycle riders still do today. Especially when a rider is moving slowly, he follows a visibly serpentine path. Using turns of the handlebar, he ensures that an imaginary line connecting the two **contact patches** always runs nicely under his own center of mass. As long as he is able to do this, he won't fall over.

Incidentally, it doesn't matter whether he swings more or less widely or whether an individual curve turns out to be larger or smaller. The main maneuver by which he maintains his balance are the continual steering changes to the right and left, which themselves balance each other out. As long as both sides are affected equally, it's okay for a rider to overcompensate now and then, but he should never undercompensate.

Balancing a bicycle is a lot like balancing a broomstick on the palm of one's hand. Better still, let's imagine a shovel as in Figure 12. Upside-down it not only has a nice high center of mass but also a handle perpendicular to the shaft. Because of this, just as with a two-wheeler, to

Figure 12. The spade balances as long as its "footprint" is directly under the center of gravity. A higher center of gravity makes balancing easier.

balance it we only have to worry about the **lean angle** from side to side—the **roll angle,** in the terminology of the chassis engineer. The "footprint," whether for a shovel, a broomstick, or a bike, should remain directly under the center of mass to the greatest possible extent. The larger the deviation of the footprint from the center of mass, the more obvious it will be that the shovel is falling over, and as it falls, that same deviation will become larger. Therefore, corrections must occur in the direction of the center of mass. If the correction is too small, additional correction will be needed. If the correction is too large, a reverse correction will be needed. If one is very adept at balancing, he will move very little.

The broomstick example gives us a good basis for a discussion of riding corners. At this point, we can go no further without considering centripetal force, which plays a role in the sequence of tiny curves that keeps a bike upright while moving slowly in a straight line, but we don't yet need to consider gyroscopic forces. What does the hand have to do if one wants to take that balancing broomstick, at a decent walking tempo, around a right-hand corner? It starts by moving a little to the *left* so that the broomstick begins to lean toward the right and into the curve (Figures 13 and 14). This concept is often called (with good reason) "countersteering." Once the broomstick has just about reached the proper lean angle, the hand moves along the envisioned path of the curve so the broomstick does not fall any farther into the curve. As the hand moves around the curve, a steady state is achieved, with lean angle, speed, and corner radius in balance. The resultant force on the broomstick, which is based on the centripetal force and the force of gravity, is exerted on the hand through the footprint, or "contact patch," of the broomstick. In principle, it's the same as with balancing in a straight line, as described above. At times, the footprint needs to be moved to the inside, and then it needs to be moved a hair back to the outside. When this occurs, it influences the centripetal force, which grows larger or smaller as a result of these small movements.

If the lean angle of the broomstick is too large, either at some point in the corner or simply because the end of the curve has been reached, the contact patch must be brought back under the center of mass in order to stand the broomstick back up. There are two ways in which this can be accomplished: either the hand has to make a slightly tighter curve, or the curve radius can remain the same and the lean angle that is now too large can be de-

With a two-wheeler, the path taken by the contact patches corresponds to the tracks that would be seen on the road surface as two lines, very close together. The front wheel travels farther on the outside (dependent on wheelbase and the radius of the curve), while the rear wheel "cuts corners."

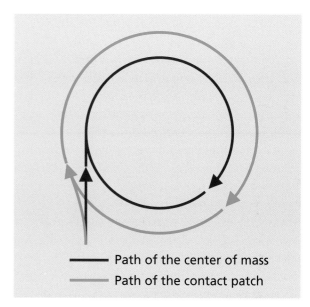

——— Path of the center of mass
——— Path of the contact patch

Figure 13. The center of gravity of a body moving along a circular path shifts toward the inside of the curve. For this reason, when riding a curve is initiated, the footprint must be pushed to the outside (see "steering impulse" in the glossary).

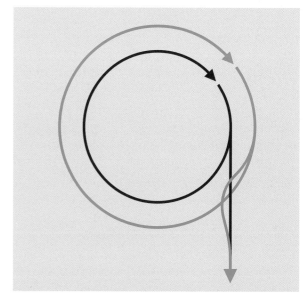

Figure 14. To end the curve, the radius must first be reduced so that the footprint can again be brought under the center of gravity.

creased through an increase in speed. This is just what the motorcycle rider does when rolling on the throttle in a corner.

Also, it should be noted that long broomsticks are much easier to balance than short ones, due to their higher center of gravity. This is why a light enduro with a high tank and high motor makes such a wonderful bike for darting around in traffic, and why it's unbeatable in slow riding exercises, even though the substantial weight shift under braking and acceleration can be bothersome.

The desirable high center of gravity is *one* of the reasons why it's easier during slow riding to stand on the pegs: at a walking pace, riding is primarily about balancing. In these situations, centrifugal forces (and especially gyroscopic forces) provide no additional help keeping the bike up.

Note that the term "manageability" can be understood in many diverse ways. As described above, a *high* center of gravity might result in easy manageability in slow riding, but much more often a motorcycle's manageability is attributed to a *low* center of gravity, which affords good handling through quick lean-angle changes in serpentine curves, thanks to a lower roll inertia.

The amazing foray into single-track

We know that with the foray into the brave new world of single-track vehicles, falls and crashes were numerous. In addition to users' lack of familiarity with two-wheelers, certain refinements based on the physics of these vehicles had not been considered at this early stage of design. For example, "trail" had not been implemented as we do today, but nonetheless—even with a vertical steering axis—it had *caster* (a form of trail) like a shopping-cart wheel. On top of that, the steering was light and there was no play in the steering-head bearing, so the design of these early bicycles was simply not optimal. Still, according to letters from the time, when they were successfully ridden, there was a sudden and incredible feeling of liberation from the Earth's gravity, and the rider felt free as a bird.

Was the penny-farthing really such a foolish idea?

Once people realized that they could balance on the two-wheeled "running machine" and use their legs merely as outriggers when starting and stopping, it was only natural to look for ways to keep their feet entirely off the ground and to propel the whole thing with pedals rather than by pushing off the ground with the feet. But it wasn't quite as simple as it seemed, because chains that would be delicate enough and move freely enough—such as the roller chains we have today—were not yet available. The only other option was to put the pedals directly onto the axle of one of the two wheels, and it clearly made the most sense to put them on the front wheel. But since transmission ratios were well understood by that time, it quickly became clear that bearable revolution speed could be attained only if the size of the drive wheel were substantially increased. It was made as large as possible, and the penny-farthing was born (Figure 15). However, with the relationship between the road and the number of rotations of the pedals, the best people could do was a gear ratio similar to the lowest gear of a normal bicycle today. The limit was dictated by the leg-length of the rider. Bicycle makers advertised "bicycles to fit your legs," and this is the only reason why women's penny-farthings were much lower (although that seems like more than enough risk with an ankle-length skirt).

The fact that the low, single-track vehicle came first, followed briefly by the penny-farthing, and then came to dominate once again (after the development of the chain drive), brought some writers to view the penny-farthing as an aberration. But the penny-farthing, as we can see, was not so misguided after all, growing as it did out of technical necessities. It was with good reason that special "velodromes" were set up all over the place: the challenge

Figure 15. The penny-farthing—today it appears rather whimsical, but the oversized front wheel was really not all that silly!

of learning to ride the penny-farthing was especially difficult and considerably more dangerous than the later "safety bicycle."

It was not until the drive chain was developed that a return to this safer model became possible; however, once that happened, a highly perfected vehicle quickly evolved, which later could be improved only in tiny details. It possessed a level of efficiency unsurpassed, even today, in either nature or technology.

MAN-MACHINE SYSTEMS

The "spontaneously" acquired ability to ride a bicycle

We now know what complicated steering moves are required to maintain balance, to initiate a curve, to get through the curve onto a desired path, and then end the curve at a planned point, but the larger mystery is still unresolved. That is, how did a rider on the "running bike," without any instruction and with no previous knowledge, manage to figure it all out!

It was certainly not through observation, thought and consideration, or planning (such as, "when A and B happen, then I have to do X and Y"). As with every child who learns to ride by himself today, the early rider perceived feedback from the vehicle (some more helpful than others) after minimal and coincidental steering inputs. Although he was not consciously aware of either the individual steering inputs or the feedback, he was evidently able to incorporate the complicated relationship between input and response into a new **action program.**

The development and fine-tuning of action programs

The learning process most certainly didn't happen overnight. On his first ride, his alternating push-offs would have been made such that he had almost uninterrupted contact with the ground, because one or the other foot was always pushing off. At most, for a brief moment, when switching from right to left, contact with the ground would be interrupted. The bike would have swayed noticeably from side to side, from one foot of the rider to his other foot. However, with a little more practice, the interruptions in ground contact became longer, the swaying was reduced, and the pushes off the ground became more confident. If the rider pushed powerfully enough with one foot, as the vehicle gradually leaned toward the other side, he could enjoy a free ride for a few moments until it was time to push off again with the other foot. During this riding, he would be able to feel the influence of the steering,

with which the leaning to the other side could be slowed and even stopped for a short time. But even though this was "practice," the rider would not have noticed or sought to understand the details of it.

It would not have been long, however, before the rider attempted to lift both legs up at the same time and leave it up to the art of steering to decide which foot would make the next push off the ground. With this, the new action program was complete. It was not a very refined program, but it was good enough. If there were deviations from the expected state of the vehicle (lean angle, speed, direction), the rider could elicit a very specific reaction to correct the actual state and return it to the nominally ideal state through a continual, moment-by-moment comparison of the two, without any conscious effort, that is, "automatically."

Two subsystems meld into a new system

When a series of actions occurs automatically, it always means that there is a program behind it, either inborn or acquired. With the help of the program, linkages are formed between the parts that create a "new" whole. This is exactly what man managed to do with the two-wheeler: it wasn't just the sum of man plus bicycle, but rather a new, functionally complete creation, a "new unit," or "man-machine system," into which he integrates himself as a subsystem. Man succeeded in this **integration** thanks to his ability to adapt (his formability and plasticity), as evidenced by the fact that a stimulus—in this case a particular movement of the two-wheeler—did not trigger some fixed program but instead led to the emergence of a new program that could continually be perfected, and within a very short period of time. (See the sidebar "Greater than the sum of the parts.")

Drais' "running machine" was still a relatively simple man-machine system, but the basic principle of balance must have been fully available to those early riders. The way in which people can spontaneously make use of this principle borders on the miraculous. The man-machine system that exists in motorcycle riding today is just vastly more complex. The sophisticated integration between the two subsystems is so extensive that the two cannot easily be separated. The **interface** between the two subsystems is not simply the point at which the seat of the pants meets the seat of the bike.

The creation of a superior new system out of two subsystems can occur more easily and more perfectly the more each subsystem has been optimized and adapted for the other. During Drais' time, the level of adaptation of the machines to humans was still extremely minimal, and even today it's still far from perfect. This adaptation is chiefly the task of the designer, but the user can also contribute by adjusting the machine to his needs as, for example, when he pulls out wrenches to adjust the position of the handlebar, footrests, and all the levers to be more suitable. Unfortunately, he soon exhausts this strategy, and then his only option is the opposite: to adapt the man (himself) to the machine.

In a general consideration of man-machine relationships, quite apart from the specific case of motorcycle plus rider, there is plenty of evidence that adaptation of human beings to machines has flourished more than adaptation of machines to human beings. The questions of mutual adaptation lead deep into the complex of problems surrounding the interface between the two. These issues are discussed further in a later section on the use of tools (see p. 88).

The man-machine system: a complicated matrix-patrix relationship

The term **"interface,"** especially as it is commonly used in data processing, refers to the junction (or region of contact) between two units that are or could be connected to one another. By contrast, the term **"matrix-patrix relationship"** connotes an intimate interaction and mutual assimilation or adaptation between two subsystems.

The profile of a subsystem can be represented as a "matrix" describing whatever dimensions (variables) the subsystem offers, along with the range of possible values those dimensions can take. The profile of a partner system—a "patrix"—should complement the matrix profile as cleanly and completely as possible. The more sophisticated each of these profiles is, the more multifaceted the mutually offered and accepted dimensions, and the more completely enmeshed the "matrix" and "patrix" are, the tighter the integration of the system will be. As the subsystems become more and more tightly integrated, their individual characteristics dissolve into the jointly created new system, and they exhibit increasingly the characteristics of the new system.

To put this concept into more concrete form for a motorcycle subsystem and a rider subsystem, let's consider a clutch lever and the amount of effort it requires. Even for this very simple detail, the adaptation processes can be quite varied.

⬤ Greater than the sum of the parts

"Man-machine system" is not a very "pretty" concept, even though it is in widespread use in anthropotechnology. The term arose at a time when it hadn't yet been adequately recognized that the "machine" portion of the man-machine system didn't have to be a machine at all. The same problem exists for the concept "man-machine interface," a formulation that is not improved when transformed, as it frequently is these days, into "man-*system* interface" (or "man-*system* relationship," etc.), because then the *man* component remains outside of the *system*, despite the fact that he, along with this other (sub-) system, constitutes a *super-ordinate* new system.

The concept of the man-machine system is most commonly used to express that it is not just an aggregation of the characteristics that each part brings to the new whole, but rather that the combined unit shows new system characteristics that are not present in either subsystem alone. This is the case with almost all tools, particularly the kinds of machines that require a person's use of only minimal exertion to control and regulate them.

The best example is the classic system of horse and rider, which easily fulfills all conditions of a super-ordinate system that subsumes its two subsystems. It is not only an ancient system, but its special nature has long been recognized.

In any case, once one has recognized that the concept of man-machine system goes far beyond what is expressed with the word "machine," he will easily find additional examples. Entirely "un-machine-like" devices, such as the cello, are united with a human being to form new systems with the highest degree of **integration.** Even the complex interconnection of four rowers to their boat or of a conductor to his orchestra can be described in this way.

Every competitive rower in an eight who has ever had the sudden feeling, *"Now* she's really running" and finds out later that the other rowers had that same feeling at the same time (even though none of them could really say exactly what this **evidence experience** was based upon), knows immediately what is meant by concepts such as assimilation, fine intermeshing, and integration. ∎

~~ Hand training

The hand gripper is a good training instrument for motor-cycling (see Figure M16). On a long ride, even a light clutch can become fatiguing after a few hundred squeezes, especially in the spring when your hand may be weak from disuse. In addition, with a lot of motorcycles, the clutch may become incredibly stiff after a long ride in the rain.

Figure M16. Use of hand-grip strengtheners such as these provides good exercise for untrained hands.

The force level required by a hand gripper should be between 180 and 200 Newtons (which equals about 40 to 45 pounds). It's enough to practice just once a day, perhaps while you're on the phone, or regularly during routine activities such as shaving or brushing your teeth—whenever your hand is free. Squeeze the hand gripper together and hold it for six or seven seconds, then release it. Repeat the squeezing and releasing a few times, then shake your hand out well.

The amount of effort required by an average clutch might be about 70 Newtons (about 16 pounds), but increases a bit when it is engaged slowly, because during this slower pull, additional breakaway torque is required. For this reason, if you start to feel pain in your clutch hand, don't make the mistake of squeezing the clutch more slowly to protect your hand. ∎

For example, in preparing a new line of a particular motorcycle in which the clutch has previously required too much hand effort, the mechanism that transfers power from the lever on the handlebar to the disengagement lever on the transmission housing would have to be re-engineered. This change would be an adaptation on the side of the machine and would lead to a lasting improvement in the integration of both subsystems.

On the machine side, though, design and engineering changes aren't all that can be done. Maintenance measures—for example, cleaning and regreasing the clutch cable—can also be effective. This also leads to an improvement in adaptation of the two subsystems; however, it is not a lasting improvement, but rather one that gradually deteriorates.

The gradual accustomization of the rider to relatively stiff levers would be an improvement in **adaptation** on the human side, and one that is usually lasting. Systematic training of particular muscle groups—for example, with a hand gripper to increase hand grip strength—would also be a human adaptation, and a lasting one. Impending tendonitis, on the other hand, would represent a *deterioration* of the human side of adaptation, which would hopefully disappear after an adequate rest and recovery period. All of these are adaptation processes of very different sorts; the last is actually a negative one.

Particularly interesting is the type of adaptation described above as "gradual accustomization," which consists of a progressive leveling out of deficiencies. If we notice that the clutch lever feels stiff, it means that, within some **action program,** an "expected norm" has developed. Only then is it possible to have a comparison between the actual and expected values, and only then is it possible to experience a difference that manifests itself as a vexing or disturbing deviation. This norm, however, is influenced by continued operation of the clutch. If we operate the clutch reasonably often (but not constantly to the point of fatigue), the norm will gradually align itself with new conditions encountered, increasing in value, and the deviation (stiffness) will no longer be noticed. But if subsequent operation of the clutch lever corresponds to the value of our earlier norm, we experience the operation as "wonderfully easy and light."

One could reasonably suggest that without this process by which deficiencies are gradually accommodated, human life would be virtually unbearable. This kind of adaptation is most striking when changes in a machine sneak up on us very gradually, such that we are conscious neither of the changes nor of our own continual adjustment. When there's an opportunity for comparison, however—perhaps when we get a chance to swap our own bike with a friend's of the same type—we realize instantly how much has actually changed during this time in both man and machine. Not only do we then notice all possible flaws in our own bike, but we also notice numerous other irritating quirks, which are often hard to describe or put into words. What we're experiencing are sudden disruptions in the matrix-patrix relationship—gaps and "pressure points" in the integration of the subsystems. The more we have bonded with the bike and the more perfectly we have mastered it, the more complicated is the integration of man with machine—that is, the more multifaceted and intricate is the interaction between the two subsystems.

The spontaneous and unnoticed adaptation to *disturbances* is especially evident in off-road riding, where it's rather common for a tipover or crash to result in a bent handlebar. The rider who just keeps on riding may complain about the crooked handlebar but won't notice in the least how much he's already adapted to the new situation until the handlebar is straightened or replaced or he gets on a different bike. Then, although he can see that everything is straight, he'll insist that "the handlebar almost seems bent somehow," and the whole bike "just feels a bit crooked," and it will take a while before everything really feels straightened out.

The human ability to adapt to deficiencies is simply a special example of the continual refinement of adaptation. In more technical terms, it is the continual **self-optimization** of certain action programs. (See also the discussion of interface displacement, p. 88).

INBORN PROGRAMS

Program acquisition without insight

With programs that arise spontaneously (inborn **programs**), it cannot be emphasized enough that this occurs not only without conscious effort but also without either rational thought or insight into the factual connections. The best example of this is how some children learn to ride a bicycle without any input from others. Earlier discussion suggested that the cerebrum could be viewed as an "aftermarket accessory." As with every such addition, it carries new possibilities, but the addition of the cerebrum certainly does not make the original structure or any parts of it superfluous.

There are also many human functions, even very sophisticated ones, that are clearly controlled by biological processes entirely outside of our intellect. It can be difficult to "wrap" our minds around this, because we are aware of so little of it, in contrast to everything that we consciously control and manage. Another hindrance to grasping this is that we usually regard with reserve, or even with mistrust, actions that we don't manage consciously.

Therefore, it seems that it can't possibly be true that balancing on a bike occurs with any appreciable participation of one's consciousness and intellect; otherwise, knowledge would be required—at least a basic knowledge of how to achieve some nominal condition, and by what means—and it is precisely this knowledge that is not present. We "know" this because the average motorcycle rider, as described above, knows next to nothing about the physics of riding. For example, if asked how far he must turn the handlebars to steer the motorcycle, he almost always overestimates (often extremely) the magnitude of his **steering input.** (See sidebar, next page.)

The passionate motorcyclist may already know a little something about very small steering movements; he may even know something about **slip angle** and the negative steering input that results from it. He may have heard that, as speed increases and the curve radius remains the same, the necessary steering input becomes smaller, and for some speed—depending on the radius—it becomes a negative input, becoming more negative with increasing speed. What even the passionate motorcyclist does not know is *when* he's actually cornering with negative steering or cornering with positive steering; there's no way he could know, because he doesn't notice any of this at all.

Flawless actions without conscious "how-to" knowledge

Because the motorcyclist is not conscious of steering angle, no matter how much he tries, we can say that he doesn't know *and does not need to know* when (or why) he's using a negative steering input nor that there's even such a thing as negative steering input. And he'll be better off, at least while this is happening, if he doesn't think about it too much. There are entirely separate and far more reliable functions of his person at work. We can illustrate vividly, with an everyday activity such as drinking coffee as an example, the complicated behavior patterns that occur without any "how-to" knowledge:

I'm thinking of drinking coffee, which many do every morning. No matter how sleepy we might still be, the act of drinking from a cup (which we had to learn, with some difficulty, way back when) works just fine. Although drinking from a cup is quite a simple matter, no one really "knows" how it's done—something that will become obvious if one is asked to describe the process. The person will either soon get stuck, or his description will remain completely superficial. Then one must follow up with ever more precise questions. It might go

The immovable handlebar

These are the actual movements of a motorcycle handlebar:

If we're just rolling comfortably along on a country road that meanders a bit but wouldn't be described as twisty, the approximate movement of the handlebar is between 0.5 and 0.8 degrees. In a car, one would have to turn the steering wheel about 45 degrees to follow the same curves! On the highway, a motorcycle handlebar rarely moves more than 0.2 degrees. But at highway speeds, even this small movement results in a surprisingly tight curve; the radius would be under 500 meters, a dimension that today's highway planners prefer to avoid. If at all possible, they opt for a radius of at least 1000 meters. A movement of 0.2 degrees for a motorcycle means the change in direction of the front wheel is practically invisible, and the movement at the ends of the handlebars, depending on bar width, is barely half a millimeter.

But take a corner that we all know well: a modern interstate cloverleaf. It normally has a radius of 50 meters, measured at the middle of the lane. This is a pretty tight curve, but the the amount of steering required at moderate speeds is still just under two degrees: about 10 millimeters of movement at the ends of the handlebar, and much less at higher speeds.

If handlebar movement should ever come to five degrees or more—one or two thumb-widths at the bar ends—this would have to be a hairpin corner on a twisty road. The remaining 35 degrees of steering typically available are used only for very tight maneuvers, usually at a walking pace and most often while parking or in the garage. So it is hardly surprising that race bikes, where there's not much room between the clip-ons and the tank, are limited to 20 degrees of steering or even less, and no one gives it a second thought. The limited movement of race-bike handlebars means that **kickback** that can occur under certain suspension conditions is constrained. ■

something like this: "So tell me again, how did it work, drinking from a cup this morning?"—"Well, the coffee has to be swallowed."—"Well obviously," one might continue, "but how does the coffee get into your mouth?" A frequent answer: "It gets poured in," which is certainly wrong. For this to work, one would have to tilt his head back pretty far. So maybe the next answer would be: "The coffee has to be sucked in." Our interviewee means that the coffee would have to be lifted by negative pressure, as in a vacuum. Next question: "So how does the sucking work? How is the negative pressure created?" A frequent and wrong answer: "With air." He means to say, by pulling air in. This can work but only for a very specific type of coffee-drinking, namely slurping.

The correct answer would have to be: "The coffee is lifted by means of an increase of the volume within the mouth, which causes the liquid level in the cup to rise higher than the small opening in the mouth (watch this sometime in a mirror), and this increase in volume happens mainly as a result of a slight drawing back of the tongue, and also, when one is drinking quickly, through a simultaneous lowering of the chin. It's only the very last little sip that's poured into the mouth."

So why can't we be serious about making these kinds of observations? Simply because, even though they may all be true, this pedantic precision of detail (which could be expanded considerably) doesn't contribute in the slightest to the action or practice of drinking coffee. This adds more evidence for what we've been talking about all along: that man, this initially unprogrammed regulator, manages to balance on Drais' machine and even on a motorcycle without comprehension and without knowledge of precisely how it's done. (For more about the many cultural developments that occur without insight, see von Hayek 1983.)

Riding a motorcycle is a completely amazing achievement. This can be seen most clearly when a person rides through a very twisty stretch, with continuous, fine **coordination** of muscle movements, continually changing lean angles and speeds, with nearly invisible movements of the handlebars and even negative steering inputs, and with all the other actions and reactions about which one does not necessarily have to *know* anything in order to perform them correctly. It is obviously the work of something other than conscious thought or action.

We should recall once again that it's not only direction that is determined by steering inputs, but also, before cornering really starts, setting the lean angle (Figure 17), which is actually the first step in cornering. This process has nothing to do with "putting oneself into the corner," "shifting one's body weight," or "pressing with the thighs," as one often hears!

The reason for these unfounded descriptions of one's own behavior lies in the fact that, when we ride through corners, the act of *leaning* with our bodies (that is, the active shifting of body weight), is the dominant experience we are aware of. In this regard, these *subjective* descriptions are absolutely correct, described precisely as they are experienced by the rider. This kind of description does not acknowledge the unnoticed movements of the handlebars and minimal steering inputs that are required by the physics of riding (compare sidebar, p. 44). Some riders press the outside knee and thigh more or less firmly into the tank in the direction of the inside of the turn. Naturally, this influences the lean angle, but not because the knee pushes the motorcycle into the lean. Rather, this is primarily because the rider actually braces himself with his hands on the bars, thereby initiating the necessary **steering moment.**

This feeling of leaning the motorcycle with one's body is so universal that one constantly finds motorcyclists who cannot be convinced that they are actually initiating the lean by shifting weight. This perception is related to the fact that experienced riders, whose **action programs** are characterized by a high level of **integration** (that is, they don't know exactly how they carry out a particular action and no longer perceive a sharp differentiation of where the rider ends and the machine begins (see discussion of interface displacement, p. 88). (This, by the way, is certainly a part of the fascination of motorcycles.) Thus, it becomes true that in the overall, super-ordinate *unity* of the man-machine system into which the rider dissolves, he does actually initiate the lean into the corner but he is not aware of this.

The less a person knows about physics, and the less authoritative the physics are for him, the more convinced he will be that handlebars contribute little to directional control. At this point, only a practical experiment can help, so for extreme skeptics, I have a motorcycle with a throttle that can be locked so that the desired speed is maintained even after the bars are let go. The candidate is invited to ride it with no hands on the bars in a deserted parking lot—a very large one, but not large enough, as soon becomes evident. It is indeed possible to ride with hands on knees or even pressing on the tank, but cornering, in the sense of authoritative change of direction, is possible only with gigantic radii and not the slightest degree of precision. When the edge of the parking lot gets too close, if not before then, the rider will seek salvation in the handlebars, and he'll see—gratefully—what tight, precisely controlled corners he can achieve with their help.

Once the correct lean angle is achieved, the curve achieves a static or stable condition, when gravitational forces and inertial forces are in balance, no roll movement is produced, and the existing lean angle remains

Figure 17. If cornering were really a matter of shifting one's weight, then an enclosed motorcycle such as the Ecomobile would be practically unrideable (Ecomobile from Peraves, Winterthur, Switzerland).

The usefulness of handlebars

Otl Aicher, in his controversial but nevertheless incisive book, *Critique of the Automobile* (1984), wrote a few wonderful sentences about riding motorcycles. In one passage (p. 59) he states: "From this standpoint there is hardly anything as pleasant as riding a motorcycle. One is constantly in motion himself, leaning into this curve and then that, and *can determine the direction of the machine by shifting his body weight.* The road comes to the rider like a flowing ribbon, and forests and hills and fields and trees surround the rider with a continually changing rolling motion." (Emphasis added by the author.)

This is a very concrete description of a phenomenon quite familiar to motorcyclists, but how is it that Aicher (who was well versed in motorcycling) describes the shifting of one's body weight—a technique that doesn't actually exist as such? He's not alone. To use another example, a renowned motorcycle tester had excited praise for a 1000cc bike: "It handles steering corrections and lean angle changes effortlessly. The handlebars are *only there as something to hang onto,* because lean angles can be achieved *simply through slight shifts in one's upper body weight.*" (Emphasis added by the author.) ∎

unchanged. This condition can be brought about through minimal additional steering input or by accelerating a bit to stabilize the bike, or by doing both together with the finest coordination. The desired curve radius can be achieved only when everything is in perfect balance.

The Physics of Riding 2: Motorcycles and children's scooters, the "skibob" and the "velogemel"

In our earlier discussion about the physics of riding (p. 37), we initially considered the stability of a single-track vehicle moving slowly, but when the discussion turned to stabilizing the bike by accelerating in the curve, we addressed the peculiarities of the motorcycle, which is the topic of this section.

To recap, we discussed two ways to reduce the lean angle (for example, at the end of a corner): either by steering or by giving it gas to increase the speed. A capable rider uses the throttle not only for corrections in the lean angle but also much more generally for stabilization. This is referred to as **"stabilizing throttle."** After the rider initiates a corner and achieves proper lean angle, he stabilizes his lean with throttle input; the handlebars can remain in their original position as he takes the corner. This is why racers usually place such high demands on throttle cables: the twist grip should have essentially no play so that riders can feel precisely when the throttles are opening. To achieve optimum control, they adjust gas input with razor-sharp precision at exactly the right moment and then modulate it minutely.

The initiation of a turn, however, is actually a bit more complicated than the physics of riding previously described, but it's only more complicated for the observer, not for the rider, who is hardly aware that he's performing finely tuned actions. First, one cannot overlook the fact that there is a constant stream of disturbances that act on the vehicle. Most are external, but some are caused by the rider, for example, if he overcorrects (p. 37). These disturbances do not upset the bike as long as they are absorbed by the inherent stability of the vehicle (here's where gyroscopic forces enter the picture) or cancel each other out. But the rest are the responsibility of the rider, and these disturbances are reduced as the motorcycle goes faster.

Unless the rider chooses to make a sudden change in direction of the sort needed in street traffic (in a swerve to avoid a surprise obstacle) or in races (in chicanes), he should endeavor not to add steering inputs to oppose the constant stream of normal road disturbances. To achieve a desired lean angle, all the rider has to do is take the constant stream of road disturbances and suppress only those that are in opposition to the desired lean angle. All that is required is a barely noticeable pressure on the inside grip. The pressure isn't enough to move the handlebar, but instead suppresses the minimal movement the handlebar is already making on that one side. Viewed in terms of physics, the rider "leans on" a gyroscope (the

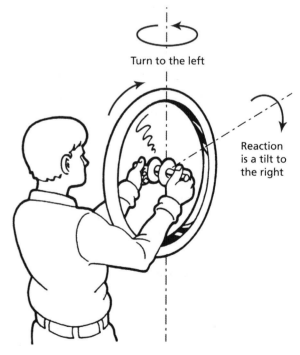

Figure 18. A motorcycle wheel behaves like a gyroscope. As you steer toward the left, gyroscopic forces cause the motorcycle to tilt (lean) to the right and turn to the right, tending to cancel the steering input. This effect gives motorcycles great stability when they are moving.

The proof is in the arm muscles

The Ecomobile (new edition called the "Monotracer"; termed "cabin motorcycle" for official registration purposes in some places) is not the only concrete proof that a motorcycle is steered with the handlebars and not with shifting body weight. Otherwise it would be impossible to explain why, after a half-day's ride in a twisty area on a stubborn, corner-phobic "beast" that seems to only want to go straight, the rider has sore muscles in his arms, shoulders, and upper back. ■

Figure 19. The Skibob (basically a scooter on skis) shows that the significance of gyroscopic forces is often overstated.

front wheel), and exerts a force on it (by way of the handlebar). There is no visible movement of the handlebar, but the force is enough to get a response from that gyroscope with a subtle "precession movement," and the motorcycle leans over.

So, how importance are gyroscopic forces? They are certainly significant, but they are nonetheless often overestimated. For example, mention of these forces is always popping up in various explanations, with claims that it's thanks to the gyroscopic forces of a spinning wheel that riding single-track vehicles is possible or that a motorcycle (as opposed to a car) has "countersteering" characteristics because of its gyroscopic forces. These notions are simply wrong, at least if they're considered absolute and without exception. However, the *principle* of countersteering shows us why it is necessary to achieve the requisite lean angle before a corner. The path—or more precisely the contact line—must be moved via a steering impulse toward the outside of the upcoming curve (page 38).

Up to this point we have not only bee how single-track vehicles can remain stable without gyroscopic forces, we were even able to adequately explain countersteering without them—using the example of a broomstick, no less! Other helpful, practical examples of this exist. One must simply look around. There are, in fact, single-track vehicles *without wheels!* Could one of the gyroscopic-force proponents out there explain to me how a person on a skibob (Figure 19) can ride straight or in curves, manage lean angles of all sorts, carve slaloms,

The usefulness of throttles

As it requires substantial mechanical complexity to manufacture a throttle without play, such throttle action is likely to be found only in unaffordable exotic motorcycles. Ordinarily, service and repair shops are happy to leave some play in the throttle, with the idea that otherwise, when the handlebars are turned to lock, the idle speed would increase. Then when entering a corner, the motorcycle would suddenly begin to pull, or at least the motor would not be able to help as much with deceleration. To check this explanation, one should test for himself sometime, with all the play adjusted out of the throttle, how much the bars have to be turned before something noticeable happens with the rpm. Then, remember from our earlier discussion how small the steering inputs actually are for cornering!

Still, one can make the best of even a large amount of play in the throttle by adopting the following habit: every time you close the throttle, especially before or in a corner, immediately go back to a "waiting position" by turning the grip back away from the throttle stop and through the play to the point at which you feel resistance. The gas is thus "prepared" but not yet applied. Then when it is needed—for example, for cornering stabilization—one instantly has at his disposal the desired degree of power which can be applied very precisely at the exact point in time and with the exact modulation.

The technique of stabilization with the throttle (**stabilizing throttle**) reaches the height of perfection in some Alps riders, who can ride through even tight hairpins remarkably fluidly, even on wobbly supersport bikes. Among riders who have not yet received higher "consecration" from the Alpine "lords," such hairpin-corner turns often take a somewhat angular or even shaky course, because of the slow speeds involved. The experts, however, keep their rear brake lightly engaged through the entire corner. This slight drag is balanced with a little bit of throttle. With fine control applied by throttle and brake actions, the steering input precisely follows the **movement plan** and thus remains almost unchanged. If the lean angle needs to be corrected a little bit, this can be adjusted with the throttle—the handlebars remain still and calm. Reducing the amount of gas causes the bike to lean more; increasing the amount of gas causes it to stand up more.

Once one has practiced this a few times, riding in a circle in an empty parking lot, the result will be beautifully round and fluid corners. ∎

etc.? And how about the razor scooter? With the minimal rotating mass of its tiny wheels, where would sufficient gyroscopic forces come from?

One may see the skibob as not the most appropriate example here, because at least in normal cases, a skibob rider supports himself with short skis on his feet. The two wide, in-line runners of the skibob also rarely track exactly together, because it can (and actually should) **drift** considerably, with lean angles that people riding two-wheelers only dream about. But there is something else called the *velogemel* ("bicycle sled"), which is very similar to, and much older than, the skibob. The locals of Grindelwald, Switzerland, use it not so much for sport but rather in everyday transport, on downhill paths with firmly packed snow (Figure 20). It has relatively short and almost skate-like (narrow and sharp-edged) runners. The rider's feet are lifted, and he meets the challenge of riding without help from his legs for support, forming a precise track without noticeable drifting. When agile young people in town ride these down the narrow, icy paths, they can reach breathtaking speeds.

So what is it that gyroscopic forces actually do on a motorcycle? Two things:

First, they ensure that as wheel speed increases, it becomes less and less easy to push the wheels out of their rotational plane. That is the (speed-dependent) stability advantage that all rotating bodies possess because of the so-called "angular momentum"; its effects are easy to see in a flying frisbee. The motorcyclist can feel this inertia in helpful and not-so-helpful ways. The skibob, more so the velogemel with its exact tracking, and also the razor scooter, all become increasingly unpleasant and frightening as speed increases. On these devices, one can feel very clearly that he won't be able to manage the ever finer steering inputs that are required for balance at higher speeds, at least not with the required precision. By contrast, motorcycle stability *increases* with speed. At high speeds on a motorcycle, it's almost as if someone else were holding the handlebars steady with Herculean strength. This feeling quickly becomes disagreeable, though, if we are forced to make a sudden change in direction; that same Hercules is still there, and he's hanging on relentlessly. It's true that a sportscar at its highest speed (over 250 kph or so) is also not easily brought into a swerve—it becomes a "prisoner of speed." However, this is much more evident with a fast motorcycle: it is not only imprisoned by its speed but is also *shackled* by it.

Figure 20. The Grindelwalder Velogemel (Grindelwald is an alpine village in central Switzerland.)

Second, gyroscopic forces provoke very strange movements. The basic idea is easy to demonstrate with a bicycle that's standing still, although the movements that a standing bicycle shows don't result from gyroscopic forces. If I put my hand on the seat of the bicycle and push it over to lean a little to one side, say to the right, then the handlebar also turns to the right because the front wheel drops to the right. If the amount of lean is slight, the turn at the wheel and handlebar are slight, but if I lean it more, then the results at the wheel and handlebar are also greater. Gyroscopic forces create exactly this effect from the so-called "gyroscopic precession" that occurs in a front wheel that is spinning fast enough. Every disturbance around the longitudinal (lean) axis, even the slightest hint of a fall to one side, will be answered with an equivalent deflection of the handlebar to steer toward the same side—in other words, with a curve. As a result of leaning, the vehicle's center of mass falls toward the inside of this curve, but because the steering moves the contact patch in the same direction, the vehicle stands itself back up.

The gyroscopic movements are responsible (more significantly in TV detective shows, alas, than in reality) when a motorcycle with a locked throttle continues to ride along, even after its rider has climbed into an airplane or fallen off. This, in fact, is something that can be ascribed only to gyroscopic forces. It would not work with the velogemel.

WHAT DO WE TRUST?

Mind or gut: is that the question?

Before we move to the second part of the book and consider more fully the *inborn* aspect of ourselves and its capabilities, we should clear up a potential misunderstanding that has two manifestations, each of which can seriously interfere with our comprehension of the complete man-machine system. The danger arises from our tendency to trust one's mind or one's gut more fully and to ignore the other.

The "believing" reader—for example, a prospective elite athlete in a training camp—might assume that all this theory, especially the physics with which he's being "tortured," really isn't worth much in practice and might sometimes even be a hindrance; one should just be able to "sense" things and act based on "gut feelings."

On the other hand, the critical reader—for example, a knowledgeable trainer—might wonder if I actually expect him to believe that theory (the rational explanation of a course of action; the analysis of the components of the action; the dissection of an action, possibly with some corrections of the parts, followed by reassembly to a whole) is "for the birds." All of his training experience tells him that this kind of analysis is useful.

The power of insight . . . and its uselessness

By no means do I want to discount the value of rational analysis. I have faith in the power of insight, especially as it is used to optimize an action. It is no accident that the very best practitioners (at anything) almost always show interest in theoretical backgrounds. A top sailor knows a lot about aerodynamics; those in top-tier motorsports have the capability to drive or ride almost with an engineer's sense during the fine-tuning of their vehicle; a world-class glider pilot can fly when necessary like a test pilot guided by the mutual dependence of certain data points. The list could go on, well beyond the realm of sports.

Still, when a person is learning a complex skill, theoretical analysis is of little help. At the moment in which an action is carried out, the knowledge of *why* is simply unnecessary. In the learning phase, a few brief and possibly greatly simplified highlights of key ideas are often more useful than theories.

Moreover, when a person carries out a particular action, even after it has long since been mastered, conscious attention to the process is more likely to be a hindrance. "You don't get far with thinking," Franz Klammer once said of rational involvement in an action. In fact, in recent years, whenever I've had a moment of panic on the motorcycle, it has often been because I wanted to see, by self-observation, how, exactly, something mysterious and almost invisible actually occurs. My concentration on a single action, as strange as it may sound, was not only an incredible *distraction,* but there was also the constant danger that reason, by its very nature, would meddle in the control of the process, even though it was only supposed to be observing it. We'll return to this issue later and become keenly aware of self-observation as a special problem in practicing and training.

PART 2
Mind and Gut

THE WORKINGS OF THE BRAIN

The brain, a rather strangely constructed organ

Let's start by taking another look at the brain and its parts. After this, we'll leave the examination of physical aspects aside and make do with a much simpler description.

The brain is quite a strange organ. It is the *only* organ that has arrived at its present form in a way that is completely different from all other organs. The other organs, over the course of their evolution, have been revised or reshaped, enlarged or made smaller, and have changed in function to greater or lesser degrees. For example, fins became forelegs, forelegs became wings, or gills became lungs. But the brain has used a completely different solution to the problem of further development and growth: one might say that an *ad hoc* addition was undertaken (or even that an "aftermarket accessory" has been added).

This was necessary because of the tremendous speed of the brain's evolution, especially in its later stages. In just 2 million years, the volume of the human brain doubled from 700 to the 1400 cubic centimeters of today. Using the time scale of evolutionary history, this is an almost explosive growth.

Let's consider a popular, if somewhat overly succinct, model: first there was the truly ancient brain, the brain stem, which, by far, has changed the least over the course of evolution compared with the new parts of the brain. Then came a second structure, the limbic system (sometimes equated, not quite correctly, with the interbrain or thalamencephalon). To top it off, at the "last minute" of brain evolution, a mighty "thinking cap" was added: the cerebrum. In humans, it is enormous, compared to the older parts of the brain, and quite literally covers them like a cap.

The newer parts of the brain did not *replace* the older parts, such that these became useless but had to be dragged around anyway. Instead, the functions of the older parts of the brain remained fully intact. The new parts of the brain, however, expanded and comple-mented or completed these functions when the older functions were no longer sufficient under new external circumstances. In this respect, the new parts of the brain are not entirely novel; rather, they are improvements toward achieving the age-old goal of assuring survival, which, since the beginning of life, has meant nothing more than the stabilization, over generations, of the internal, physical system. The newer brain parts were copies of the older parts, in whose service they stood to some extent, but they were much more comprehensive and extensive, and they had improved neural circuitry. The new parts took the brain to an entirely new level, such that now it's possible for many parts of the brain to be involved in a single function. This approach to development led to a characteristic **redundancy** in the human brain structure (which, in this regard, corresponds to modern computer design), so that now, without risk, a progressive specialization of the redundant parts can take place.

Ancient, but not obsolete

In verterbate species the very oldest parts of the brain, which are at least 300 million years old, grow directly out of the spinal cord and are responsible for the regulation of the basal bodily functions that are fundamental to the preservation of life and thus have inborn programs. The older the individual parts of the brain, the more fundamental the functions that they control. They are responsible for the maintenance of a large number of physiological norms that are key to life. Because they manage such basic functions as breathing, circulation, water and electrolyte balance, and core body temperature in simple, fixed programs, these parts absolutely cannot be replaced. The destruction of the brain stem results in instant death; this is not necessarily true for damage to other, newer parts of the brain. Even vertebrates' behaviors in response to physiological events, such as responses to extreme cold or heat, are stored as relatively fixed programs; other examples of fairly fixed, inborn behaviors include the care of chicks, ranking in the pack, orientation, choice of living spaces and their contain-

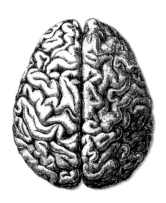

✐ The nitty-gritty on parts of the brain and their functions

The cerebrum is actually a *two-part* cap, although the connection and cooperation between the right and left halves of the brain don't need to be discussed further here. Sperry's theory about the two halves of the brain has been, to his own chagrin, overinterpreted badly enough in popular science (see Gazzaniga 1989, pp. 9 and 63). Likewise, at this point, we do not want to discuss the cerebellum, which is not responsible for any "higher" brain functions but is instead responsible for such things as the position and **coordination** of the limbs and the body in space. (Thus, it is a part of the brain that is strongly developed in birds.)

The representation of the brain that was used earlier in the book is based on the well-known model of the "triune" (three-part) brain put forth by Paul MacLean (for more, see Restak 1981, p. 41; more briefly summarized by Hampden-Turner 1983, p. 80). However, one can't take the autonomy of the three parts of the brain too literally. This limitation applies to a number of models of this sort. It's more the case that the cooperation is so close that, for example, there is no thinking that occurs without some tinge of feeling, and no feeling without at least a corresponding hint in one's thoughts. There are far too many immediate connections up and down that exist between the cerebrum and the lower (older) brain parts for this not to be the case.

There is a whole group of models that one could just as easily select for our purposes. What's important is simply that they all stem from the fact that some parts or regions of the brain are older than others and all show this "space-time entanglement." If the models are set up in this way, they allow a concrete representation of how courses of action occur on different levels of consciousness.

For example, von Hebenstreit (1993), who studies reactions in traffic situations, also uses a representation of separate levels, namely three clearly differentiated reaction circuits: first the reflexive reaction circuit on the lowest level, then the subcortical, and finally the cortical reaction circuit. In the reflexive reaction circuit, the processing of an external stimulus occurs in the spinal cord, on an extremely short pathway and thus very quickly, such as when one reflexively closes an eyelid or pulls away from sudden pain. These are inborn behaviors. The subcortical reaction circuit is where all acquired and long-since automated **programs** run (see p. 28). Although this is no longer reflexive, it also does not yet involve conscious awareness, like knowing the shift pattern of a transmission or braking when a traffic light turns red or when we see the brake lights of the vehicle ahead. Finally, the cortical reaction circuit is involved in all cases in which, for purposes of proper processing, a stimulus has to not only be perceived but also be interpreted to determine its meaning before an action is initiated in response—for example, when a child's ball rolls across the road in front of your car and you brake.

Acting and reacting within the cortical reaction circuit takes time and is strenuous, at least when there are many stimuli to be processed; in addition, it's not a particularly reliable process. All three of these disadvantages are easy to observe in a student driver or rider in the first hours of practice. The more experienced the rider, the more processes he will have moved into the subcortical level of the brain. ■

⤴ The pros and cons of redundancy

Redundancy is always beneficial when there is a failure somewhere and one can either jump over or fill in the gaps with relatively few problems. This is also the case with the human brain. But when harmony is lost and contradictions arise, redundancies can be extremely irritating; instead of (redundant) affirmation, a person will *simultaneously* also experience fear and doubt. Among athletes, this problem is readily evident in the form of "action stutter," whereby, in the last stages of decision-making, one finds himself very quickly jumping back and forth between two mutually exclusive actions that might be initiated; or in the phenomena of "action mixing," such as when a new rider, under certain stressful circumstances, gets on the throttle with his hand (with the intention of giving it gas) but is also already braking with his foot.

When action mixing or action stutter occurs on a decision-making level, however, it belongs instead to the realm of "blockades," something we can observe at sharp and fast interchanges, when a driver who is obviously reading the sign depicting the interchange is in such a hurry that he can't pick one direction or the other and, in the worst case, resolves the conflict by running over the sign.   ∎

ment, etc. Thus, a hunger pang elicits a very specific type of search for sustenance. A feeling of fear leads to the initiation of a sophisticated escape program or to some other kind of defense behavior. These genetically transmitted (inborn) programs are always concerned with the survival strategies that have been best preserved in the evolutionary experience of the species or genus. They are also, because of their inflexibility, minimally useful when it comes to reacting to new environmental factors and adapting to new challenges.

For this reason, a superior brain structure developed; this is the mammalian brain, with its cortical region, which emerged about 100 million years ago. With this brain came the capacity for lightning-fast decisions, for reacting to new environmental situations, and finally also for learning. It is responsible for emotions and for initial blanket differentiations between friend and enemy, useful or hurtful, and "good" and "bad."

A wonderful latecomer

Of utmost importance, finally, is the cerebrum, the seat of our consciousness. It first emerged several million years ago but did not reach its current volume until about 200,000 years ago. In terms of evolutionary history, that's not much more than a moment or two. With the advent of the cerebrum, we gained the ability to think analytically and to find causes, even from a great spatial and temporal distance. With the help of the cerebrum, we can reproduce a likeness of the external world as a model (much simplified) in our heads. This inner representation of outside reality allows us to "test" things in our thoughts without having to act. This is what Konrad Lorenz meant when he stated that thinking is "tinkering in imaginary space." It's quick, without risk, and saves effort and is therefore an incredible competitive advantage for humans. With this thought-based testing, we can unlock the future for ourselves—an amazing and exclusively human capability. We can imagine objects that do not yet exist, situations that have not yet occurred, start to "work" on them, and even change them if we want to. We can conceive of how something could be built; we can play through how something might happen; we can anticipate things that might occur unexpectedly—whereby we can also remove the element of surprise to some extent. This is the ability to build hypotheses (**hypothesis construction**), an ability that we'll consider in connection with a particular behavior (and it always enhances safety).

Furthermore, thanks to the cerebrum, we can not only bring the world *into our heads,* but conversely, humans can also *step outside of themselves* and take a good look at themselves to see what they're like, what they could be like, or what they would like to be or should be. This is the "actual" versus "ideal" comparison, which is important for all behavioral change and is therefore also important for systematic training (see p. 116). The ability to make this comparison requires the presence of *self-consciousness;* the perception of a *self* is a human capability that, once again, relies on the functions of the cerebrum.

Thus, with the cerebrum we have a unique brain component that unlocks almost infinite possibilities for us. However, because of its relative complexity, the cerebrum not only works measurably slower than the older parts of the brain, but it also has a disproportionately smaller "channel capacity" (or bandwidth). These older parts manage multiple tasks across the board continuously.

When things get crowded in your head: limited channel capacity—in sensory perception and in actions

"Channel capacity" is a concept from the world of telecommunications. Only a certain amount of information can be moved through a particular path at one time— only a limited number of telephone conversations over a particular line or over a carrier wave of a particular bandwidth. A computer has capability for only a limited number of calculations per unit of time. One can imagine this as a canal, like a pipe with a particular diameter, through which only a limited quantity of a liquid can pass in a given time.

This is true to and from, in and out, for the transport of stimuli, or—one could also say—data. The same goes for the processing of stimuli or data. We cannot really think about two problems *simultaneously*. We might come close to this by quickly switching from one to the other, such as a "simultaneous" chess player does (as he is not really playing simultaneously), but we cannot really consciously monitor and continuously manage two separate systems at the *same* time. For example, as motorcyclists, we cannot perform optimal braking (that is, maximal braking without wheel lock) with both the front and the rear wheels at the same time. It would be nice if we could, but the human regulator simply cannot manage this, so we're better off concentrating on the front wheel (Eberspächer 1991).

These are tasks of the conscious self, and therefore tasks that involve the cerebrum and neocortex. But when it comes to processing stimuli, the capacity of the cerebrum is very limited. Take driving, for example: while we chat with our passengers, we can, at the same time, not only engage the clutch, shift, and accelerate appropriately, but also steer, providing that these courses of action are adequately "automated." In this instance, the conscious self, with its limited capacity, is not burdened, because these are activities of the subconscious self, whose channel capacity is greater.

You have probably experienced overstepping your personal channel capacity, although you may not have interpreted it this way. Example: you're listening to the car radio without paying particular attention, but the news comes on and you listen more closely. You may not be all that interested in the news itself, but you know that the weather forecast will come at the end, and you're very interested in that, because you're planning a big ride for the next day. After a while, you reach a multi-lane highway junction with heavy traffic, have a bit of trouble merging, then change lanes several times, and hear loud horns. A truck ahead to the left suddenly gets in front of you and forces you to brake, and you have to be careful to get to the proper lane at the right time to get the exit you need. You breathe a sigh of relief once you're back to a relatively normal road, lean back and relax, and then hear the radio again: "That was the news with the weather. Now back to the program." You did not catch a single word of the weather report!

It's not only incoming *sensory* data that are affected, but also outgoing *motor* data. The greater the required amount of self-conscious attention, the more readily we can see our limitations. For example, the ski instructor wants you to put more weight on the ski tips as you slowly ski across the face of the slope, and shouts, "Stand more on the balls of your feet!" You do this easily, and then the instructor shouts, "And with knees forward!" because you're now standing too stiffly on the balls of your feet. You can still follow this direction pretty well, but then you may get yet another hint, such as "Uphill shoulder forward!" and you notice that it's already getting a bit complicated. You have to concentrate hard to follow all three directions at the same time. Before the next turn, you review the three points once more and correct your body position a little, but then, immediately before the gate that you're supposed to ski around, the instructor calls out, "Push with the heels and unload the *uphill* ski!" Although you know exactly how this is supposed to work, it occupies all your attention. After the turn, when you have to put conscious effort into re-collecting yourself (the balls of your feet, your knees, and your shoulders), you can suddenly feel exactly what limited channel capacity is. But then the instructor comes up with yet another hint: "More weight on the downhill ski!" You promptly concentrate fully on that downhill ski and resolve to pay special attention to it because, after the next turn, it will be the other ski, and you will have to think quickly once more about your feet, knees, shoulders, and heels. And then the next turn comes!—and you unload the uphill ski . . .

Everything worked, but the disappointed ski instructor says, *"But you forgot to plant your pole!"* This was something that had worked just fine up until then, but that part got tossed out because there suddenly was no more channel capacity available for making it happen. The pole-plant was neglected because you were fully occupied when the time came. That skill might have been the least solidified of all, maybe because it was learned in the previous season and really hadn't been sufficiently automated yet, at least not such that it could be done spontaneously and without burdening the available channel capacity.

What can one learn from this scenario?

1. Don't be surprised when there are suddenly "blank spots" on the map; instead ask yourself why one particular task was dropped out and not something else.

2. Don't change everything at the same time in training and practice, and try not to pay attention to everything at the same time. Instead, build your skills into sensible, not-too-large groups (action complexes), to which you can pay attention separately. For example, practice the entire braking process, including downshifts, rather than just the throttle action in-between all by itself.

3. Only when a particular action complex is solidified—that is, when it has become automatic— is it time to take on the next one.

4. An action complex that has already been solidified can only be changed or improved through self-conscious awareness, the same conscious awareness that, in most cases, will initially decrease your proficiency with a course of action. This is why it is so important to let things "sink in" once you've learned them. For this, relaxation techniques can help (see p. 124).

Cerebrum and spontaneous action

From all this, we conclude that we cannot expect the cerebrum to be responsible for spontaneous actions—and riding a motorcycle requires a large amount of spontaneous action! We can make this immediately clear with an example: passing on the highway, let's say in the car. The first and most visible of the primary activities we seek to carry out is the lane change, which begins by pulling out of our existing path. Experienced drivers will execute this spontaneously, without much thought about what the exactly correct moment is in relation to the distance and the difference in speed compared to the car ahead, and without thought about the magnitude of the change

in direction. Then there's the important glance into the rearview mirror—followed by activation of the turn signal, which should happen before the move is made.

But as everyone knows, reality is often a little different. The driver starts to pull out and signals either at the same time or sometimes even after pulling out—occasionally the driver does not signal until the car reaches the lane marker. The "announcement" signal has degenerated into a "confirmation" signal. Why is this reversal of the sequence so common?

It is not that the driver almost *forgot* to signal and is getting it in at the last minute. If it were, it wouldn't happen the same way every time or several times in a row. Instead, it's because the pulling out is happening *spontaneously*, without specific conscious involvement. The additional actions must to some extent be initiated and run on a substantially more conscious (less automated) level, and this takes more time. Recognition and elimination of such errors are discussed later in this book.

The conscious self and the subconscious self

From this point on, let's leave aside the brain parts, with their different ages and working speeds, stacked as they are on top of each other and bound together in complicated ways. Let's actually leave aside the entire physical substrate, and agree on two terms or concepts, which may not be very precise but are actually extremely useful: the *conscious self,* and the *subconscious self,* which describes a deeper aspect of ourselves that is less subject to conscious attention and manipulation. These concepts are actually somewhat familiar in everyday terms, when one speaks of doing something deliberately, or conversely, of acting on instinct or a "gut feeling," meaning that something was done spontaneously, without careful forethought.

The conscious self is concerned with everything that one is consciously aware of and everything that involves thinking, imagining, and deliberate actions.

The subconscious self is responsible for all actions that are not planned and managed by the conscious self. We aren't aware of the activities of the subconscious self, or we notice very little, and what little we do notice is only vague. Sometimes we aren't aware of these activities until after the fact, when, for example we realize that some spontaneous response must have been triggered from deep within us.

Despite these distinctions, we must nip in the bud the possible misunderstanding that the conscious self and the subconscious self are sharply distinct from each other. Rather, imagine that there are very fluid transitions and that the concepts simply accentuate the main focus of the different regions of the brain and their distinct functions. This fluidity is important and it would be wrong to simply equate the older parts of the brain with the subconscious self and the cerebrum with the conscious self.

In this regard, the picture of a floating iceberg that is often used to represent the human conscious and subconscious is a bad image. Nine-tenths of the iceberg lies invisible under the surface of the water, and this is said to correspond to the subconscious. At best, this image illustrates that such a thing as the subconscious remains invisible and that its volume should not be underestimated—but that's as far as it goes.

Almost everything else suggested by the iceberg analogy is misleading. For example, things related to the mind cannot be understood as firmly formed and inflexible, like a monolithic block. In reality, the mind is a matter of constant and highly dynamic *processes*. In addition, with its sharp border between water and air, the iceberg picture can foster the misunderstanding that both aspects of the self (subconscious and conscious) border directly on each other (water and air) and that the shift from one to the other is immediate, with no transition zone. This would lead to the misconception that what belongs to each aspect of the self has been permanently and immovably set. Everyday experience shows how this picture is incorrect; for example, there are certain psychological processes that we are ordinarily unaware of but can become aware of after the fact. Sometimes we experience insight into these processes immediately; sometimes this occurs only with great difficulty and substantial effort; and sometimes we can only do this with the help of an outside expert (e.g., psychologist or psychiatrist), if we can do it at all.

Close to, and further from, the self

Beyond everyday experience, the exchanges between the conscious self (air "above") and the subconscious self (water "below") are brisk, and thus I am avoiding all too-fixed models. However, I do not want to give up the fundamental idea of a *depth dimension,* which is a scale with the terms "self-oriented" and "self-distant" at the ends. This representation allows us, entirely in agreement with the reality that we can experience, to categorize mental processes into different levels. Some processes are very

Depth dimensions of the subconscious self: feelings and moods

Language is a good "psychologist" and allows the "self-distant" origins of certain experiences to shine through clearly by the expression of feelings, such as when grief *"overcomes" us* or fear *"grips" us* or when anger *"rises" within us,* whether we want to experience the feeling or not. Sometimes these feelings are accompanied by automatic actions, of which we say, "that happens by itself," which is to say, without involvement of the conscious self, sometimes even against its intentions.

The moods we are subjected to also show the autonomy of the subconscious self. Certainly they always affect the entire person, but they arise from the subconscious self. We can, of course, go on in spite of our moods, but we cannot just push them aside or wave them away. They take on great meaning in competitive sports because they determine the tone of what is perceived and thus influence the performance brought about in response to that perception. At times, everything might be steeped in a dismal and pessimistic color but, surprisingly, after just a single night of good, deep sleep, the world can have brightened up completely.

Although the many cognitive processes often generate far greater interest, especially in light of important discoveries in recent years, some behavioral theories argue that there are also courses of human events that occur outside of consciousness because they are automated. The works of behavioral theorists reflect very little interest in consciousness and the cognitive processes, dismissing these topics with the caveat that it all tends to be illusory anyway. Instead, the subconscious is credited with high levels of activity and is sometimes described as if it were actually a complex, extremely clever, independent person, which can lead to a misunderstanding of the concept. ∎

self-oriented, such as reasoned thinking. Other process are not quite so self-oriented but are still a long way from being subconscious, such as any general or nondescript feelings. There are still other processes that resist being brought into consciousness (that is, processes that are **self-distant**), such as highly automated actions, which is our topic. The label "self-oriented" is placed on the upper portion of the scale, and we ascribe that part to the conscious self. The transitions between each type of process are fluid as the progression moves from one extreme to the other. The label "self-distant" is placed on the lower portion of the depth dimension, and we ascribe that part to the subconscious self.

Let's look at an example using these concepts of the conscious self and the subconscious self.

The ball toss as a key example

The ball toss, which appears to be a fairly simple activity, lends itself well to making clear the special capabilities of the subconscious self and the hopeless inferiority of the conscious self for certain tasks.

In a group experiment, the participants—usually students in a lab—are instructed to each toss ten balls into a bucket four meters away. There's a line on the floor that cannot be crossed. Because the balls are relatively light for their size, the task is really not all that easy. The best in the group manage an average of about seven hits. The worst tossers average between zero and one hit. After an increasing number of turns, the average number of hits begins to stabilize for individual participants. The tossing is halted when the first significant improvements in the averages occur because of the increased practice.

Then the best tosser is told, mind you: "What you have accomplished wasn't exactly stellar. With all that ef-

The parable of the centipede

After observing a centipede for a long time, a natural scientist finally asked, "Dear centipede, how do you move each of your many feet so nicely in sequence, always putting the one into the footprint of its predecessor, without ever getting fouled up?"

The centipede looked up and paused. "I've never thought about that before! Just a moment, please! First I need to do it very slowly for myself," answered the centipede. He tried out one foot after another, and the more he paid attention to his many legs, the more he kept stumbling and the more confused and mixed up they got.

From then on, he could no longer walk, and died a very miserable death. ∎

fort, you managed only seven hits in ten tosses!" In truth, that was an outstanding achievement, and the discouraged participant almost always counters with something like, "But . . . the others were even worse!" To which the experimenter responds, "And they *are* even worse off! But you are actually not entirely ungifted in your motor skills. I could clearly see that your poor results were caused by the fact that you don't have the slightest understanding of ballistics. But we can change that!"

So then this participant has to complete a rigorous and extremely compressed audio-visual seminar on ballistics. For 15 minutes he sees one slide after another in quick succession, frequently interrupted by multiple-choice questions to test what he has recently learned.

After this brief quarter of an hour, he knows far more about ballistics than the average high school graduate. He knows about the ballistic curve, how it differs from a parabola, and where the vertex lies. He knows what "v_0" is, namely the initial speed at which a bullet leaves the barrel, or in our case, the speed at which the ball leaves the hand. He knows that the speed decreases after that point, and at a constant v_0 the ball will go farthest if he throws it at about 45 degrees—that the shot will be shorter if he throws it at a steeper angle and it will be shorter if he throws it at a flatter angle.

Confident about this new knowledge, the participant feels that he now *knows* exactly what the key to success is, and he makes the excuse that at first he basically just didn't know enough about the ball toss. To which the leader of the experiment replies, "You'll see that it will now work much better. So try it again!" And just as the participant gets ready to make an easy first toss, the experimenter calls out, "Wait! We need a *countdown!!*"

Another participant then counts down the seconds out loud, "10 . . . 9 . . . 8," etc. At the same time, the experimenter calls out to the tosser and starts quietly repeating all sorts of concepts from the preceding ballistics course as if to remind him and admonish him. During the few seconds of the countdown, the tosser, who had been standing relaxed and comfortably loose, becomes increasingly stiff, with more tightly controlled movements, like a poorly handled marionette. Finally he commits the cardinal sin of the ball toss: instead of looking at the target (the bucket), he looks at his hand.

The countdown has now reached 3 . . . 2 . . . 1, and the experiment leader says yet again, "The v_0, remember the v_0!" "Zero!" shouts the counter, and our participant throws . . . the balls land everywhere but in the bucket.

✎ Complex precision movements and successful movement plans

In the existence of the movement plan (of which we have such minimal conscious awareness) lies one of the explanations for the phenomenon of an experienced person who can, more or less, "see into the future"—not very far into the future, but with surprising reliability. What is meant here is the certainty with which an experienced tennis player—especially a virtuoso—knows, from the moment in which his racket contacts the ball, whether or not it is going to arrive at the spot he intended, because he *feels* it in his forearm, hand, and racket. Long before the ball lands he perceives whether or not the executed action aligned with his movement plan.

This phenomenon occurs for all kinds of sports, but it is most apparent with sports in which a ball, a shot, or some other object is aimed at some target, because these are situations in which there's a time lapse between the last influence (action) by the athlete and the arrival of the object in the area of the target.

Netherlander Ceulemans, many-time world champion in billiards, was once asked in an interview: "At which moment then, does an experienced player such as yourself feel whether he has ruined a shot? As soon as the ball begins to roll or earlier?"

Ceulemans: "Much earlier! Often exactly at the second in which the tip of the cue touches the ball. I can feel the error immediately in my fingers. Then I don't really even need to look any more."

That such highly concentrated precision movements are possible at all is related to a special characteristic of the human central nervous system. It's true that highly developed mammals such as chimpanzees are entirely capable of pounding on something with a stone or club, or throwing, or other

individual movements that follow each other in quick succession. However, the control of these movement complexes is carried out in a noticeably coarse manner, compared to the corresponding process in humans (compare also the limited training successes of bicycle-riding chimpanzees or bears, p. 35). The neural control system in animals is too slow for the kinds of quick, precise movements that are required of humans, for example, in a fast passage on the piano, when hitting a tennis ball, or even when speaking. But the acquired programs of the type already discussed are not adequate for these actions. These actions must instead be prepared and stored at the ready in a type of "high-speed generator," to be managed in the human neural system by "sequencers," which, in principle, behave like the caches in a computer that are used for the interim storage of data strings (as with virtual "clipboards"). Within these sequencers, entire chains of commands are lined up, as if on a launch pad, ready to be called up when needed.

The more such caches there are (with switches in parallel), the more likely it is that even when several actions are concentrated into a short period of time, the required precision will be achieved, particularly with respect to timing. Neurons, in both human and animal systems, can precisely control movements in the range of hundredths of seconds, but for particularly demanding human activities such as language, which involve highly concentrated precise movements, the required exactness of the timing is greater by a factor of ten. This is only possible with the additional measures in the organization of the neural network mentioned above (see Calvin 1993). ■

So what happened? This ball toss was a complicated course of action, well-suited to the particular activities of the subconscious self, but the process was then brought more fully into conscious awareness by means of all kinds of gimmicks. Thus, it was given over, ever more firmly, to the control of the conscious self, which then thoroughly spoiled the course of action. We will often be reminded of this example in the following pages of this book.

BRAIN ACTIVITIES "TRANSLATED" INTO ACTIONS

A key concept: the movement plan

In all of this, there's a relatively invisible process at work: the **movement plan.** It does not have to occur consciously and, in fact, only leads to a perfect outcome if it is created without much self-conscious involvement at all.

The skilled ball tosser looks at the target, weighs the ball for a moment in his hand, and then instantly has a complete movement plan. The absence of verbal coding of the movement plan is the reason why it is so difficult, if not impossible, for our ball tosser to put this "action instruction" (instruction on a series of actions) into words—a curious contradiction to the high level of certainty that an expert brings to a task, in this instance, tossing the ball.

If we accept the idea that a movement plan is an action instruction without words, then we recognize that it is simply an imaginary **action program** (see page 28) to be copied into reality. The ball tosser tries, with his actual throwing motions, to come as close as possible to his imaginary plan (program).

The principle of the movement plan can be readily understood with the very simple example of a telephone keypad. If you call a particular number very frequently and get really good at that sequence of numbers, you develop a complete movement plan for that number and can dial it very quickly, much more quickly than would be possible with individual commands, even if they occurred in rapid succession (along the lines of "first this button, now that button, etc."). If, in the course of this very quick action, you make a mistake, you will sense the error immediately. Or, consider a pianist who makes an error playing a passage that he has otherwise completely mastered; he will notice the error right away because he has *heard* it. However, if he were to play a silent piano, the *experience* of the error would be similarly instantaneous,

because at that particular point, the actual movement of his fingers had deviated from the movement plan.

No movement complex without the movement plan

In training and practice, it's not just the execution of an action that should be developed and improved, but also the movement plan itself. With beginners, the plan is only vague and fragmented, but with increasing practice, it gradually becomes more complete. Finally, when expert ability is attained, the movement plan is highly sophisticated and comprehensive. As a movement plan nears perfection, it is informed by an increasing amount of data about the sensory feedback expected to result from the action: information that can be used to make corrections and refinements to the process *while* it is being carried out. This goes for tossing a ball, for playing the piano, for kicking a ball, and most anything else.

Likewise, innumerable movement plans are required of the motorcyclist, continuously active and overlapping one another. An excellent example is riding on the "right" line, sometimes called the "ideal line." Let's now cover this topic more fully.

The ideal line: the razor-sharp divide between confidence and terror

Responses to the question of what the **ideal line** is can vary widely, from "riding really close to the left side" (usually used to mean making use of the entire width of the lane); to "hugging the corner;" "taking the shortest possible line;" "cornering with the greatest possible radius;" and "following the safest path."

All of these answers are, at most, only partly correct. The first two—"using the entire width of the lane" or "the corners just have to be tightly hugged"—are the most naive: they are only a coarse description of what can be observed more or less from the viewpoint of the onlooker.

The "shortest line" sounds a little better as a description but is still not quite correct. The length of a stretch of road is measured at the centerline (Figure 21), so the description of a race track might be as follows: length 4.542 km, ideal line 4.494 km (this was the original Grand Prix course at the Nürburgring, before the various renovations). Thus, the ideal line is indeed shorter but is in no way the shortest of all possible lines. Only a very slow vehicle would be able to follow the shortest line (Figure 22); from one corner to the next, it takes the shortest path, which is a straight line, and each corner, from start to finish, is traveled as far inside as possible. This is sometimes called the "minimal ideal line." The faster a vehicle travels, the wider it has to swing for a corner (Figure 23) until finally it reaches what is called the "maximal ideal line." The track would not allow a vehicle to go any wider. If someone were to ride on or near that maximal line at a slower pace, he'd be going wider than necessary and would luxuriate in all that space. He'd be taking a longer path than needed, and in everyday street riding, within the bounds of the available lane, this is recommended because it protects the rider's safety reserves. However, if one really were to ride at the proper speed on the maximal ideal line, then certain stretches that one had considered pretty harmless, while moving more slowly, become corners that have to be taken seriously and must be approached with precision (compare, for example, the **turn-in points** E1 and E2 from Figure 22 with those in Figure 23.). So much for the idea of the shortest line!

Thus, the ideal line, with increasing speed, actually becomes *longer* up to the point of the maximal ideal line. Not very much longer, but still longer. Although everyone talks about *the* ideal line as if it applies to everyone in the same way, it exists only as a general principle. The ideal line depends not only on speed but also on other factors, such as particular local conditions and even to a certain extent the style of the rider.

And what about the "largest possible radius" mentioned above? It doesn't look much better. The largest possible radius is used only in corners that are isolated from other corners by sufficiently long straight stretches (Figure 24). That is, *the ideal line in any corner is influenced by other corners,* both before and after. This is what makes the issue of the ideal line so difficult and so fascinating. And it's not a matter of tiny, invisible shifts, either. It is absolutely possible that a corner, because of the influence of its neighbors, would have to be entered from the far right edge rather from the far left edge, and vice versa.

The basic strategy for a series of corners is always to ride the fast corners at the expense of the slower corners. That means that for corners that are slow anyway, one can certainly choose a slower line if it means that, in using this line, one can use a faster line through an inherently faster corner. Races are won in the fast corners, not in the slow ones. Five km/h lost in the exit of an 80 km/h corner can literally be made up in the blink of an eye . . . it's a matter of a few meters. However, in a 200-km/h corne r, recovering the same 5 km/h would take a small eternity, since there is less reserve for acceleration at high speeds.

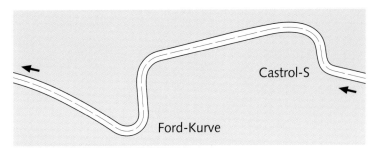

Figure 21. The length of a track is measured at its centerline. The ideal line is shorter. This depicts a segment of the Grand-Prix circuit of the Nürburgring before the 2002 configuration change.

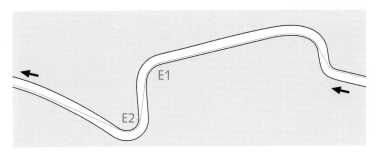

Figure 22. The shortest of all possible lines, the ideal line, of a relatively slow-moving vehicle.

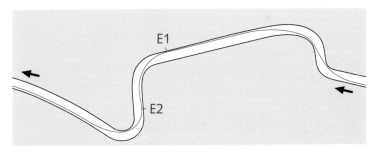

Figure 23. A faster vehicle swings more widely and has a longer ideal line than a slower vehicle. Note the different turn-in points (E1 and E2) compared with those in Figure 22.

The Nürburgring Nordschleife controversy

The old argument about how many corners the Nürburgring's Nordschleife has is actually an argument about the speed at which those corners are taken. So, although we always hear about 72 corners, some come up with more than 90 by counting each individual kink separately in double- or multiple-kink corners, even if these are ridden with one single, unchanging radius. Crucially, they also include a few very fast corners, which are the most difficult and, in races, the most important. For slower vehicles, however, these fast corners don't exist at all.

■

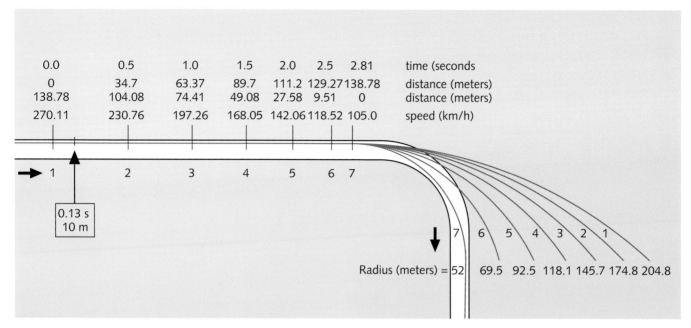

Figure 24. An isolated right-hander, not influenced by a previous or subsequent corner. This representation shows how incredibly precise one has to operate to really go at full speed, whether on a bike or in a car. Shown here are data from a race car. The track is 8 meters wide, and the 90-degree right-hander has a midline radius of 36 meters. The car approaches the curve at 270 km/h. The driver must begin optimal braking by the time he reaches Point 1 in order to slow the vehicle to 105 km/h by the time he reaches Point 7, the turn-in point. That is the fastest speed at which the corner can be taken if the driver stays precisely on the ideal line. The driver has 2.8 seconds in which to brake (top row of numbers), and the braking distance is about 139 meters long (second and third row of numbers). The deceleration is therefore significantly more than 1 G, which is due primarily to the aerodynamic pressures on the vehicle. If the driver brakes just a tenth of a second (!) later, he will lose almost 10 meters of braking distance. This is almost exactly the distance between Point 6 and Point 7. This means that he arrives at Point 7 with the data from Point 6, which means that instead of 105 km/h, his speed is about 119 km/h, and that the smallest possible curve radius is not 52 meters, but rather 69.5 meters. The driver will have to call on some impressive magic to still make this work.

The smallest possible corners for the speeds listed in the individual Points 1 through 7 are shown on the right. Corner 1, with a radius of 205 meters, would be required for the speed shown at Point 1, that is, at 270 km/h, etc.

One could also look at it this way: if the driver approaches the corner at 270 km/h, he's pushing along in front of him an invisible smallest possible corner with a 205-meter radius. While the driver brakes, the corner's radius will decrease steadily with decreasing speed until the invisible corner fits the actual corner exactly. In the ideal situation, this occurs exactly at the turn-in point—that is, exactly at Point 7, and no sooner and no later.

This is the great artistry of really fast riding: not to ride every corner, one after the other, as fast as possible (there are many who can do that), but to consider a longer series of corners as a unit and to feel immediately where one can sacrifice a few hundredths of a second in order to gain a few tenths someplace else.

Before we go further, we must remind ourselves that we are concerned not only with the racetrack but also, and at least as much so, with everyday street riding. In rider training courses, practicing on the racetrack is helpful because it is free from the dangers of opposing traffic and one can ride an ideal line that stretches from one edge to the other. For this also to benefit our street riding, nothing fundamental has to change. Of course, the entire roadway is not available, so one must stay within the proper lane, bordered by the centerline and the edge of the road. There's one matter that deserves special attention, however: a motorcycle and rider can occupy amazing width when cornering. Although, at the racetrack in a left-hander, we can truly ride all the way to the left and hang our upper body and head far over the edge of the track, we could never do the same thing on the street. Otherwise, we'd be hanging far into the path of oncoming traffic, and although a collision with an oncoming vehicle can usually be avoided at the last minute, this requires a very sudden and substantial correction,

Acceleration capabilities and the ideal line

Many a participant in a training course who has had trouble finding the **ideal line** has asked his instructor in exasperation why the ideal line is not simply painted on the course. But that just wouldn't work because even changing tire temperature has an influence on the ideal line as well as on the location of the braking points!

After a change in the regulations in 1989, Gerhard Berger had to get used to an unsupercharged Ferrari after having driven the turbo. Even a driver of his caliber was surprised after his first laps at how everything was different, despite almost the same amount of power: not only was the sound different, he said, but also throttle response and acceleration. Because of this, the ideal line had changed as well.

That the acceleration capabilities of a vehicle can influence the ideal line is readily evident in the "notchy" line that riders of especially powerful motorcycles take in certain corners. Anyone who observes the great 500cc racers in training, in order to try to learn something about the finer points of the

ideal line, will often be disappointed. When others might approach a corner far on the outside, these 500-racers sometimes ride right in the middle—a far cry from what most people would understand as the ideal line. What they're doing is trying to keep the motorcycle relatively upright for as long as possible to allow braking at the entrance to the corner, so that after a tighter and slower segment they can start to accelerate again as soon as possible in order to maximize their exit speed.

These days, when it's possible to measure speed very precisely at certain points along the track, it's hardly surprising that in certain short segments of some corners, riders in the 500cc class often take their corners a tiny bit *slower* than the 250s (the 125s, with their far smaller acceleration reserves, can afford even less deviation from the classic ideal line).

The greater the available acceleration reserves when leaving a corner, the more advantageous it can be to use the highest possible corner exit speed, at the expense of the overall cornering duration. ∎

which can lead to a very precarious line on the exit of the corner, possibly resulting in a crash. Unfortunately this is a fairly common cause of accidents.

Figure 25 shows two paths of negotiating a series of corners, one with an ideal line that does not represent the largest radius in each corner and another with an ideal line showing how each corner would be ridden if it were an isolated corner. Clearly, the individual lines do not connect with each other.

Now let's turn to the notion that the ideal line is *the safest of all lines*. Some experts, to whom "ideal line" sounds too much like racing, do in fact call it the safety line, but there's one thing to remember: at the same speed, the ideal line is the one on which the least centripetal force develops. To express it more precisely: on the ideal line, the sum of the **lateral acceleration** in all corners is the least. In fact, regardless of whether corners are negotiated at race speed or at a comfortable pace, less lateral acceleration reduces wear and tear on the motorcycle and, above all, increases traction reserves. More reserves mean greater safety. While the everyday rider wants to minimize lateral acceleration (and thus maximize safety) with the help of the ideal line, the racer

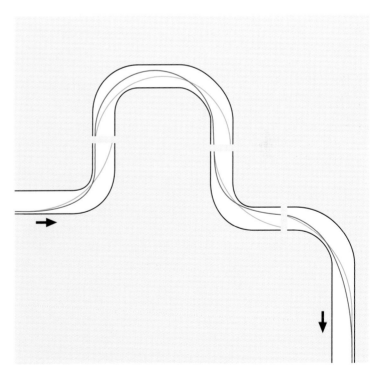

Figure 25. The ideal line of a sequence of corners (red) can differ significantly from the ideal lines for the individual corners (blue).

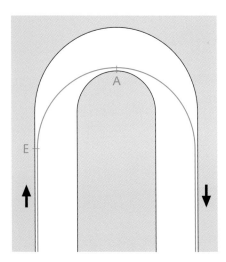

Figure 26. The line with the largest possible radius.

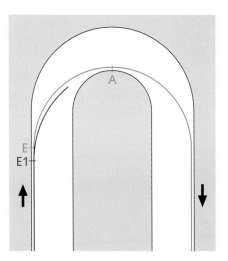

Figure 27. Even a slightly premature turn-in point (E1 instead of E) creates big problems.

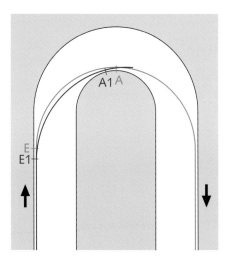

Figure 28. There's no sign of trouble up to the apex (A1), but the problems become evident in the second half of the corner.

wants to achieve the highest possible speed with the help of the ideal line.

In practice, however, the matter looks a little different. It soon becomes evident that the ideal line is not so safe after all. If one deviates from it only slightly, the line can suddenly become very dangerous. Let's take a look at how one *can* ride; how one, for safety reasons, *should* ride; and what one would be better off to avoid entirely. For the sake of simplicity, we'll consider all corners under the conditions of the greatest possible speed (that is, without reserves).

Figure 26 shows the line with the largest possible radius, drawn inside of an artificial 180-degree corner. This is the ideal line which, according to our definition, is the line with the least lateral acceleration, and thus with the least **lateral force.** Thus, it's the fastest line and the one that creates the least wear and tear on the motorcycle: width 8 meters; radius of the centerline 12 meters; traveled radius approximately 15.3 meters; E the turn-in point; and A the **apex,** that is, the point at which the traveled line comes closest to the inner edge of the lane.

But, if one makes even a slight error with the turn-in point and initiates the turn prematurely, then everything immediately becomes intensely uncomfortable. Figure 27 shows a premature turn-in, at E1, which is just two meters short, but because of this, in the next phases of the turn it becomes especially clear how precisely one must adhere to the ideal line if he is riding very fast.

If one is watching all of this from the side of the road, at this point nothing appears too remarkable. Even in the

next phase (Figure 28), everything still looks pretty good: the vehicle has moved nicely to the inside, and it's hardly evident that the apex (A1) has been reached a little bit early. However, seeing the direction the vehicle is pointing, one can recognize (at least in the figure) that something is not quite right. This becomes more than obvious in the next moment (Figure 29): the rider doesn't necessarily have to continue on the original arc, but instead, from the apex, can switch to a line with the same radius as the ideal line. But even with this correction, the line simply no longer fits into the road, at least not if one is riding at the limit (without reserves). At the very least, a great deal of "magic" is needed at the exit of the corner, and not only does this cost time, it is also risky.

And now for the rider who turns in late. So that things are easy to see, we'll have him turn in late by a considerable amount. Figure 30 shows the turn-in point E2 just over 10 meters after the turn-in point on the ideal line (E). This is basically how one would ride down a pass in the Alps. The rider does have to follow a tighter line in the beginning of the hairpin, but in return, he has a much longer braking distance available to him. Since he won't have to use all of that distance in order to **decelerate** to the lower speed necessary for getting around this tighter line, he could brake a little later if he wanted to.

If we were standing at the apex to observe this, we'd notice that the apex has moved in the direction of the exit (Figure 31). We'd especially notice that the rider could accelerate before he reaches the apex, because he has long since "opened" the curve a little (that is, he was able

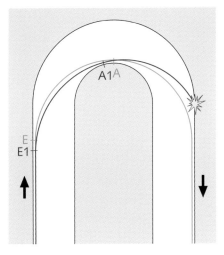

Figure 29

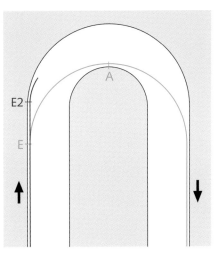

Figure 30. A substantially delayed turn-in, with a correspondingly late turn-in point (E2).

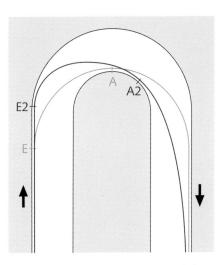

Figure 31. The apex moves toward the exit of the corner, and the vehicle can be accelerated again early and with minimal risk.

to enlarge its radius again). If he's very experienced, he could even **drift** a little in the corner without much worry, or if he suspected that the road might be getting slick, he could test how much **grip** he still has at the rear wheel. These are things that the rider on the classic ideal line would be advised not to do—with full lateral acceleration, he's about to come very close to the outer edge of his lane.

This very early acceleration, which can be powerful only if, from that point on, the radius is larger, is a very decisive point in racing. It's only in this way that the rider can achieve a substantially higher exit speed, which means that he can easily afford to take the slightly slower corner that he built into the beginning of the curve . No one has mastered this better than the top American racers. But it's not just a matter of speed; it's also a matter of safety. For everyday riding, it's at least as important, if not more so, that a rider who turns in late as he approaches a blind corner can see into the upcoming stretch of road sooner. Thus, reducing speed at the beginning of a curve is a safety advantage that cannot be overestimated.

As we can see, this is simply a refinement of the old rule about cornering: *enter slowly, exit quickly.*

The turn-in point

This is very easy to see in training, especially in riders who are not yet familiar with a track: although corner-exit speed on the chosen line may very quickly approach the rider's personal best, improvements on corner entry require much more work. In the beginning, the rider is still far too slow, but he gradually increases his speed, resulting in a gradual delay of the braking point and an ever more exact determination of the **turn-in point.**

Depending on the corner, however, there can also be a gentle modification of the line, as shown in Figure 31. The decision to reach a high corner-exit speed—a critical concept in racing but important also for street riding—is made *at the beginning* of a corner. A rider who consistently enters too fast will never achieve a first-class lap time.

The value of a late turn-in is even more striking when one considers a real curve, such as that shown in Figure 32, rather than an artificially constructed one. This is a decreasing radius turn in reverse; thus, it gradually opens up. The rider on the line with the late turn-in (E2) has very favorable conditions for acceleration just after the apex at the latest. The rider on the ideal line is still circling along, with full lateral acceleration, and approaching the outer edge of the lane, where he'll have to ride for a considerable period on this part of the road that's usually covered in debris—not so ideal after all. After all of this, the rules can only be repeated over and over:

Linger on the outside! Use a late turn-in! Push the apex toward the exit!

These simple rules are truly a form of "life insurance," but they have to be practiced systematically: not because the late turn-in is technically all that difficult, but because it goes against our instinct. I have seen innumerable cases in which riders have turned in too early, and not

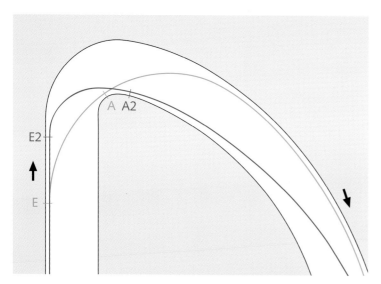

Figure 32. The line with the largest possible radius makes for high lateral acceleration, takes the vehicle dangerously close to the outer edge of the track, and keeps it there for a dangerously long time (blue). The line with the late turn-in point (E2) allows a much earlier acceleration and offers greater safety reserves (red).

Figure 33. The rider is already very close to the inside at the very beginning of the corner, and at first glance, everything looks perfectly fine.

Figure 34. Even here, nothing remarkable catches the eye.

Figure 35. At the exit of the corner, however, things can become dangerously tight if there is oncoming traffic.

Figure 36. This rider stays on the outside for as long as possible.

Figure 37. The rider is still not all the way on the inside. He has pushed his apex out almost all the way to the end of the corner.

Figure 38. As the rider exits the curve, he has a substantial safety cushion.

just in rider training courses. Only very rarely have I seen an instance in which the turn-in was truly too late. Having studied the schematic representations of different corners, one can glean a lot more from the multiple variations that are encountered in reality, even though these may differ in many ways from unambiguous models (see Figures 33–38).

A postscript on the ideal line: the "racing line" and the "fighting line"

Once in a while, one has to listen to objections when discussing the topic of the ideal line in great detail. The safety contingent will protest that it's only important for racing and has no place on the street. The response is simple: if one always tries to stay on the ideal line within the confines of one's own lane, this will provide constant practice in finding and using the largest possible radius when cornering. For this reason, when the ideal line becomes natural and obvious, even during everyday riding without particularly sporty ambitions, there will be enormous gains in safety.

Nevertheless, we should take another look at what's happening with the **fighting line** that some swear by.

Although the ideal line is not necessarily the fastest of all possible lines, that does not render it obsolete. Rather, it is the foundation that must be mastered first. It is the basis from which more specialized lines are developed,

Figure 39. The challenging entrance into the Kallenhard curve at the Nordschleife (Nürburgring).

Late turn-ins and the ideal line: a prime example

To illustrate the issues connected with late turn-ins, let's look at Kallenhard on the Nürburgring's Nordschleife, a descending 120-degree right-hander, which requires an extremely late turn-in and combines all the elements that can entice a Ring novice to turn in too early (Figure 39).

Since the beginning of our experience with riding, we have had **conditioning** not only to ride more or less on the right side of a lane but also to follow the actual path of the road. As a result, we orient ourselves—much more strongly than we realize—to the edges of the road, especially the right edge. When a person learns to look for the **ideal line,** this becomes less of a fixation; when riding with an emphatically delayed turn-in point, our habit has to be abandoned entirely.

In training courses at the Ring, an instructor will lead his pupils through the Kallenhard by doing the exact opposite of what our conditioning demands of us: he approaches the corner relatively close to the *left* edge of the track, and instead of abruptly making for the right edge at the last minute, he calmly continues to ride straight ahead, toward the left edge of the track, which bends ever more tightly toward the arrow-straight line of the instructor. To Ring novices, this looks rather threatening: the track is going downhill, the instructor brakes and brakes, while the distance between his front wheel and the left edge of the track is rapidly dwindling, and a wall of gloomy trees is looming ever larger in front of him. From the observer's viewpoint, this can't possibly turn out well . . . but then the instructor turns off to the right and lets himself fall into the curve that drops sharply down to the inside.

With such a large number of apparent risks, the uneasy novices behind the instructor abandon all their good intentions and cease to follow him, moving farther to the inside and turning in earlier—which leads to a horrible line farther back in the group.

It seems that the scariest moment occurs shortly before the turn-in, when one hardly has any straight braking distance left in front of the front wheel. An early turn-in brings some relief, because there is instantly a lot of space between the front wheel and the left edge of the track. This is deceptive, however, because on this line the rider is all the more likely to end up in "hot water" at the corner exit.

However, even with all the advantages offered by the late turn-in, the picture is a little different in racing. A racer who knows that he's being followed closely by a competitor would never use this kind of line, because the other rider would immediately ride through the gap that would open up. In the smaller classes, he would likely ride through the corner a little slower, with a smaller turning radius, but at least he did stay in front. But if he has a large acceleration reserve, he could afford to brake much harder, which would allow him, with or without an adversary, to use a sharper approach to the corner. This produces a more or less distinct **racing line,** which is in any case, shorter than the ideal line. However, the racing line must be expertly executed for it to be faster, and it puts a disproportionately greater strain on the rider and the motorcycle. ■

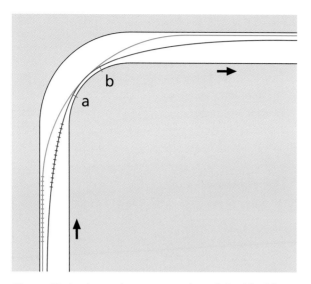

Figure 40. A schematic representation of the ideal line (blue) and the so-called racing, or fighting line (red).

and these can certainly be faster in certain cases. It is also a reliable recovery strategy for a rider who, for example, is exhausted in an endurance race after a few sprints and too much dicing with competitors; or whose vehicle is not performing well or has been otherwise compromised by some other misfortune.

Among the specialized lines, there is frequent talk about the fighting line, by which is meant the more challenging (that is, faster, but also more strenuous) line. It is the **racing line** that is useful for passing in a one-on-one battle; strictly speaking, however, it should really be called the "fighting line" in this situation.

These lines represent a massive renunciation of the safety principle that advocates using a late turn-in (see p. 62). For this reason, they only come into play on well-practiced stretches of racetrack that a rider knows perfectly. These lines are based on the fact that there are substantially shorter lines than the classic ideal line, with its wide swings and arcs (compare Figures 22 and 23). However, a rider on the shorter line will have to use smaller radii (that is, tighter arcs) in some sections of some corners and thus will be slower than he might have been if he were using the ideal line.

The schematic representations in Figures 40 and 41 show that the rider on the racing line (red) is not taking a notably shorter path than the rider on the widely swinging ideal line (blue). We can also see that the rider on the racing line rides much longer without leaning or with only a minimal lean, and thus not only can initiate braking much later but also can accelerate much earlier when

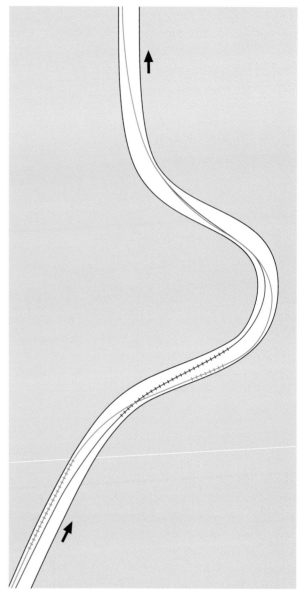

Figure 41. The racing (fighting) line, as opposed to the classic ideal line, in a series of corners (braking zones cross-hatched).

he exits the curve. Only the segment *a–b* becomes tighter and therefore slower.

As we can see, the rider on the racing line can work more with longitudinal acceleration (with braking and acceleration) and minimize lateral acceleration, which means that he can use correspondingly tighter radii for the curves. Given all of this, the classic ideal line is the one with the least loss of speed, which is readily evident from data recorded in real time. The greater the acceleration reserves, the more easily one can afford the shorter racing line and the more pronounced this line can be. Correspondingly, the faster a curve, the less can be

Figure 42. Wide approaches and late turn-in points on the classic ideal line (Nürburgring-Nordschleife, Wehrseifen).

Figure 43. Compare the substantially sharper approach to the left-hander, as shown on the racing line (Helmut Dähne).

achieved with the racing or the fighting line (unless the "kink" is so minimal that one can approach it very acutely). Alternatively, the slower a series of curves, and the more technical the individual curves are, the more important the racing and fighting lines become, and the advantage that they bring will be greater. In this respect, for example on the Nordschleife at the Nürburgring, the classic points for the racing and fighting lines are Hatzenbach, Adenauer Forst, and Wehrseifen (Figures 42 and 43).

While the classic ideal line leaves relatively little room for variation, the story is substantially different for the racing or fighting line. There's the extreme racing line with its very acute approaches to the curves, harder braking upon entry, and smaller radii, but there's also a line that differs only slightly from the classic ideal line. This line frequently requires no additional braking because it can be managed with only a slightly increased lean angle—and there are any number of lines in between!

What makes the racing line so difficult is that if one doesn't catch it right—for example, because he has misestimated the acceleration reserves or because he braked too much or too little—then he would have been better off had he stuck with the trouble-free ideal line, which is less stressful on both the machine and rider. A study was conducted with eight well-trained and engaged sport riders (who were not racers) to compare their times on the racing line with their times on the ideal line through

the Hatzenbach series of curves on the Nordschleife (Nürburgring). Only one rider was slightly faster on the racing line than he had been on the ideal line. That says it all.

The actions of the movement plan and their execution

Even for the ideal line and its variations, the implementation works all the better if the rider's movement plan remains spontaneous, that is, without conscious involvement in the actions—to put it another way, if the conscious self "gets out of the way" of the subconscious self.

The novice rider, however, must experience this line himself, and for this, there has to be some deliberate intent. The ideal line then becomes the conscious model for the subsequent action. This is a good thing, because it's only after continued and conscious examination of the path of this line that following it gradually becomes self-evident and requires less and less conscious attention. Then, as shown in experiments with top riders, the line is instantly *available* to determine the course of action, without any effort on the part of the rider to plan out, step by step, the process to be followed. By contrast, a less-expert rider who is figuring out the ideal line with much effort, must deliberate carefully about whether the line at a particular point should have been a little farther to the inside or outside, or whether the **apex** should be here or better a little farther along. Of course, these are considerations that an expert rider makes as well—for example, in a complicated series of corners. Riders actually study a racetrack on foot quite frequently. For the expert, track analysis usually has less to do with the movement plan as a whole; instead, it is a matter of ferreting out a few details.

But coming up with the ideal line, in a timely manner and with as few errors as possible, is not quite enough. The implementation of the movement plan into real actions must also be trained. It is a complicated task for **coordination,** but it is much more easily done without self-conscious control than the development of the movement plan. If the plan was sufficiently defined, performing the action that should copy it is much more likely to be successful the more "automatic" the implementation. Then, the action is no longer self-consciously controlled, but is only *monitored* and examined by the self after the fact.

The coaster experiment

With a very simple experiment, one can get a good picture of the extent to which an action can be harmed by all-too-conscious and deliberate implementation. Find a quiet parking lot and set an index card or drink coaster on the ground. Then try to ride over it as precisely and perfectly as possible. One rolls toward the coaster, keeping his eye on it. It quickly comes closer, then disappears behind the front wheel, and the bike goes past without touching it. Even very good riders usually cannot do this, at least as long as they continue to stare at the coaster. In contrast, one immediately has a better chance of hitting the coaster when one quickly figures out where it is and, as he gets closer to it, moves his gaze beyond it, so the coaster is only visible as a white spot in the lower periphery of his visual field.

Why? Because looking directly at the coaster means that the whole thing happens with far too much involvement of the conscious self. In other words, it's happening at a far too self-conscious level, resulting in a large number of continuous corrections (of which most are overcorrections) that follow each other quickly and build up unnoticeably, especially as the distance to the target gets small. A more fluid, spontaneous approach on the part of the rider would be much more successful.

The results of the coaster experiment often prompt someone to question why then, a beginner bicyclist might run into the only tree in his entire practice field even though he's trying to avoid it.

Every intensely imagined movement (here: crashing into the tree) contains the tendency to become reality through minimal suggestions of movement. This phenomenon can also be observed in novice skiers, although they typically do not deviate from the planned path nearly as much as bicyclists can. On a bicycle, the tendency to try to steer away from the obstacle leads to a slight lean toward the obstacle, which can be corrected only by another steering input toward the obstacle—a vicious repetitive cycle whose effect is intensified with every repetition.

Motorcyclists with relatively little experience occasionally complain that they have trouble with riding close to the edge of the road or along a curb, because it seems to magically pull them to the edge. Offroad, a rut or ridge that we really want to just ride around, or a rock that we don't want to run over, can have the same effect. The more experienced the rider, the less he will feel this kind of "magical pull."

Helmut W. Bönsch drew my attention to a very similar situation that nevertheless does not have its basis in the head of the rider. In strong crosswinds, when a rider approaches a truck, he will prepare to pass it with a slight rightward lean to counter the pressure from the crosswind. At precisely the moment when he gets into the lee of the truck, however, this will turn into a right-hand curve toward the truck that can be stopped only with an even stronger and sometimes frighteningly conscious steering effort toward the truck.

Why it's a good idea to look far ahead

This coaster experiment leads directly to a practical recommendation for better riding: do not stare at the apex of a corner as if hypnotized! However, the further one goes with systematic instruction and practice with corners, the more likely he is to do this. Until the process is fully automated, one should take only a quick look at the path of the ideal line as he approaches the corner, essentially as a review of the movement plan, and then look far ahead down the track. The movement plan will then prevail all the better.

The beginner off-road rider is told something similar. Almost the first thing a new rider is told "in the gravel" is not to look right in front of the front wheel, but instead to look farther ahead. It never ceases to amaze people how much better the riding suddenly works.

Also note that whenever a rider thinks he has to really put in an effort, he has a tendency to stare fixedly at the

⚞ "Decoupling" one's gaze from a focus on the road

A common recommendation advocates separating the direction of the gaze from the direction of the road. This may accomplish a lot, but it can't be easily monitored by the rider, to say nothing of the fact that on a straight road, this "separation" is not even necessary. A better formulation would be to "decouple" the direction of one's gaze from a focus on the road, although this sounds slightly complicated and still does not ensure that one's gaze falls far enough ahead. Eberspächer separates perception with: "Feel the motorcycle with your rear end; let your view reach far ahead."

Gazing far ahead does not mean staring *fixedly* off as far as possible into the distance. Instead, it means letting the focus swing easily between far and near, to "read" the road. ∎

front wheel so that he can very carefully see which groove or crevice he's about to land in and which stone he's about to roll over—and then, as everything immediately becomes much more difficult, he will see this as is confirmation that the section really is tough and that he really needs to work hard and concentrate. A whole lot of practice is needed before he will be truly free of the bad habit of constantly staring at what's directly in front of the front wheel.

On the street or at the track, the same phenomenon occurs whenever things get difficult, such as when one is approaching a complicated series of corners: there is the same tendency to shorten one's sights. This kind of error is almost the rule among inexperienced riders, but it can also surface in experienced riders, when, for whatever reason, they become distressed. The rider then looks only at the very next kink in the road, although he could be looking far beyond it; or he only looks at the apex of the next corner; or, still closer, he only looks at the **turn-in point** at the entrance to the corner, and his attention remains there until he's just about to reach the entrance. Then he seeks the next object that he will stare at, which of course is also far too close. And it all seems to be happening incredibly fast. The result is a rider's concentrating only on very short segments, individually and firmly in sequence, making it impossible to achieve a smoothly flowing line.

True experts always look surprisingly far ahead. On track courses, the instructor looks far ahead and his head is almost tipped back because of the forward lean of his upper body—and his "brood" follows behind, heads down. When it starts to rain, often a rider does not even look beyond the rear wheel of the rider ahead, something that is obvious just by observing the position of his helmet; because of how far the helmet sticks out just above one's eyebrows, it's impossible to look far ahead if the head is lowered even slightly. This is also the reason why, for example in races, the head leans counter to the body instead of with it (see cover photo). One might hear from time to time that this is done in order to keep the horizon more or less horizontal, but this is, at best, only half of the truth. More important, keeping your head up makes it *much* easier, with large lean angles and a forward lean with the upper body, to look far enough into and beyond the corner. Even the average rider on public roads can reap these benefits by keeping his head level.

Look far ahead. I can think of no recommendation that leads so quickly to a palpable and visible improvement of one's riding style. But I also can't think of one that, in spite of it all, is more often forgotten and takes so long to become firmly "seated" (compare p. 150).

Throwing a ball and riding a motorcycle: closed and open action programs in movement plans

The starting point of our observation was the ball toss, a simple game containing many of the same concepts that play important roles in motorcycling, which is far more complicated. It is easy to get an overview of the individual phases in the ball-toss example, not only because the course of events is simpler, but also because it's a matter of an individual and a "discrete" process, with a clear beginning and end—that is, it is a more "closed" **action program.** This is entirely the opposite of motorcycle riding with its "open" courses of action (open action program): not only does one action lead into the next, but there are always several processes going on at the same time, many of which become mysteriously linked to each other. Sometimes these processes may even influence each other, even if they are happening independently.

But even with the relatively simple ball toss, we could see that sophisticated movement processes were obviously being controlled from an area of the brain that is inaccessible to the conscious self, to say nothing of the much too limited channel capacity of the conscious self and its inability to manage lightning-fast fine-tuning and **coordination.** Thus, performance progressively worsens the more self-consciously one gets involved. Too closely focusing one's attention will hinder the process (the movement plan), as was evident when the ball-tosser looked at the ball (rather than at the target) and also in the rider who fixed his gaze on the coaster. When one concentrates only on a very particular part of the action, he loses sight of the whole.

Trigger movement and response movement

In the implementation of a movement plan lies one of the secrets to the fascination of riding a motorcycle: First, a movement plan is set up, largely without conscious input, let's say for riding through a corner. But the movements the rider *himself* carries out to implement this plan appear to have little connection with the resulting movement process of the *overall system,* that is, *the rider plus motorcycle.* At least, the connection between the two is not readily apparent to an observer.

Mirror Neurons

Although these statements about thoughts and forces were based originally on observation alone, a century and a half later, the discovery of the "mirror neurons" shed some light on the mysterious phenomenon. There are particular nerve cells that not only become active for the initiation and control of a goal-oriented action, but also fire during the imagination of that action or simply by the perception of such an action being performed by another person (Gallese & Goldman 1998). Thus, it's not an action that is carried out but rather an action that is *reflected,* hence the term "mirror neurons." Some neuronal activity is also necessary to make sure that the execution of the activity being reflected is indeed blocked—but this is something that evidently isn't always successful.

The mirror neurons play a decisive roll in learning by imitation, which is one of the most important types of learning in humans, and they are especially important in the movement plan (p. 58). ∎

This requires further explanation. In a jump, a toss, or a punch, the movement plan has a very direct and obvious connection with the movement that results from it. But this is substantially different with a motorcycle. While the rider's movement plan (as in riding through a corner) is related to the subsequent movement process *of the overall system,* the muscular movements of the rider to bring this about are of an entirely different sort. For example, tiny movements in the handlebar initiate countersteering; minimal changes in the position of the throttle influence the lean angle; or even—and this can have enormous effects—the *suppression* or the complete *omission* of a movement can influence the overall dynamics of the man-machine mass (see "Thoughts are forces" below).

The controlling muscular movements are not only of an entirely different sort than the resulting movements of the motorcycle, and they are not just distant physically from the movement of the overall system, but more than anything, they're unimaginably small. They are so small that in most cases, we don't even register them anymore, and they occur without any conscious awareness (compare sidebar, p. 44). For this reason, with an especially "corner-happy" bike, you can get the impression that—as is often half jokingly stated—*All I have to do is look into a corner, and the motorcycle just goes in by itself,* exactly following the line in the movement plan.

Even though I know all about what's actually happening, sometimes when I am riding a particularly sensitive motorcycle, I suddenly become convinced, once again, that there simply are bikes that have somehow learned to read the minds of their riders. Or, is it actually possible that forces arise from our thoughts?

Thoughts are forces

The slogan "Thoughts are forces" is often used in the world of the occult. There's only one thing certain about it, but it is respectable enough: a conceived movement does not remain an image in isolation. These imagined movements "jump over" or "break through" to the physical side, even if only to the slightest possible extent.

The facts about the initiation of minimal movements by simple imagination has occupied academic psychologists for quite some time. Every imagination of a movement, as they put it, releases a tendency to carry out this same movement. Taking this a step further: it's not just the imagination of movement of one's own body; becoming aware of a movement of another person releases the same urge for physical movement.

To test the idea that a conceived movement does not remain an image in isolation, we only need to look for something in which even very minimal forces can lead to considerable movement, such as undamped oscillations in a pendulum. Very small impulses, provided they occur at the right moment, can "build up" and lead to an ever-widening swing.

Because the results of this experiment are so astounding, the effect is exploited in all kinds of magic tricks. Hang a button on a thread above an X marked on a table top (see Figure 44); allow the button to swing back and forth between A and B. Support your elbow, try to hold your hand as still as possible, and say under your breath, in the right rhythm, "A" and "B" for the end points. The button (pendulum) will not stop swinging. Your first insight should be that the impulses are still getting through, unnoticed, even though you don't want to pass them on and are trying to suppress them. But there's more: if you start to concentrate on C and D, even while still trying to hold your hand as still as possible, it will not be long before the pendulum starts to swing along the other axis.

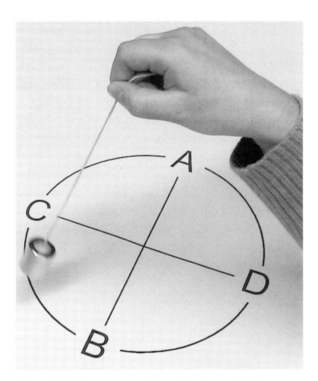

Figure M44. Hocus pocus? Even the thought of a particular direction can influence the pendulum.

Soon, you can also manage to elicit the circular path A - D - B - C (whereby the letters have to be spoken twice as quickly). And finally you'll manage, after only a slight period of renewed swinging on a single axis, to get the pendulum to follow the circle in reverse (A - C - B - D).

As already shown, the whole thing is a bit more complicated with motorcycles. The rider not only *inputs* fine impulses into the motorcycle, but even more frequently, he also does the opposite. Out of the constant barrage of small and large disturbances to which the motorcycle is being subjected (irregularities of the pavement, wind buffeting, and so on), which might be described as mechanical "noise," the rider filters out the impulses that he doesn't have any use for, so that the others (that he is not suppressing or is actually aiding) can win the upper hand. This does not preclude him from giving stronger inputs, such as might be needed for a rapid transition from one lean to the other (see also p. 138).

DANGERS AND RISKS

Dangers of riding too spontaneously

Of course, something that happens "by itself" to the extent we've discussed is not only fascinating but also potentially dangerous. While everything may work more easily and more in accordance with the course of action, this riding entirely under the control of the spontaneous, subconscious self is also completely *uncritical* riding in the sense that the conscious self has only minimal involvement in it. When this is the case, one may act in ways that he never would have if he had been thinking clearly. For example, after a blind corner you suddenly see a few construction workers in the right lane. On the left is heavy oncoming traffic. Between the opposing traffic and the construction site, there's still a bit of space, but this starts to close as the workers move around. You can tell immediately—you can practically *feel* it physically and with great certainty—that there's still plenty of space and that you won't need to stop. As you ride through at full speed, a worker leaps backward. Everything works out fine, but afterward you ask yourself how you could have done something so reckless and inconsiderate.

In this example, the **movement plan** was *spontaneously* and directly turned into immediate action, unmodified by the hesitant, conscious self, with its cumbersome cerebrum; it also happened without consideration and without any thought about its possible consequences. This spontaneous kind of riding is extremely effortless and it is the only way to get through re-

🏍 As if riding in a trance

The effortless experience of riding from the subconscious self (spontaneously) can be described as riding "as if in a **trance.**" For this same reason, it also tends to be uncritical and uninhibited, in the sense of being "unrestrained," or free from strict self-control.

The sensitive Count Berghe von Trips, an accomplished German Formula-1 driver who died in a fatal crash at Monza in 1961, understood this early on and worked unremittingly to internalize this understanding. He spoke of a "quasi animal-like driving" (which was not meant pejoratively at all), and once he achieved this driving state, he could manage unbelievable amounts of pressure.   ∎

ally long stretches, but it takes a lot of practice to strike and maintain the right balance between spontaneity and direct control.

The effortless feel—the direct implementation of a plan without the active involvement of the conscious self—is part of the fun of riding a motorcycle. It can be downright euphoric. Very young riders, the first few times they step into this new dimension, usually experience this heady sensation. This kind of feeling is reflected in many common cliches: "I was on rails;" "Suddenly I was riding like *never* before;" "It all seemed to be happening by itself;" "It was like a dream;" "It was as if I were my own passenger." Those who know better will shake their heads and just hope that this is not the beginning of a tale of an accident. When a rider experiences this kind of euphoria, and everything suddenly seems to be happening with an all-too-playful lightness, alarms should go off. (See "Flow, Simultaneously Helper and Enemy," p. 107)

Paying attention without getting involved

It's true that spontaneous riding, completely under the control of the subconscious self, is both our goal and the basis of truly perfect riding, but at the same time it requires special vigilance. This is a job for the conscious self, which, even though everything is going along so nicely, shouldn't leave the scene entirely; it should not, however, get directly involved in the processes either. This alert watchfulness, without meddling, is a fairly unstable condition, which degrades all too easily into either a complete lack of watchfulness or too much involvement. It demands, as stated above, continuous practice, even for the expert.

In any case, when left entirely alone, the subconscious self will be overtaxed. It's not that this will lead to a breakdown in performance; it is actually more dangerous: very

specific errors can creep in, which can easily become disastrous. Almost all errors of this type can be summarized in one way: the rider lacked insight into what *could happen* in a particular situation. We are reminded of the example on page , describing the rider who crashed right into a logging truck around a blind corner. Dangers that are not directly observable remain hidden from the subconscious self, unless the rider is specifically prepared to recognize particular risks.

Eons ago, in the dim, dark past, on wide-open hunting grounds, these kinds of risks didn't often arise, because in most cases there was plenty of time to adjust one's circumstances and avoid the danger. Under our present motorcycling environments, however, situations with surprising, unmanageable risks do arise.

Example of a threat that's hard to visualize

A good example of an entirely abstract but very real danger is a blinding, low sun in front of you. The problem is that when you experience reduced vision because of the blinding sun, the person whom you see poorly, if at all, is very much in danger—deceptively so, since he has particularly *clear* vision of you with the sun behind him. Driving in the fog also reduces visibility but poses quite a different situation, since visibility is reduced for parties going in both directions, making all drivers more alert to the danger.

Seeing your own shadow directly in front of the bike on the road should therefore trigger an alarm of the first degree, especially if the shadow is long. This is especially important when the shadow points in the direction of other traffic, either opposing traffic, or a person waiting to turn, or a person waiting at an intersection or entrance. This danger is one that not all traffic participants are aware of, and only very few (such as professional riders in tests) are conditioned to pay attention to. They are so strongly oriented toward this invisible danger that seeing their own shadow in front of them immediately sets off an alarm; the initiation of appropriate safety measures occurs almost automatically. You should register the highest level of alert when you are blinded by the sun from your own rearview mirrors (compare also p. 161).

One simply has to *know* about some situations before behavior can be adapted on the basis of this knowledge. But even then, it's still possible for this knowledge to remain too faint or abstract and thus to affect our behavior only a little bit or not at all. The motorcyclist who crashes into a logging truck around a blind corner on a familiar road most certainly *knew* about the possibility of hidden obstacles, but he did something that is very characteristic of the subconscious self. In the approach to the corner, he obviously made no differentiation between the perceived picture and the imagined picture—that is, between the first part of the corner, which he could actually see, and the hidden part of the corner, which he knew as well as he knew the first part but could not see.

Actually, it is more complicated: even if a rider realizes the risk inherent in relying completely on the imagined picture, it still doesn't mean that he will select a speed at which he could easily and safety deal with an obstacle that suddenly appeared at the exit of the corner. Instead, he's more likely to do something very strange: to ride *just a little more slowly* because there *might* be an obstacle there, but he'd still be going *far too fast* if there actually were an obstacle there.

Lying to ourselves: the risk composite

The so-called **risk composite,** whereby the rider calculates a sort of risk average based on the severity of the possible event (which could be fatal) and the likelihood that it will actually occur (which, in fact, is rather small) is a form of self-delusion.

Our everyday lives are full of nonsensical "middle-ground" solutions that are completely inadequate. In these situations, rational control has to step in and make improvements. The subconscious self does not have access to all the right kinds of **programs** for a behavior appropriate for risky situations.

TRUST IN THE SUBCONSCIOUS SELF

Even though we have had occasion to cast doubt on certain capabilities of the reasoning mind, I do not want to project the false impression that I agree with those who see the root of all modern evils in cold, calculating rea-

Figure M45. Nürburgring, Nurberg Germany, considered by many to be the most challenging racetrace in the world.

Riding from memory

At the Nordschleife of the Nürburgring, there are a few segments of the track that must be ridden in accordance with the rider's mental image of the course, not merely what he can see. In these segments the rider must *initiate* action according to the "perceived" image (the image he can see but is insufficient for completion of the action); thus, the action must be completed or complemented according to the rider's mental image of the track that follows the portion he *can* see. Corners that can't even be seen yet are approached with precision, and sometimes the motorcycle is pushed into a turn at a point at which the track seems to still go straight (such as a turn on the other side of a rise).

What's remarkable about this is that if one knows the course well, he can ride according to his mental image rather than just the perceived image. Another remarkable thing is that one can add to an incomplete perceived image with a mental image. When this happens, the transition occurs so smoothly that one hardly knows that it has happened. Many experiments in the psychology of perception have shown that the perceived image and the mental image can't always be differentiated—therein lies the danger. For this reason, one should never ride based on a mental image, except on a closed track where one can rely on the alertness of the corner workers and their flags.

In any case, there must be a strict differentiation not only between perception and imagination (which is not so simple in practice), but also between the mental image and the *expected* image. The mental image is acquired by means of intensive practice on a track. Only then can it become precise and reliable enough, even as it becomes gradually more and more difficult to differentiate from the perceived image. Before such training, there is only an *expected* image, which is more or less just a vague presumption about what the perceived image might look like. ∎

son. Such people are suspicious of "Western thought," mistrust all rational ideas, and see rational, scientific research as a dangerous aberration, which they would just prefer to end with a general about-face. But in a difficult period such as the one we live in, there could be nothing worse than undertaking a sort of mental self-mutilation by giving up our capacity for rational thought. This was also an important concern of von Ditfurth (1992): "These days, there are many signs that indicate that we are approaching an epoch not only of increasing animosity toward science, but also one of increasing propensity toward irrationality. But if we want to re-emerge alive from the crisis into which we have fallen because of the uncritical application of scientific insights, then we need more rationality than ever before, not less."

This book is anything but a plea against the mind. Indeed, we have just seen that there are situations in which rational control by the conscious self is *urgently* needed. And we will encounter still other tasks of rational thought that cannot be delegated to the spontaneous, subconscious self.

My only goal in expressing reservations about the powers of reason is to make people aware of how effectively our subconscious self can help us. Since we are all raised in an environment that is oriented toward more cerebral activities of the conscious self, an appreciation of the hidden, subconscious self must be cultivated.

I want to instill in the reader a feeling for the capabilities of this subconscious self, which will stay faithfully by his side and without which he could not exist at all. In short, I want readers to learn to *trust* this powerful helper. Although humans rely on the subconscious, in our lack of understanding we all too easily disturb it by means of interruptions and constant skeptical surveillance.

It is easiest to foster the necessary trust with a few examples that we can easily relate to. They have purposely been taken from outside the world of motorcycling, as it would be very odd indeed if all this did not apply to many other aspects of life as well.

A window to the unknown

Lars Gustafsson, in his short story "The Tennis Players," writes:

> In world championships, like for example the Australian Open, it can happen that a player makes three double-faults in a row.

> This is a testament to the degree of difficulty. No one really knows how to serve a tennis ball. Of course we have basic ideas of how it works, but no one who's actually in the process of serving can be certain that it's going to work. There's really only one possibility, and that's to entrust the whole thing to that dark, silent side of our personality; to rely on it, and under no circumstances to disturb it. Only then is one in a position to carry out the dizzying feat of muscle coordination, ballistic calculations, tiny adjustments to the positioning of the joints in the hands and feet, precise motions of the back muscles, et cetera, that go into a serve.

> The serve is a window to the unknown.

Gustafsson is an unsuspicious witness, because he's reporting from a completely different world, but tennis is nonetheless full of examples that relate to our topic. While it's true that there are substantial differences between tennis and motorcycling, the human being that performs them is ultimately the same.

Gustafsson recommends one to "hand oneself over to the dark, silent side of one's own personality" (the subconscious self), and to "trust it entirely, and not to disturb it under any circumstances." What kinds of disturbances could he mean?

Self-observation as a disturbance

There are a number of things that could be disturbances. We'll discuss the disturbances of *fear* and *tension* in more detail later (p. 134), but in the present context we're mainly interested in the way in which we become *conscious* of our own activity while the action is being carried out. The mildest form of this conscious awareness is self-observation, in which we pay attention to our own doings, but even that can be enough to cause a lasting disruption of the activity.

Another example from the world of tennis relates a mean trick that one can use in club matches or games with friends, whereby a few pointed words can create an insurmountable advantage. During a break, one says to his opponent, "Your backhand is looking fantastic today! . . . Absolutely perfect. Nobody in the whole club has such a great backhand. It looks incredibly elegant, too!" And then, "So tell me, how are you holding the racket? Show me exactly how you position your hand . . . And show me your stroke, really slowly . . . And just how are you positioning your shoulder?" and so forth.

Our opponent will of course feel flattered, and he'll show us everything and demonstrate willingly. *But he won't have a single successful backhand for the rest of the day!*

Attention and conscious awareness as disadvantages

Every competent golfer knows how much of a disadvantage self-observation can be while the activity is being carried out. Golf, it appears, is *also* played in one's the head. He's prepared to explain all manner of things to an interested bystander—what the most important rules are, which clubs one should use for this or that situation, why the wind has to be taken into account here and not there, the effects of dew on the green, etc., but our golfer will fall silent as soon as the execution of the actual action comes up; the stroke comes entirely "from the gut." He would never dream of announcing or explaining all the individual, sequential phases of the stroke as he performs them. He has at least some vague notion that this kind of conscious awareness would lead to failure.

It's true that there are specialists who can actually take the stroke and simultaneously talk about it. Furthermore, they can deconstruct the stroke and perform one phase, then pause and explain, and then repeat it again slowly, then continue with the course of action, then pause, back up, and finally hit the ball. These are *golf instructors*. They had to learn a double activity: acting "from the gut" and simultaneously explaining things in a mindful manner.

The golf instructor might add that his stroke is better when he's not doing it as part of a demonstration. Sometimes, one even hears a golf instructor say that he used to play better before he became an instructor, because he had then played by feel and without much thought. By now it will have occurred to the reader why this would be so: the explaining involved in the instruction raised the entire course of action to a far too conscious level. The conscious self suddenly becomes involved, meddles in the activity, and usurps the subconscious self's control. As a consequence, the course of action is compromised, and may even be disrupted to the point that it becomes impossible to continue.

Self-awareness and verbalization as hindrances

Such influences of consciousness are evident in all aspects of life, even to the most demanding of human activities. Consider an established painter or sculptor who has been called to join an academy, only to find that this

The Arlberg method

The deficiencies of oral instruction became enduringly clear at the end of the 1920s when Hannes Schneider put skiing and ski instruction on a more solid basis (the Arlberg method). He did not rely exclusively on the *"testimony"* of the ski instructors (and also not on his own ideas). Instead, with the help of Kruckenhauser, he was the first to turn to more exact methods of movement analysis by *filming* particularly successful skiers. The discrepancy between the completely subjective description of the movement process and the objective movement analysis was considerable and justified the Arlberg method, which at the time was not an easy undertaking. ∎

appointment takes a big bite out of his creative work. In the worst case, his productivity will dry up; at the very least, the change reflected in his oeuvre will be noticeable. What happened? Now that he's playing a teaching role, the artist is suddenly forced to pay attention to his own creative process—that is, the germination and brewing of an idea in the subconscious self must be observed while it gradually takes shape. Prior to this, an idea had been relatively spontaneous and had manifested itself as a work of art without the central involvement of the conscious self. Now, the artist must not only rationally *observe* this process but is also forced to put it into words to explain it to academy students. He has to talk about it all, and this is something that often goes against the grain of a visual artist.

Kleist, in his essay "On Marionettes," described "the youth in front of the mirror," whose graceful movements became ever more stiff and deliberate the more he gazed narcissistically at his image in the mirror and the more he tried to come up with ever more pleasing movements. It's hard to come up with a better description of the negative consequences of self-observation.

The influence of an audience on self-observation

Self-conscious self-observation is the clearest form of "heightened attention." However, heightened attention can also mean having a strong accompanying will to perform an action especially well and to really "pull oneself together" when carrying out the course of action, as sometimes is brought about by the presence of an audience.

◆ Zen in the Art of Archery

The Japanese archer's motto is known among many Western archers in its abbreviated form: "Hit the target without thinking about the target." But there's more to the motto: "Because all desire limits the spirit." Once one understands the shift between thinking about the target that he wants to reach (by means of a very specific action) and mentally internalizing the achievement, one can recognize that the motto is an admonition against supervising oneself during the execution of an action, which would invoke meddling by the conscious self.

In his book "Zen in the Art of Archery," German philosopher Eugen Herrigel (1979) tells of several years of instruction with a Japanese master. One day, after years of training, the instructor called out with respect: "Just now, 'it' shot."

This fits well into our picture, as does the constant reminder that Herrigel heard: "Don't think about what you have to do; don't consider how it is to be done"—at least not at the moment of execution of the action.

However, it's not just incorrect thoughts and images, but also purely physical things that can cause problems in archery, a discipline in which performance is so easily disturbed. Muscle tension is enough to ruin a shot, even when these muscles are not directly required for the movement. Anyone who plays tennis can demonstrate this through a simple experiment, by balling his free hand into a tight fist in the middle of a play; it will then no longer be possible to predict where the next ball will end up!

This is why motorcycle training courses strongly urge riders to always stay *loose* when riding, especially after hours in the saddle or after experiencing a frightening situation. ■

For a long time, the influence on performance caused by the presence of others was a favored research topic of both social and sports psychologists. The results, however, were initially frustratingly contradictory, since it could lead to either an improvement or a worsening of performance. R. B. Zajonc finally resolved the contradiction by proving that after the level of consciousness is raised, the prevailing behavior will be the one that has the strongest **habituation,** has been practiced the best, and has sunk in the deepest either because it was inborn or is highly automated; whether it leads to an improvement or a worsening depends on the situation. (This, by the way, has a lot to do with "relapse," when an old behavior returns even though it was thought to have been eradicated through training; for more detail see p. 117).

Thus, the more reliable a command the "performer" has over the required courses of action (that is, the more automated they are), the greater the chance that the presence of an audience will lead to an improvement in performance. Therefore, a confident, well-trained athlete will likely experience an improvement in performance in the presence of an encouraging audience. In contrast, a nervous or uncertain musician in an audition is more likely to experience a worsening of performance due to the influence of critical judges. (An overview of this effect can be found in M. Rosch 1985.)

Archery might be the most disruptable of all human arts, a "sport that takes place half in the soul and half on the field," as described by Manfred Sack (1987, p. 48). Every consideration of how to hold the bow, how to place the arrow, when to let it go, etc., will reliably block a good performance, if it happens during the action. A skilled archer looks intently at the target and is with all of his thoughts, there *in* the bullseye, so it's correct to say that he "thinks" the arrow into the target. The correct action that goes with it is handled by another part of the brain.

The acquired **programs** are not necessarily always the shakiest, or the most likely to fail or easiest to disrupt. Inborn programs that have been transmitted genetically also are not unshakeably solid in all situations; they are fallible even under such gentle influences as self-observation (see "Programs that control actions," p. 28).

Thus, *swallowing* is a very basic function that is important to survival and is therefore all too easily seen as unchangeable, but it is actually highly dependent on whether one leaves it up to the subconscious self and just swallows without deliberation or the conscious self, which deliberately meddles in the action.

Almost everyone notices that swallowing is oddly difficult when taking a tablet, that is much harder than "everyday" swallowing, and there is always someone who professes to be utterly unable to swallow a pill in spite of how much he might want to. However, the same person, hurrying off to work, might swallow a sizable piece of unchewed bread in the midst of a whole mouthful of poorly chewed food, but he's thinking about the traffic, the time, and not being late—not the act of swallowing. If he concentrates on the swallowing, because he absolutely *wants* to swallow something at a particular moment, he can't.

Disturbance by self-conscious awareness—does this make any sense?

With these strange and diverse examples, the question becomes all the more insistent about why the focusing of one's attention on the execution of an otherwise automatic and flawless course of action disrupts it, sometimes to the point of failure. What is the biological reasoning behind this? What is it about a human being engaging his most valuable and unique organ—his cerebrum—and "switching on" his conscious self, that it ruins the whole thing?

Quite correctly, it is always emphasized that the cerebrum developed as an "instrument" to aid in survival (and not as an instrument for philosophizing or solving mathematical problems) and this general development strategy of "insight over biceps" seems to have been a great success. But in our examples, this instrument fails to help when it gets involved. Worse still, it doesn't only fail to help but also *dramatically* worsens the whole situation, something that is especially evident with sports that carry some level of risk, such as motorcycling. To make biological sense of this, we must figure out what meaning this paradoxical phenomenon might have had under circumstances that existed long ago.

Too-strenuous desire

With a child who has the hiccups, one can elegantly exploit the interference with automatic actions that can result from attention and deliberation. Instead of trying all kinds of home remedies, one should instead offer a reward for continued hiccups. "So, one more hiccup, and for each one after that, you'll get a quarter for your piggy bank." The child puts in a lot of effort, but for this very reason, the hiccups stop.

Ability and knowledge: their limits

Our everyday lives are full of similar examples that can be examined in this context. Thus, at a job interview, if one wanted to find out whether the applicant could type, it would be silly to ask him: "Tell me please, *quickly,* which finger you use on a keyboard for the 'p'!" With automated actions, one doesn't even have to know this, but a skilled typist would come up with the answer by starting to "type" on an *imaginary* keyboard. He's telling the subconscious self: "Type something that has a 'p' in it so I can see which finger is used."

Clearly, somewhere, there's a precise bit of information—the finger used to type the 'p'—*that the conscious self obviously cannot access.* Our self-conscious **memory** has saved nothing. Only during the learning process, during the **acquisition** of an automated action, was something stored there for a short time. The information still exists, but it is now part of a **program** that's being stored in a completely different location, one that falls within the domain of the subconscious self.

Thus, if one accosted a motorcyclist with the question, "Tell me quickly which hand—left or right—do you use to brake?" he might first move his hands a little to test and would then answer hesitantly, "The right hand." However, one would be drawing the wrong conclusion if he were to say: "I'll never be *his* passenger again. Did you see how long it took before he could say which hand he used for braking?"

It's quite clear in this case that there are two aspects involved: one that performs the action and one that answers. By trying it out, the rider was able to determine the answer—but that doesn't necessarily have to be the case.

Let's say someone lets his friend drive his car and gets into the passenger seat. When the friend asks where reverse is, the owner replies, "Left front." The friend shifts around a while but cannot get it into reverse. The owner advises: "Okay, keep your foot on the clutch," and tries it himself (with his left hand, of course), but cannot engage reverse either. Eventually, the owner of the car and his friend get out and trade positions. And as soon as the owner puts his *right* hand on the shifter, he suddenly feels as if his memory were seated in his hand. Reverse is actually *to the right at the rear,* and he feels absolute certainty about this even before he puts it into gear. Surely this is something that he *knew* at some point, maybe from reading the owner's manual when the car was new, but it is something that has long since been dropped from memory. Why? Because it has long since been moved to another storage area, the contents of which can no longer be brought to the surface just by asking (as can be done with things stored in our "normal" memory), because the conscious self has no access to this other storage area. This seems a little strange to us, but the lack of access by the conscious self is in no way detrimental to these functions. In fact, it's quite the opposite: the path from this storage to the centers responsible for controlling these actions is far more direct than it would be if it went by way of the conscious memory, and it is much more stable, something that is related to the much larger channel capacity of the subconscious self (p. 50).

The reader can experience just what is happening with this mysterious storage area with an everyday activity: hand clasping. There are two ways to clasp the hands together: either the left thumb, index finger, ring finger, etc. are respectively on top of the corresponding fingers on the right hand, or the opposite is the case. In all people, one of the two possibilities is preferred, and some are hardly even aware of the other because they always do it in their one and only way. If they try clasping their hands together the other way, they feel strangely vexed: their own hands feel slightly alien to them, and they feel with great certainty that this is not the way in which they clasp their hands.

However, most people are unable to answer, without trying, the question of which of the two options he prefers—this happens even when the person has just tried both of the options for himself! There's hardly a better example than this to illustrate that the cerebrum, seat of

Figure 46. The simple act of clasping one's hands is actually the work of a complex built-in program. To clasp your hands with the opposite fingers on top requires conscious attention and feels very odd.

our consciousness, is in fact an "aftermarket accessory," as described earlier. Somewhere there's an exact action instruction in the form of a program, because we can clasp our hands together instantly, without attempts and corrections, under all conditions, even with our eyes closed or our hands behind our backs.

The procedural memory: a rather inaccessible repository

To clasp one's hands, a large number of finely harmonized and precisely coordinated muscles have to be activated, so it's hardly a simple program. Here we see it again, this enormous repository, distant from the self, ancient in terms of evolutionary history and not verbally coded. Sometimes called "procedural memory," this repository has a direct line to the brain centers that control actions. It was already outstandingly functional at a time when there still was no self-consciousness. When self-consciousness finally arrived as a function of the cerebrum, there was still absolutely no reason for its insertion in between the existing control centers.

Certainly, these ideas have been greatly simplified, but they explain why our conscious self has no direct access to this gigantic storehouse. There is only one way to retrieve what is contained in this storage area and that is to just try it, as in our hand-clasping experiment. This trying out is a much more cumbersome process than it appears to be at first glance, and it reveals yet again this remarkable hierarchical structure. After the conscious self can't find anything in its own memory to answer the question, it essentially gives the subconscious self an order to clasp hands. The latter has direct access to the procedural memory and thus can initiate and manage the hand-clasping process, and the conscious self can get the answer by looking at the results, after the fact, as if they were someone else's hands.

The inaccessible procedural memory is contrasted with the self-conscious memory; both belong to different regions of the brain. The self-conscious memory includes, for example, the "declarative" (or explanatory) and the "narrative" memory. The declarative memory is the factual, cold, knowledge memory, including vocabulary, names, formulas, functions, and all kinds of other information, from important dates in history to telephone numbers. The narrative memory is responsible for the memories that are much more colored by feelings, such as from one's personal life history with its more autobiographical or episodic character (thus, it is also called the "biographical" or "episodic" memory). The self-conscious

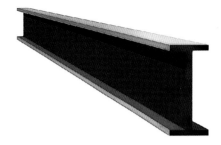

⟶ Case study: the raised beam

For many years at my institute, I had a testing facility that allowed one to preset the degree of experienced risk: on the gray floor, a 10cm-wide black strip ran across the room, not quite from wall to wall. At one end of the strip was a short, perpendicular landing. The subject was told to walk on the black strip, neatly setting one foot in front of the other as if he were on a balance beam. At the end of the strip, the subject had to turn around and come back. The task was so simple that the subjects couldn't really see the point of such an easy "test" and listened only casually to the instructions, just as a favor to the investigator.

In the next phase of the experiment, however, it became evident that the black strip was the top of an I-beam that could be raised up out of the floor. At a height of three or four centimeters, the task still came incredibly easily to the subjects, even if they were much more likely to watch the placement of their feet; any suggestion that this task was more difficult than the previous, however, would elicit protest. In spite of this, there was an obvious increase in the conscious self's involvement, and the action was no longer being carried out fairly spontaneously, as was evident in the subjects' glances at their feet. During the first phase, there was always at least one subject who performed the task with one hand in his pocket or on his hip (a demonstration of absolute effortlessness), but this was no longer the case during the second phase.

If the beam were raised to 45cm—about the seat height of a normal chair—the scenario became substantially different. Unlike previously, the subjects all put their hands on the landing behind them (which had been raised with the I-beam), or leaned on it with their bottoms, and looked in front of them at the beam before setting out. Upon starting, the subject's gaze would usually sink still farther, and each footstep was carefully watched and controlled. Eyes and attention were fully focused on the tiny area immediately in front of the feet—something

that any tightrope walker or gymnast would tell us is extremely detrimental. The arms became somewhat spread out from the body, and the hands were slightly raised. If the subject was told, "Earlier you were moving your head much more freely, and once you even looked over toward me when I talked to you. But now you're looking fixedly at your toes," he would turn his head toward the investigator for just a moment, literally in the blink of an eye, and would look back at his feet on the beam just as quickly.

At the daunting height of 1.5 meters, the scenario became substantially worse, and there could be no doubt about whether the subjects were experiencing risk. In addition to the heightened level of attention already seen, there was now a physical tension that bordered on cramping. Before setting out, the subjects not only held onto the landing, some actually clung to it. When they started, they usually took a deep breath, spread their arms wide, and pressed their lips tightly together—a picture of extreme focus. But in spite of this, most subjects only made it a few meters before they lost their balance and had to jump off.

The same task, which had been so ridiculously easy at first, had become more and more difficult with each phase and became impossible for the subjects. The increased subjective feeling of risk spawned increased attention, conscious effort, and focus, which led to stress, tension, and finally failure.

Over time, some subjects achieved a remarkable ability with the balance beam and gradually moved with greater certainty on it, but as the height of the beam was gradually increased, the characteristics of increased conscious attention gradually increased as well, and they never reached the same level of confidence that they had when the height was zero.

The goal of "danger training" like this is to reduce the subjective risk without underestimating the objective risk so that the experienced level of risk has less effect on the execution of an action. ∎

memory is what we generally understand as our "memory." It's the memory from which we reproduce the contents of our knowledge and that which helps us explain things we encounter and tell stories about our experiences. It is not the memory from which automated action processes are controlled (see also Gazzaniga 1988, p.124).

When a question is asked about how a basic action works, the self-conscious memory is useless as a repository, as the process was not recorded there. In order to give an answer (which is a job for the conscious self), the action process first had to be *initiated* (by the conscious self) and then *executed* (by the subconscious self) out of the procedural memory. During this time, through self-observation, the self-conscious memory is temporarily supplied with the information necessary to give the answer in the form of a report or narration.

The disruption of automated activities' becoming conscious ones

When automated activities are made conscious activities during their execution, it can lead to major disruptions in the process (action programs). This prompts us to

Figure 47. Learning to ride a bicycle illustrates vividly the gradual process of transforming conscious physical actions into programs that help us perform automatically to balance and turn.

question what kind of biological purpose this could possibly serve. To find the answer, we first need to examine the circumstances under which this highly unwelcome disturbance occurs. As a key example, let's look at a child learning to ride a bicycle and observe the changes in the way he's thinking and feeling while this is going on.

One Sunday morning, the father removes the training wheels from the bicycle because he's decided it's time for the child to learn to ride. The child has already mastered the pedaling and can also steer a little; the only thing left to learn is balancing. Initially, the father will keep the child balanced by holding onto the seat, and he'll probably give the child a few simple suggestions, like, "When the bicycle falls to *this* side, then you have to steer toward the *same* side that the bicycle wants to fall. Then it will straighten back up. If you steer *away* from it, you'll fall right over." They might practice this a few times standing still, and then, saying nothing about more refined **coordination** of the **steering inputs,** the father starts to push.

The child can tell immediately and obviously that his steering movements really do have an influence on which way he leans. For a few moments, he consciously applies his father's advice and is successful. Then a very immediate form of unconscious learning begins to develop in the form of an ever more sophisticated input-output scheme in the **program**.

The child might lapse again at some point and make the wrong movement, and the father had better be ready to hold on tightly. But even this kind of negative experience contributes to reinforcement and helps to further solidify the proper scheme for processing the fault messages that are arriving in a constant stream.

There's not yet much to see in the way of refined coordination or calibration. The movements still look a little choppy and don't flow smoothly together. In particular, the magnitude and speed of the steering movements are not quite yet properly matched to the lean angle deviations to which they are reacting.

The child soon notices that it's much easier to balance if he rides faster. The father, reassured by the child's improvement, lets go of the bicycle and runs along behind, just in case. But as the distance gradually increases, the child suddenly shouts, "Hey! You're not there!" and falls over at the same moment. The father might just barely manage to catch him.

The experience of heightened risk

What happened here? Something dramatic, as can be seen from the feelings of the child and the way they changed so quickly. At the very beginning, he felt a mixture of curiosity and fun, and maybe even excitement. Then, this turned into slight anxiety when he got onto the bicycle during the simulation. When he actually started to ride, it turned into an anticipating, anxious tension, followed by a joyful feeling of flying as he rode faster, which suddenly stopped because he felt fear. The growing feeling of freedom and assurance was immediately replaced by an abrupt increase in the experience of heightened risk (father is gone!), which instantly provoked fear and led to a collapse of the automated program that was being constructed. The instructions that had been so consciously followed at first, "when A and B happens, then I have to do X and Y," were just sinking in—just being passed on to the subconscious self, and just becoming automatic. The program was anything but solid, and this is why it was so easy for it to collapse. At the moment of perceived danger, the conscious self jumped into the breach, grabbed the whole action back from the subconscious self, and failed.

When it comes to our question about the biological purpose of this mechanism, the experience of risk is much more important than fear. Fear is only a particular case. There are other triggers that lead to stronger involvement of the conscious self, but some kind of increased experience of risk plays a role in every situation.

Note that the increased experience of risk can also manifest itself in other ways and can even sneak up gradually. As one thinks of an upcoming exam (or audition or speech), he is increasingly robbed of his composure as the date nears. There's no sudden or frightening event that has occurred, but there is certainly an experience of *risk,* even if it is not a physical one. It might be the risk of failure, of not passing, of embarrassment, etc. And almost always, when there's something we *really* want to do well, such that we exert a conscious, deliberate effort in an attempt to control an action—basically whenever we observe ourselves—it's always linked to a situation in which we are attempting to confront an increased level of risk.

By now we have a better idea of the circumstances under which an increased involvement of the conscious self can arise even in an otherwise automated process. But the biological purpose of this mechanism is a question still unanswered.

Self-blockade: an extreme case

Let's imagine that a balance beam were positioned between two skyscrapers standing close together, maybe 300 meters above the ground. Hardly any of us would be prepared to walk across it. There might be one person who would would climb over the railing, spurred on by ambition within the group or by a foolish dare, but he would stop there as if paralyzed, looking down fearfully. His knees would knock, his brow would sweat, and he would hold on so tightly that his knuckles would be white. He would be *completely blocked* and thus unable to carry out the action of walking on it, from one skyscraper to the other.

Could it be that there's a barrier, a safety mechanism, that prevents man from getting himself into situations that are far too risky? It would be biologically useful as an aid to survival and would work according to a simple scheme: an experience of great risk could indicate a high likelihood of an objective threat, which might easily be avoided with a complete inability to act (for example, a severe dizzy spell at high altitude). For a long time, this was the dominant opinion.

I would like to try to disprove this without invoking the language of probability testing. Some industrious person has determined how common such total self-blockades are and also, more importantly, how commonly the milder forms of disruption occur in the form of uncertainties and deteriorations in performance. The resulting accumulation of errors are sometimes called "creeping blockades," and they can range from a mild, nearly invisible irritation during an action, all the way to a heavily compromised course of action that is poorly or barely managed. Using numerous examples and descriptions of processes, experts came up with an estimate of how great the physical endangerment was for each activity that was accompanied by greater or lesser degrees of uncertainty.

Regardless of whether he selected the more optimistic or the more pessimistic estimates of all the data for further analysis, our expert always came up with an extremely negative result. The total blockades, with their implicit survival function are so rare, and the milder creeping blockades, with their milder detraction from the activity, so common, that this safety mechanism, if it existed, would be a horribly faulty design. To be protected from great danger by a total self-blockade *maybe* one time in our entire lives, we would be subjected to unnecessarily increased danger (through diminished performance and increased errors) in an immense number of everyday situations. In individual situations in which creeping blockade might arise, the increased endangerment may not be considerable, but because of their great numbers, in sum they carry a greater weight than the extreme danger that would be mitigated by a total blockade. In other words, as a safety measure, this strategy has many risk-increasing disadvantages that outweigh its rare benefits.

So, there was no biological purpose and no survival advantage to be found. But why do these blockades (total and creeping) happen? At this point, we must free ourselves from the widespread notion that everything in nature has a reason or purpose or *had* a specific function in the past. It is much more likely that impractical or unhelpful characteristics or behaviors remain, despite evolutionary adaptations, provided they did not become *impediments* in the competition for survival.

THE PRICE WE HAVE TO PAY

Certainly a creeping blockade, provoked by the conscious self and its cerebrum, has caused harm to many people, but this has been bearable because one is compensated by the other tremendous competitive advantages that the cerebrum gives us. So, a creeping blockade is nothing more than an acceptable disadvantage that comes along with an immense advantage; it has no biological purpose. It's simply that under certain circumstances, the cerebrum gets involved and meddles in some things that are none of its business. One could say that the creeping blockade is the price we have to pay for having such a superior and miraculous brain at our disposal.

People sometimes accuse motorcyclists of having "turned off their brain"—not always an unjust accusation if we once again consider the rider who flew around a blind corner into a logging truck. But on the other hand, it's true that the motorcyclist is constantly plagued by ill-timed cerebral meddling. In subsequent discussions, we'll see how best to manage this.

Creeping blockades

Authority figures are among the factors that can trigger creeping blockades, such as when a ski coach stands purposely half-hidden on the trail and surprises the skier. The successful veteran racer might be unfazed when he spots the coach, but the young new team member might react with an error; the degree of associated danger is then dependent on the seriousness of the error. Because this has led to crashes in the past, most coaches have given up these games of hide-and-seek and are more likely to announce in advance where they plan to stand to watch the skier's descent.

The sensitive Dr. Giuseppe Farina, one of the Ferrari aces of the 1950s, drove measurably more slowly when his friend and rival Alberto Ascari was behind him in a race. Then, as he himself said, errors that he otherwise never made would immediately creep in. If Farina saw Ascari's car in the pits, he immediately drove distinctly faster until he saw that Ascari was back in the race. This subtle creeping blockade may have lost him only a few hundredths of a second, but in the accumulated laps, it was a noticeable difference.

Exactly the same thing is happening when a woman protests to her husband, who constantly critiques her performance from the passenger seat, that she drives much better when she's by herself. Because he sees his advice as important and correct, he may think the opposite—*but she's probably right.*

Of course, similar things can happen entirely without the presence of others. Sports journalist Günther Isenbügel, a capable endurance driver in his younger years, reported on a long overnight drive in a car in winter, in which it kept raining off and on. Despite the fact that the roads were shiny, wet, and slick, he kept up a healthy pace. He stopped and got out for a stretch at a closed railroad crossing, however, and slid quite a ways on the first step. The road was no longer wet, as he had believed up until then, but had long since been coated with ice. From then on, the drive was torture, not only because he

had to drive much more slowly, but also because he had the feeling that, in contrast to his earlier experiences, he could hardly keep the car on the road. The car would slide out after even the most minimal braking and even turned sideways in a corner.

Before science had even recognized the problem of severe blockades, Charlie Chaplin had already depicted it masterfully in his classic *The Circus,* one of the greatest comedies of the silent film era, which shows a relatively severe partial blockade. As a stray tramp who works as a helper in a circus, Chaplin falls hopelessly in love with a beautiful and celebrated circus rider. When the high-wire artist unexpectedly can't go on during a tour, he tries to impress the woman he loves by jumping in as a replacement. He secretly attaches himself to a thin wire that runs over a pulley to a hidden stage hand whom he has bribed. The whole thing starts out well and Chaplin's climbing up on a rope—using only his arms—goes quickly and almost without effort because his helper is pulling so strongly. At dizzying heights on the high wire, he initially moves somewhat timidly, but his helper holds the safety line tight, and whenever Chaplin gets a little crooked, the helper gives the wire a strong pull to straighten him up. The bizarre movements look like a difficult clown act, and as the audience reacts with excitement, he gradually becomes more courageous. Unfortunately, however, he slides out of his harness. His despairing helper bounces up and down above him as a warning, but Chaplin is so absorbed in his daring feats that he doesn't notice. He becomes ever more confident and makes ever more daring jumps and leaps as the audience cheers. However, when his gaze happens to land on the harness floating above him, he instantly loses all his confidence, and his movements suddenly become awkward and tense until he finally falls. ■

PART 3

The Question of Karl V

THE CONCEPT OF INTEGRATION

The warmup for the "upper half" after a long break

Every rider has had the experience of resuming his riding after a long winter break or perhaps riding a bike that he's never even sat on before. The feelings of general foreignness generated by this are not nearly as noteworthy as the observation that these disturbances disappear after a while, often rather suddenly. Clearly, there's a certain process of adaptation that's happening unnoticed. Sometimes the rider realizes this only after the fact, when things have started going much better and, once again, riding feels natural. He gets a feeling of having *absorbed* the bike, as if it has become a part of him, or, conversely, as if he has become part of the bike itself—its "upper half." In effect, a new unit, with new system characteristics, has been formed from two separate subsystems (see p. 41).

On merging driver and vehicle

Otl Aicher always had very high standards and at least *dreamed* about such standards for automobiles. In 1984 he wrote, "My dream is a car of the highest quality; a car that is tailored for me; one that is so good that it becomes a part of me, and that driving becomes one of my physical processes." The legendary Jim Clark, Formula-1 world champion in 1963 and 1968, didn't merely dream about it; he had apparently long since experienced such a vehicle. He said, "I don't drive the car around the corner, but rather I bring myself through the corner." The driver as part of the vehicle or the vehicle as part of the driver—three decades later this issue is still an important topic. Immediately before the start at Imola in 2000, the loop that kept the seatbelt tight in his Ferrari was torn, and Rubens Barichello said, "I was no longer part of my car." ∎

This new unit becomes all the more perfect and capable the higher the level of **integration.** That is, the more multifaceted the control circuits are between rider and motorcycle, and the more sophisticated, the better the new unified system will be.

A new unit with a higher level of integration

When a rider experiences a high degree of integration, he might feel like he's a part of the vehicle or that the vehicle is part of him, and he can easily relate to either way of looking at it. Along the same lines, Karl V, who seemed almost more interested in horsemanship than in state affairs, asked *whether the horse was a part of the rider or the rider a part of the horse.* This kind of question would never even occur to an awkward vacationer lifted up and *loaded* onto a horse like a sack. However, everyone who can really ride understands the question immediately and has an almost physical feeling for the nature of the question. The statement that the vehicle has become like an *extension* of one's own body ("as if it were a part of me") is one way of expressing the apparently well-known feeling that arises when riding at a high level of integration.

More than just words and sayings

The different ways we express the feeling of integration are remarkable in their similarity: an "extension" or a "piece of one's own body"; a "part of myself"; being a "part of the motorcycle"; "absorbed in the motorcycle"; "having slipped entirely into the motorcycle"; "becoming one with the machine." All are expressions of a particular experience of the seasoned or expert rider. Bystanders are more likely to see these as mere images and overly exaggerated metaphors. This third part of the book is, in essence, all about how Karl's question and all of these related expressions are predicated on a particular feeling in the body and are much more than simple images or sayings. Instead, they're physical intuitions about a largely hidden reality.

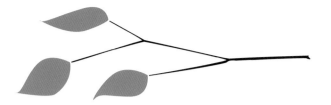

Are tools the exclusive province of human beings?

Prehistorians and anthropologists find tools extremely interesting. To the extent that they are made of durable materials, they are some of the only remains, aside from bones and teeth, that we have from early human times. The discovery of fossilized skeletons along with tools, especially those made of stone, has played a decisive role in determining whether or not they were the remains of human civilization, but over time, as the base of knowledge grew, ever greater exceptions had to be made about what exactly set apart and identified the *human* use of tools.

At first, the use of tools was the substantial criterion in the differentiation of human versus animal, but numerous exceptions were soon discovered. The use of tools even by insects was eventually observed; for example, there are wasps who use tiny stones to tamp down sand to close off the cells of their nests.

One would therefore have to demand an *insightful* use of tools as the definition of their use by humans, because the use of tools based on a genetically transmitted **behavior program** is not intentional, thus not insightful and presumably not human. However, we see that chimpanzees and pygmy chimps are undeniably capable of insightful tool use, for example, when they find new ways to use tools to resolve challenges in new situations. So the bar has to be raised even higher: it's not simply their use of tools or their insightful application of them that differentiate humans; instead, it's their capability to *hone* and *produce* tools.

We can see where this is going: chimpanzees, as it turns out, very carefully remove the leaves from a twig before dipping it into a termite nest. This is not only a honing, but rather more: it is the *fabrication* of a staff out of a twig. To create a longer bamboo stick, chimpanzees will also gnaw the end of one bamboo stick to sharpen it before inserting it into the end of another. This is likewise not just honing, but rather fabrication of a long tool out of individual shorter sticks.

The distinction then evolved to hanging onto or *saving* a tool. According to everything everyone knew, that much consideration and future planning was not to be expected of the primates. In fact, the saving of tools did not seem to occur among animals. However, it does actually occur (even if extremely rarely), as researchers had to admit after observing a troupe of chimpanzees who set out for an area in which there were nuts and took stones with them to crack the nuts because there were no stones in the area where they were going. This represented "saving" in the sense of preparing something for later use.

So goes the debate. Even the act of *teaching* others about the use of a tool—the final transition from biological to cultural evolution—could not enduringly remain the exclusive domain of human beings. This issue has had (and will continue to have) unheard of consequences, because the beginnings of *culture,* namely the passing along of acquired behaviors, has had to be recognized in certain animals!

A very nit-picky criterion was needed to salvage the use of tools as unique to human beings: the use of tools for the fabrication of other tools. Or, to strengthen it just a little further: fabricating tools *in order* to use them for the fabrication of other tools. And with this formulation, the succession of needs becomes so complicated that only humans can still understand it. But these last criteria are hardly valuable as a solid means of differentiation. The clear and unambiguous distinction sought at the beginning is entirely gone unless we take one more criterion into account: the human being is the only user of tools *who refines his tools for aesthetic reasons,* for example, by paying attention to the sweep of a handle or by making a tool distinctive through decoration—that is, he continues to improve a tool beyond the basic fulfillment of a function. This occurred even with some early tools, and it continues to happen today, for example, with our motorcycles. ∎

THE MOTORCYCLE AS TOOL

The use of tools

When a rider experiences the feeling of becoming one with the vehicle—feels like a part of the machine or the machine feels like a part of him—it is a sign of a high level of **integration,** an important characteristic of an especially perfected kind of "tool use." "Tool" will be our key word for this section. This word might seem a little strange in a discussion of motorcycle riding. Is the motorcycle a tool? The answer depends on how we understand the concept of a tool. A clarification of our relationship with the motorcycle—on the basis of the tool concept—offers insights that are beneficial for understanding our interaction with the motorcycle.

If one tries to come up with the most general description of the concept, most ethnologists and prehistorians would agree that *tools are objects, external to the body, that are used or implemented in a purposeful and planned manner.* This means that they are used for a particular purpose that has been conceived in advance; they are not used playfully or haphazardly.

Tool or equipment?

The proponent of a definition that includes the alteration of one's surroundings might advise us to consider the motorcycle not as a tool but rather as "equipment." Neither is wrong, but the following discussion, even if it initially appears nitpicky, actually reveals something substantive about our relationship with the motorcycle: "tool" and "equipment" are, without doubt, conceptually very close together. The words have so much overlap that they are sometimes used interchangeably, but they have subtle connotations that go beyond customary usage. Both are objects external to the body that are used or implemented in a purposeful and planned manner.

A specified purpose or
an end in itself

Equipment tends to be more complex and larger than tools (although there certainly are also highly complicated machining tools—"tools" in the strictest sense), but these really aren't distinguishing characteristics. However, language is a good guide and helps us along: we notice that the names of specific tools are most commonly associated with *transitive* verbs, but the names of equipment are not. Therefore, in a sentence with the name of a tool as the subject, we will find an *object* of a transitive verb, or a target. (The sword strikes *the enemy.* The knife cuts *the meat.*) In other words, this means that tools are oriented toward a target (an object). In contrast, nouns that name equipment (e.g., chair, bed, stove) are not so easy to use with the transitive, and these most commonly appear with intransitive verbs. This is no coincidence, because pieces of equipment have a *purpose in themselves* and *fulfill needs directly.* Much more so than equipment, tools are a *means to an end,* much less fixed in their purpose. For this reason, it's not that easy to find a particular primary need that can be satisfied with the help of a tool (for example, with the help of tools, one could build a chair that could satisfy the need for a place to sit and rest). The use of equipment is largely fixed, while tools are "open-ended" and can thus also be used to make still other tools. They are meant for a pure, purpose-oriented activity, and they are *active* (for example, a hammer), while equipment is more *passive* (for example, an anvil, which is much more like equipment than a hammer is).

The crucial concept is that tools seem to be purpose oriented while equipment seems to have an inherent purpose.

And the motorcycle?

You have probably had the image of a motorcycle in the back of your head this entire time as we have been testing out which definition might best fit the motorcycle. The result seems fairly unambiguous: the criteria above point emphatically in the direction of *equipment.* A motorcycle is clearly an object that is external to the body and is used or implemented in a purposeful and planned manner, but it is *not* used to change our surroundings and is thus more like a piece of equipment. It is more complex and larger than what is generally understood as a tool—thus, equipment once again. It isn't used on a certain target the way a tool is and thus is more likely to appear in connection with intransitive verbs—again, equipment. It has a purpose in itself and fulfills needs directly—yet again, equipment.

A motorcycle is, however, more active than passive, and the activity of motorcycling is target-oriented; in this sense, it is more like a tool.

In addition, there is the phenomenon of "interface displacement," which is characteristic of certain tools. Interface displacement, the topic of the next section, sheds clarifying light on the nature of our relationship with the motorcycle. It seems so fundamental to me that

I have absolutely no doubt that the motorcycle, even if one classifies it as equipment, has a pronounced "tool-like" character.

MAN, OBJECTS, AND ENVIRONMENT

The most important boundary

In the course of his early development, every person discovers one of the most important boundaries there is for an individual: the boundary between one's own person, the *self,* and the whole rest of the world. This personal boundary, as self-evident as it is to us, also plays a major role in evolutionary history, since its gradual formation was one of the most important steps along the way to our becoming human beings; it was a path that led to a gradual realization of consciousness.

Everything on the other side of this self-boundary constitutes one's *surroundings.* My hands, for example, although I can do things *with them,* belong to my own person. A plate nearby belongs to my surroundings or environment, and even if I turn toward it and pick it up, it is still an *object,* remaining a part of my surroundings.

Not environment and not object

Now for the strange part: certain tools—those with which we take up a close physical connection when we use them—don't conform to this apparently distinct classification. For example, a hammer that I use to shape a boulder is clearly no longer simply a part of the surroundings, *but it's also no longer the object of an activity.* If one pays attention, this can be felt physically when using the hammer. The surest way to experience this firsthand is with "double tools" such as the hammer and chisel: they start out as mere features in one's surroundings but become objects as soon as they have been selected for use. And as soon as they are being used, they lose their status as objects—the hammer slightly sooner than the chisel—as they are absorbed into one's conception of his own body (**body concept**). With that, they pass from an item in the surroundings to a part of one's self.

The more expertly someone wields a tool, the more they will agree. The more awkwardly they use a tool, the less pronounced the experience of **integration.** The example of a hammer and chisel is especially instructive, because it's not uncommon that an unskilled person might be able to "absorb" the hammer (feel like it's a part of one's self), while the chisel would remain outside, "unabsorbed" into the self (Figure 48).

But what then?

Let's return again to the consideration of working directly on the boulder with the hammer alone. The hammer is no longer environment, as stated above, and also no longer object. But what is it, then? The environment, or surroundings, during the activity of pounding a boulder, is the ground that the boulder rests on; the boulder has become the object of the activity. Both exist on the outside, but the hammer in my hand is clearly in a different camp, namely on the inside: it has been absorbed, or integrated. It has become part of my own person, part of my self, in the same way as was the hand that I used to pick up the plate. All tools can be put down, but an integrated tool can also be released from the "inside," at which point it once again becomes part of the surroundings and loses its temporary organ-like character. None of this is true of the hand. Both are organs, but the hand is

Figure 48. When one grips a hammer but holds it still, the interface that is experienced is the same as the objective interface. But if one picks up the hammer and swings it, even with the most minimal force, the interface that is experienced begins to move away from the objective interface. If one swings the hammer and hits the head of a nail, then the interface that is experienced moves as far as the pounding surface of the hammer. Finally, a second tool, as with the chisel here, can be included in one's overall body schematic. In this case, the experienced interface moves as far out as the point of the chisel.

a permanent, natural one, and the tool is a temporary and artificial one which, in the best case, can be an integrated tool.

Using tools to perfection

What is special about tools is that we make a close physical connection with them and wield them at a very high level of integration. They are, as with the hammer above, *no longer part of the surroundings and also no longer an object,* and they are on the way to becoming part of one's own person and being absorbed into the self. The more perfected the use of the tool, the more this absorption occurs. Nowhere can this be more readily observed than in the perfectly executed use of sports equipment and in the virtuoso-like mastery of a musical instrument.

Over and over again, the archer hears this from his coach: body, spirit and *bow* should be one and "the bowstring in your hand will become a part of your body." The great cello player Mstislaw Rostropowitsch uses almost the same words: "The cello is part of my body"—*no longer environment and also no longer object.*

The jazz trumpeter Dizzy Gillespie, with whom one could practically see the great extent to which his instrument was a part of him, belonged to the great era of jazz improvisation: when the musicians had an idea, they would sing it for each other and then follow the theme further together with their instruments. What's notable in this for us is that after just a few seconds, Gillespie often couldn't say whether he had sung the notes or played them on his trumpet.

INTERFACE DISPLACEMENT
Moving the boundaries between self and surroundings

With the phenomenon "not environment and not object," one raises the issue of the **interface.** The experienced interface is displaced and is obviously no longer in agreement with the actual physical interface. This is well-known to the pianist, who imagines that he's reaching deep inside the piano or dreams that he's conjuring, enticing, or pulling the tones out of the instrument and into his hands, arms, and whole body. This is also well-known to the tennis player, with his racket, and to the horseman, who doesn't *figure out* what the ground is like through rational consideration but instead feels it as if he were touching the ground with his own "hooves." In other words, he experiences the characteristics of the ground in an immediate and concrete way.

Artificial and functional organs

Such interface displacements occur whenever tools are used as artificial organs, to function like **prostheses.** This must be elucidated.

It occurred to thoughtful observers relatively early on that tools are handled or wielded like organs that a human either does not possess *or* does not possess in a form to meet specialized needs. Consider the use of a hammer or pliers, a shovel or scoop, or rudder or paddle.

Hans Hass (1970, 1987, 1994) advanced the concept of artificial organs the furthest with his Energon theory, in which he more generally refers to tools as "artificial function providers." He understands artificial organs not only as the tools and equipment with which we have a direct physical connection, but also recognizes them in all technical or organizational structures that can be viewed as functional extensions of one's own body.

Ernst Kapp (1877) spoke about tools as organs that can be "set aside." Today, after Hans Hass with his Energon theory, the concept of "artificial organs" has become accepted. Arnold Gehlen, in particular, sees the technology manifested in tools primarily as an *unburdening* of our natural organs but also as the *replacement* of our organs and the *surpassing* of our organs.

Technology of tools

Over the history of humans' use of tools—and at the beginning, the entire world of technology consisted only of tools—the first was the *found* tool (for example, a stone used to crack a nutshell). This was followed by the *honed* tool (for example, a digging stick made from a branch from which the smaller twigs had been removed). Much later came the *created* tool, which went beyond the mere improvement of something encountered in the environment (for example, the sword, which has its origins in iron ore). From that point on, it's likely that the manufacture of tools took place at the hands of specialists (for example, armorors or smiths). Frequently, with the increasing complexity of tools, there are ever-longer and ever-growing *chains* of specialists whose purpose is to "add value").

If we consider the motorcycle as a tool, these specialist chains are enormously long and are, in large part, *anonymously* connected; thus, the chains are not visible in their full extent to any of the participants. For the manufacturer of an interim product, its further use generally remains open. This is an important characteristic of an economy based on the division of labor. With increasing proximity to the end product, the numerous chains bundle themselves ever more tightly. There is no individual who produces the tool, as was originally the case (unless, perhaps, only for one's own use); there is also no single group that produces the tool. Instead, there are numerous groups with different specialties who work in sequence, and *none* of these would be capable of producing the result of this complicated cooperation without the help of other specialists.

Things we can put down or swap

The concept of replacing and supplementing our natural organs with artificial organs goes beyond the individual tools or equipment to all machinery, to the factory, to the enterprise among different factories, and all the way to the distribution organization spanning an entire market, leading to the concept of "communal organs." This is not due so much to the fact that artificial organs, such as tools, can be put down and used by several people. In-

Tools as organ replacements

Gehlen (1975) places far more importance on the "organ aspect" and thus on one's relationship with and way of handling and using tools. Before Gehlen, F. Keiter (1938) also spoke of "organs" with which humans equip themselves: "The hammer replaces the fist, pliers replace the teeth, the spoon replaces the hand, clothing replaces hair," etc. But Gehlen considered the matter systematically and constructed useful categories that were then picked up by others and further developed: the tool serves to *strengthen* an organ or to *surpass* an organ's capabilities (for example, using a stone and later a hammer instead of the fist); the tool also serves to *replace* an organ (as with a vehicle or trained animal for riding, instead of one's own legs); the tool also serves to *complement* and *improve* an organ (as when an inadequate coat or insufficient fat reserves are made up for with clothing); tools also serve as *extensions* of organs (as with diving apparatus); and as described by Gehlen emphatically, tools can also serve to relieve or reduce the burdens on organs (as with a walking or hiking stick). In any case, Gehlen breaks away from the aspect of the "processing tool" with finality and no longer asks what individual things can be produced or *done* with the tool (such as splitting wood). Instead, he asks how it serves the human being *with respect to his organs.*

Even before that, Paul Alsberg (1922) was considering the tool's reduction of the burden on organs. He likewise contrasted the tool (as an artificial means) against the physical organs. The tools didn't strengthen the organs but instead switched them off; the more powerful or capable the tool, the fewer demands placed on the organ. The ancient human took on the struggle against his environment with the tool; he was thereby forced to walk upright

and, as a result, lost all physical means for flight and fight. He became increasingly a "being of tools," "creating tools and being created by them" (Kraft 1948). In fact, tools have long since become a part of us, and we a part of them. We are simultaneously creator and creature of our tools, and this becomes all the more evident the more these tools become machines (Bammé 1983).

There are innumerable possibilities for classifying tools in their relationship to humans. This has summarized just a few that are most important in the context of this book. In any case, the following point is valid: tools are "organs as needed" (Osche 1982), and if tools are called artificial organs, then, conversely, actual organs are "natural tools," which, in contrast to the artificial tools, cannot be put down and thus must constantly be carried around. Because of this, natural tools can't become overly specialized. For example, a beak is useful as a grasping organ for picking up food, and it can also be used to kill prey and divide it into smaller pieces. However, the beak also has to be usable in building nests, feeding young, for preening, for defense, and maybe also for making sounds.

Because of the inalterability of his natural tools, the animal is tied to narrow ecological niches and requires the enormous time spans of biological evolution to adapt to changes in the environment with "reengineered" tools. However, artificial organs give the human being extreme flexibility and adaptive capability—both for very short periods for different situations and for long-term changes in the environment. He puts one tool down and picks up the other—"organs as needed." Even a single type of tool, in comparison to the animal tool, has an

(continued next page)

(continued from previous page)

amazing range. Take, for example, the artificial organ "hammer," which appears as a 20- to 30-gram hammer among watchmakers and similar craftsmen; upholsterers uses an 80-gram hammer; and the progression continues to a 6- or even 8-kg stonemason's hammer and even on to a 10-kg sledgehammer. This covers an amazing span in size: more than 1:400!

As with different tactile situations, human beings also rapidly adapt to entire environments. Humans are the only higher life form on almost the entire globe, and for this, humans have their artificial organs to thank. Among animals, evolution has taken place in the organs; among humans, evolution has occurred increasingly by means of tools and has been transferred to technology. The animal adapts his organs slowly and over a very long time to a changing environment; the human simply changes his tools. There is no more fundamental distinguishing characteristic between animal and human than these very quickly adaptable "organs as needed."

However, the human being also takes on undeniable disadvantages with his artificial organs. "Need-based" organs can be developed in an amazing variety and degree of specialization, but their proper use must first be learned. In addition, the ability to set down artificial tools means not only that they can easily be transferred to other people, but also opens up the possibility of an undesirable transfer. artificial organs can not only be misplaced, forgotten, and lost but also removed and stolen. This means that these tools have to be carefully stored, guarded, protected, and defended (Hass 1970). There are entire professions that concern themselves exclusively with storage, guarding, protection, and defense of tools, such as the guards of a factory's security services. Entire wars have been fought over nothing more than tools.

With the reduction of physical burdens by tools, Gehlen has realized a new burden of an entirely different sort, which is really a basic principle of all human development: for every advance, for every liberation, for every unburdening, there's a price to pay—witness the current topic of "technological impact assessment." The question has always been, and will always be, to what extent the price is acceptable. ∎

stead, it's mainly because very complex artificial organs (such as a factory, a railway train, or the postal service) often can no longer be implemented by a single person as an artificial organ. An animal—for example, a hound, a horse, or an ox—can also become an artificial organ. Even a human or a group of humans can be the artificial organ of another human, and it doesn't necessarily have to be the extreme example of slavery. The term "artificial" is not related to the manufacturing of the organ but rather is used in the sense of having been artificially included in the organization of our bodies.

The division between function fulfillment and the control of that function

The following statement applies to all artificial organs: *The fulfillment of a function is separated from the body of the user, but control stays within the user's own organism.* The degree of separation of the function fulfillment from the body can span all levels, from *rudimentary* (as with a shovel or paddle) to almost *complete* (as with a remotely controlled missile). The motorcycle falls somewhere in the middle of this range, but it is certain that fulfillment of the motorcycle's function is separated considerably from the rider, while control stays firmly with him.

INTEGRATION AND SUPER-ORDINATE SYSTEMS

Our main interest in tools is as artificial organs, especially when their use has been expertly *integrated* into the physical self. These artificial organs become subsystems that, together with the human subsystem, form a new, *super-ordinate system* with new system characteristics (p. 84). It's a matter of artificial organs, and specifically of a sort that involves integrated *use*, meaning that they—with many consequences—are subsumed into the physical body of the user.

Artificial organs and integrated artificial organs

The subsuming of an artificial organ into the physical body of the user is exactly the situation that distinguishes man's relationship to a tool of a very special kind: the **prosthesis** as an artificial *replacement* or surrogate. Thus, an artificial arm or even dentures are indeed prostheses, but a pair of glasses or a pacemaker are not, as some have claimed.

Prostheses that replace limbs are, quite literally, perfect examples of artificial organs because their use occurs at an especially high level of integration. The person who has a prosthesis may have lost a limb, but he does not lose the vivid and constantly present spatial conception of that limb. The absent limb is only physically missing, but there is a so-called "phantom limb" that he senses vividly and that has a compelling subjective reality to the point of tormenting him with extremely bothersome phantom aches—*outside* of his actual body! So, for example, a person who has had an arm amputated has an exact idea of the position of the fingers, the hand, or the forearm at any given time. He has, to some extent, become absorbed into the prosthesis along with his phantom limb, but it's not necessary for the prosthesis and the phantom limb to always be congruent (over several years, the phantom limb will begin to wither anyway). He finds it astonishing at first that, with the prosthesis removed, he can move his "arm" (the phantom limb) through a solid tabletop; his concept of his body still stretches unchanged all the way into the fingers of his phantom limb. And this is where he *experiences* the **interface** with the objects in his surroundings, while the *physical* interface is actually at the point of the amputation (Krech and Crutchfield 1992).

Just like using a prosthesis

For our purposes, the prosthesis is an unbeatable model of **integration** into one's own physical self: in relation to the interfaces, the circumstances are similar to those that exist when a tool is being used as an integrated artificial organ. We use tools in a manner similar to the way a prosthesis is used.

Certainly, you have has been thinking about the motorcycle this entire time, but for now, it is a far too complicated tool to consider. Simple tools will give us a better overview. The use of a plain old pointer, for example, is full of wonders. If we close our eyes and move the pointer toward a wall, touch it with the tip of the pointer, and feel it a little bit, we experience the resistance that it offers, not in our fingertips or in our hands, but rather *out front at the tip of the pointer*. More precisely, it's not so much the resistance that we experience; it's more like *an immediate experience of the wall itself*. And at the same moment, we can make further statements about what the wall is like—whether hard or soft (glass or velvet), whether rough or smooth (plaster or paint), etc. We can also locate a light switch or the frame of a picture hanging on the wall, and effortlessly determine its size and the nature of their surfaces; we could do the same with a vase

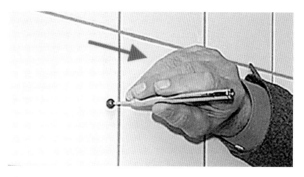

Figures 49 through 51. A touch test demonstrates that the interface that is experienced and the physical interface are not always the same. Because of the different grip positions of the hand (from the right, from the right and below, from the bottom), and in spite of the fact that the hand-held feeler is being moved in the same direction in each case, very different forces are exerted on the fingertips.

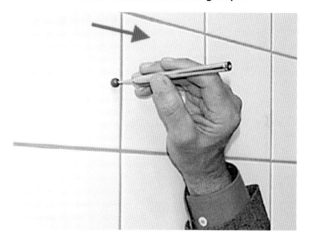

Nevertheless, the picture of the object being felt (tiles with grout), as it develops at the point of the feeler, is independent of how the feeler is held and is the same in all three cases. The interface that is experienced is not the same as the physical interface.

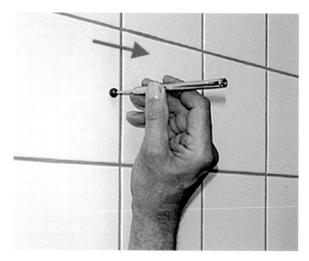

standing on a table. In addition, we can make surprisingly exact statements about the length of the pointer and, with that, about how far away the object is, even if we weren't handed the pointer until we'd already closed our eyes or been blindfolded.

Interface is not the same as point of contact

Although this high level of integration is a unique phenomenon, it's one that we take for granted to such an extent that it has become invisible in everyday life. It really is astounding: the physical interface lies between the fingers and the handle of the pointer, and that's as far as the necessary sensory receptors reach. But, the surface of the object, which is one or two meters away at the tip of the pointer, is where the interface is *experienced*. As with a "real" prosthesis, we have been absorbed into the pointer, and we've incorporated it into our own physical self in such a way that it is no longer part of the surroundings and also no longer an object.

Figure 52. When the bucket gets hung up on a lower scaffold, the man feels this not in his hands but rather far below, at the edge of the bucket.

There are many examples of this. Consider a person on a scaffold pulling a bucket upward on the end of a rope. If he feels the bucket get hung up on something, he experiences this *down by the bucket,* not in the hands and arms, where the receptors responsible for feeling such inputs are located (Figure 52).

Classic craftsman's tools

All of the "classic" craftsman's tools—the hammer and chisel, pliers, side cutters, sewing needles, planes, awls, files, and rasps, etc.—are used in precisely this way (like prostheses), and it seems so normal to us that we don't even notice it. Not only would we be highly irritated, but our projects would not turn out well if the experienced interface were to stay in the same place as the physical interface between hand and tool. The integration of the tool would be lacking.

This also goes for instruments that require more subtle handling, such as writing implements or cutlery, for a knife not only when cutting, but also in a pronounced way when scraping, and finally even for a rubber eraser. With an eraser, we all gradually become specialists in the practical evaluation and uses of "sliding friction." A cellist (and players of other stringed instruments) has a closely related experience, because he can feel it reliably when his bow begins to become too smooth and needs rosin to make it "grab" again. He feels this in the bow itself, where it lies upon the strings of the instrument, and not at the so-called "frog" where he holds it in his hand (Figure 53).

Figure 53. After a long playing session, as the friction of the bow diminishes, the cellist feels this not in his fingers that are holding the bow but rather at the point at which the bow contacts the strings.

Orchestras, flocks, and fish

With a beginning cello player, the bow becomes integrated relatively early, and much sooner than the instrument, which initially remains part of the environment. Along the way to a perfected and ultimately virtuosic manipulation of the instrument, the level of integration rises as more of the environment (the instrument) is "taken into" the player's own physical self.

Apropos of the concepts of Hans Hass, a conductor has at his disposal a mighty artificial organ: the orchestra. If he's one of the great conductors, he is also capable of shaping it into a highly integrated unit and, with respect to all substantive characteristics, subsuming it within himself—not immediately, and not always, but in a few great hours after sufficient cooperative work.

The famous conductor Herbert von Karajan vividly describes how he once felt during an orchestral performance that the oboist was about to become short of breath. It was not that the oboist had run out of air such that Karajan could hear it, and he didn't "conclude" this based on signs or past experience that there might soon be a shortage of breath. Instead, he *"felt"* it, even with his eyes closed, just as one can feel in the organs in his own body when some kind of burden or stress needs relief. Because of this, he was able to help the oboist out.

When complete unity has been achieved in an orchestra—when all 120 people have become *one* body—then a conductor doesn't really "conduct" anymore, says Karajan, because if he were conducting, the orchestra's responses would follow the conductor with some delay, and the amount of the delay can differ. Aside from rehearsals, the crucial element is the **mental** performance.

Just as happens in a dense flock of flying birds, this is an example of synchronicity among living things. The flock, consisting of a few hundred crows, not only takes off pretty much all at once but also pulls together into an even tighter group during flight. After takeoff, for example, there might be an extended right-hand curve in the ascent, which gradually tightens, and then a fluid transition into an open left-hand curve, accompanied by a simultaneous flattening out of the ascent and an increase in speed. Only rarely does a flock fly exactly straight. At some point, a synchronized descent is initiated, with curves that look as if they were the result of long planning, followed by a complicated landing in a dense group, from the middle of a curve in flight.

No lead bird can be recognized, and no member of the flock has a set position. Changes in direction are not passed along from the front to the back (which would lead to substantial delays), and the birds don't line up one after another (which would require long organizational processes). Instead, there is absolute harmony without buffering and without visible corrections, as if each animal were flying for himself, but had pre-coordinated the flight path which each member of the flock down to the minutest detail. The same is true of a dense school of fish, even when the water is so murky that each can see only its closest neighbors. Or, take the simple yet puzzling "system" of the eight-man rowing crew, which can suddenly swing into its own rhythm. ■

The dangers of dis-integration

If a tool is set down, of course, the integration dissolves immediately. It also dissolves if a person who has been using the tool for a particular purpose stops doing something specific with it but still happens to have it in his hand: suddenly, the tool goes from being an integrated artificial organ to being a dis-integrated appendage, and no more information is received by the user about its po-

sition—it has been *decoupled* from one's physical self. This is why it can be so dangerous to continue to hold onto a tool when one is already doing something else. This is why children should be told emphatically to put things down right away when they are no longer needed. Otherwise, a fork or pair of scissors that is still "along for the ride" can all too easily injure an eye. Adults who have failed to set down a hot soldering iron or a similar tool also have experienced painful surprises.

Dis-integration in racing

There is a mysterious phenomenon in racing that is a dangerous type of dis-integration: when a racer is almost at the point of completing a "half-fast" lap (perhaps because he has a large lead and victory seems assured), errors arise in great numbers and have often led to incomprehensible crashes. There are famous examples of this in the world of auto racing, and much thought has been given to whether the appropriate level of tension was lost, or the driver lost his rhythm, or something else happened. From our standpoint, it is not a complete dis-integration like that which occurs when an unused tool is still held in one's hand, but the level of integration that existed at the driver's highest level of effort and concentration has been diminished. He is no longer fully integrated with his vehicle—the vehicle is no longer as well "absorbed" into the physical body of the driver. ■

Sensing without sensors?

The rational skeptic, however, just can't "wrap his mind around" the idea that inanimate material can, in a way, become alive. One can only advise him to try his own experiment (as described on p. 91) of feeling along a wall with a pointer or by other very simple means: he could take the handle of a toothbrush and, without looking, run it slowly along the tiles and observe what happens when he comes to a groove and crosses over it. But the skeptic either won't try it at all because it's fully clear to him what he would observe and what *couldn't* possibly be otherwise, or, if he does try it, his subjective certainty would so limit his objective observation that the phenomenon would remain unobservable to him. This presumed knowledge that's standing in the way is based on the fact that even when an object is wielded with the utmost virtuosity (whether a pointer or a motorcycle), there are simply no sensors on its outer surface (at the end of a pointer or on the motorcycle's contact patches) and no neural connections to the center. Therefore, it's all imagination.

How vision works

This kind of entrenched skepticism completely overlooks the fact that our visual perception is constantly working in the same way. We can look out the window and see, with unmatched concreteness, a small grassy lawn, beyond that a low stone wall and a lawn chair in front of it, and a bush beside that. But there are also no sensors on the wall, chair, or bush! And no neural connections from them to the center! And indeed, I can already hear the retort: seeing is a sense that occurs at a *distance,* not directly: the perceived objects, in accordance with the rules of physical optics, are precisely *reproduced* as an image on the retina. And this is exactly where I want my skeptic. I can now continue: first of all, these retinal images aren't all that exact at all; there's a fair amount of complicated data preparation that has to be done to build complete information from data fragments. What's revealing about the nature of this data preparation is, however, the following detail: the two retinal images are considerably different from each other, especially for objects viewed at close range; therefore, the data are confusing and contradictory. But we don't notice this at all—we don't experience two different pictures *in our eyes,* but instead one unified perceived object *outside* (although the object is actually "re-formed" within our heads). The object is simpler, but thanks to its depth dimension, richer than both of the individual images, and it is coherent and without contradiction. The variety of incoming stimuli is thus projected back outside by means of a grandiose data cleaning process, because the object we experience is reconstructed on the *outside*. In other words, with the data that we receive *inside* (in our eyes), we reconstruct the object *outside*. As this happens, the divergence of the two pictures determines the distance from ourselves to the perceived object.

Transfer to the tactile

And how does this relate to the use of an integrated tool? In principle, tactile perception works in the same way. For this discussion, however, we should take a closer look at the experiment with the pointer that we ran along a surface.

Once again, it is obvious that we get plenty of information about the surface: how rough or smooth it is; about impediments that the tip of the pointer runs into or runs along beside or skips over; about **static friction** and dynamic friction, and the transitions from one into the other. Finally—and this can also be perceived with the eyes closed—we get information about how far away the object is from our hand, etc. Ths information can only be gleaned from the multiple kinds of forces that are being exerted on the fingertips. The convoluted, and as such, completely opaque tangle of data is sorted out and put together as a concrete experience of the object, or an "image" in the broader sense.

Separation of the experienced interface from the physical interface

What's essential in this is:

1. Although the image of the object being felt is "made in our head," it is reconstructed outside of our head and experienced outside as well. That is, the physical interface does not coincide with the experienced and visible **interface.** The former is at our fingertips, while the latter is at the end of the pointer.

2. It is only with the dissolution of the experienced interface from the physical interface that a concrete and coherent image of the object being felt can emerge.

3. Depending on the orientation of the fingers, compared to the direction in which the pointer is moving (Figures 49–51), quite different forces will be transmitted to the fingertips. That is, the individual pieces of information are very different. *However, the image of the object that arises based on the information is independent of that: it always stays the same.* One cannot overlook this evidence that the forces felt in the fingertips are completely inscrutable.

Rainey's constant reminder (and two other witnesses)

Just one last remark for the remaining skeptics, with which we can once again get closer to our actual topic: why do top riders like Wayne Rainey always say that the motorcycle is "constantly telling a story?" This is more than a metaphor! Whoever thinks it is impossible that his front or rear wheel can "tell" him something will also have a harder time actually perceiving what he does feel happening at either wheel. The saying that people can only have the experiences that they want to experience, only see what they want to see, and only understand what they want to understand is not without truth. It might be an exaggeration, but it just points out that, in order to really *hear* the story, rational obstacles must first be removed. They are easier to break down with the help of related experiences of reliable witnesses, such as Carl Fogarty, World Superbike Champion of 1995. After his incredible double victory in the Superbike World Championship race at Brands Hatch, UK, in 1995, he ex-

Hass's concepts: supplemental organs; extra-physical organs

To prevent misunderstandings, Hass later gave up his concept of artificial organs and replaced it with that of "supplemental organs," which is broad enough, and better expresses the contradiction of something organ-like outside of the body, thus covering all possibilities but, unfortunately, it is also much weaker and harder to implement. The term "extra-physical organs" probably best captures the concept, and Hass subsequently began using this term. In our specific context of tools and equipment, though, we can stick with the previously introduced idea of artificial organs.

As accessible and intuitive as Hass's concepts are with respect to simple artificial organs such as a hammer, shovel, or paddle, in the case of more complex artificial organs, especially super-ordinate systems containing multiple subsystems (discussed later in detail), it seems at first an extremely unusual way of looking at things. One might be able to dispatch the analogies inherent in these concepts as far-fetched in their application to them if it weren't for the fact that Hass shows, point by point, that from the standpoint of energy balance, the same laws apply to more complex artificial organs as apply to the more easily grasped, simple artificial organs. ∎

Dilution of the "integration" concept

Integration as a concept has been appallingly diluted in recent years. Every mail-order catalog extolling the virtues of some additional equipment added to some device crows that this additional piece is "integrated." For example, an "integrated clock" only means that the superfluous addition of the clock has been built into the device. Thus, turn signals are not mounted flush in the fairing, but rather "integrated into it." In strict usage, however, *integrated* means integrated into the *system,* not just into a housing! It means that it has been factored in and is thus a fully valued component that is *required* in the system, and the presence of which brings about a new larger *whole.*

A subsystem that, together with another subsystem, builds a new super-ordinate system with new system characteristics, is integrated into that system. The level of integration, or degree of mutual penetration, can vary, however. ∎

plained: "At the very beginning, I didn't quite have a feel for the tires, but it soon got better." Or, even more clearly, from Scott Russell, World Champion in 1993: "In Daytona you have to have a really good feel for the **grip** at the front wheel when you're riding through the banking. You just ride in and lean the bike. But it only works if you have the right feel for the front wheel."

INTEGRATION IN MOTORCYCLING
Multifaceted qualities of experience

Up to this point, we have spent quite a bit of time on the incorporation, or integration, of something external to the body into our own concept of our physical self. After the phantom limb and the pointer, after the cello and the eraser, it's finally time to turn our attention back to the motorcycle, with the new insights we've gained. It is not such a big step. The cello and eraser examples showed that it's not just dimensions that can be determined, but also even certain characteristics about the material being touched by the integrated artificial organ. We got an idea of this with the experiment of feeling along a wall with a pointer, and even more so with the horseman who gets a very concrete and detailed experience of the footing his horse's hooves are standing on. This is an example of the kind of trait that can be communicated by means of an artificial organ, as long as the organ is sufficiently integrated within the physical self of the user—that is, becomes like a prosthesis.

Static friction and sliding friction

The information about surfaces that comes in by way of such **prostheses** can, as shown in the cello and eraser ex-amples, even relate directly to **static friction** and dynamic friction. It's static friction (and its transition into dynamic or sliding friction)—particularly the integration of the **contact patches** of our tires into the physical self—that is of particular interest to the motorcyclist.

While the transition from static friction to sliding friction is easy to recognize in an unmoving object, when it comes to a rolling wheel, one has to understand the following: even with a freely rolling wheel, because of the deformation that occurs in the contact patch, local changes in the transmission of power occur (the so-called "micro-slip") even when static friction has not yet transitioned into sliding friction. Even the most minimal **lateral forces** that a rolling wheel has to transmit lead to a **slip angle** and the wheel imperceptibly starts to describe an arc. Thus, there are already certain sliding processes at work in the contact patch. Without even the most minimal slip angle, the wheel could not develop any cornering forces. Similarly, in the circumferential direction of the wheel, with increasing tangential forces (from braking or accelerating), the so-called "slip" becomes greater and greater until static friction has transformed completely into sliding friction.

Let's take a first look at friction on a sloping surface, as opposed to the **lateral acceleration** that occurs during curves. Car manufacturers have high-speed tracks with wonderfully banked curves, similar to what can be found at Daytona. If we tried to walk up the side of a track like this, on which the incline increases as one gets closer to the outside (see Figures 54–58), we'd expect to eventually reach a point at which our feet would slide out because the static friction of our soles would no longer be enough

Figures 54 through 58. The evidence experience with increasing utilization of the available static friction: the test subject doesn't finally slip but instead stops just before the changeover to sliding friction.

to hold on. But this doesn't happen. In experiments, every subject stops precisely just a hair before reaching the limit of traction, even though the activity is relatively new to them and it's certainly not a situation they've had the opportunity to practice before. The subject stops because it becomes *evident* to him that he has arrived at the limit of the available static friction and that, if he took one more step, he would slip. He doesn't have to know anything about the physics involved.

But there's a much more everyday example, one that nearly everyone has experienced: that of walking down a wet, slippery, grassy hillside. A person might just barely still be able to hold on, when it suddenly gets much more slippery. He can see that he still has a few yards before it either gets flatter or less slick, but instead of spontaneously dropping onto the seat of his pants, the person starts to run in short, quick steps, faster and faster. Even a person who has no idea about the physics involved will do the right thing. The goal is to make absolutely certain not to exceed the remaining available traction but also to transmit the minimal braking forces still achievable from the soles of the feet to the ground as evenly as possible.

Distinct evidence experiences

A person walking down a slippery hillside offers an example of an **evidence experience,** that is, an immediate insight into a situation, along with the certainty that it is correct. Immediate insight means "not acquired by means of rational thought and not acquired after discursive consideration and logical reasoning." It is extremely practical for us that the limits we encounter in all kinds of everyday situations are signaled by these evidence experiences. It's as if there are guardian angels constantly watching over us, who will immediately put up a warning sign if we happen to naively place ourselves in danger.

A person walking up the banking at a track can have this evidence experience only because he has incorporated the soles of his shoes into his own physical self, which allows him to feel the traction almost as if he were barefoot, a familiar experience. The same task is required of the motorcycle rider if he wants to become a good or first-class rider. However, the incorporation, or integration, is much more difficult. It's not just one's shoes but the entire motorcycle that must be incorporated into his own physical self. Only when using a fully integrated tool will his instinct and special touch reach all the way into the **contact patches** of the tires.

The protective nature of evidence experiences

In the world of actions, the evidence experience carries great significance. For example, for a tree-dweller, it was a substantial survival advantage if, before a daring leap to another branch, he had reliable knowledge about whether he could jump that far and should take the risk. This is what the evidence experience is capable of. It is to some extent confirmation that the **movement plan** is realistic and fits with the given situation. To our great benefit, it has been preserved throughout human evolution. A person who is even slightly athletically trained can see the evidence experience in the standing jump, a jump with the legs together, onto a platform of variable height. In the vicinity of the limit of his abilities, the athlete can report, accurate to within a few millimeters, whether he can still manage to jump to the height of the platform. Likewise, a good tennis player "knows" with certainty, the instant the ball leaves his racket, whether it will land where he wanted it to.

Sports are full of examples of protective evidence experiences that precede actions. Anyone who observes animals and is familiar with the concepts of the movement plan will quickly notice that the evidence experience exists elsewhere in the animal kingdom. How could it be otherwise? In certain critical cases—for example, with a difficult leap under cramped or otherwise difficult take-off conditions—an animal will keep rearranging itself until the evidence experience sets in, or it will simply not make the leap because of the continued absence of the evidence experience.

Of course, the evidence experience can't guarantee absolute certainty or safety. A highly subjective certainty of correctness can even be misleading, and not only in the realm of actions. Optical illusions are convincing proof of this. ■

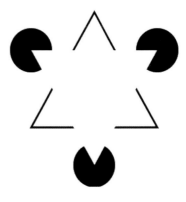

The limits of slide

Under the influence of better and better tires, the **slide** (and so-called "back-wheel steering") have become less important in recent years. It can still be observed all the same, especially when there is a decrease in the coefficient of friction on the road surface. It is most commonly deployed to test the remaining amount of available grip on the road—for example, when it's starting to rain.

Divergent riding styles had a lot to do with Cadalora switching from Yamaha Team Roberts to Kanemoto Honda before the start of the 1996 racing season. Roberts, as a many-time world champion was, in his day, the uncrowned king of **drifting**; Cadalora, on the other hand, had less regard for back-wheel steering while drifting and was more likely to avoid a pronounced slide under acceleration. ■

The impossibility of riding a motorcycle fast without interface displacement

The fourth part of the book contains a few useful practice tips for learning to "slip into" the motorcycle more easily. Successfully slipping in, all the way into the contact patches, is a prerequisite for truly fast motorcycle riding like that in racing, but it's not even necessary for the rider to be consciously aware of it. Conversely, riding fast would be far too dangerous without displacement of the interface, as previously discussed, because otherwise how would it work when racers trained on corners? Let's imagine this kind of training, maybe even on a wet track, just to make everything more vivid. What would happen?

Just like safety-conscious touring riders, the racers would be trying to avoid potentially dangerous lean angles, but since they still want to get the best possible times, they'd have to keep pushing themselves into an area of uncertainty, testing cautiously all the way. The farther they would get into these uncertain areas, the more they'd be able to "smell" success, but at the same time, they'd be getting closer and closer to the sudden crash that would be lurking somewhere at the end of this zone of uncertainty. (The whole scenario is a sort of Russian roulette being played on the roof of a tall building by several blindfolded people. The winner would be the person who, without feeling around with his feet, has walked closest to the edge of the roof without falling off.) In fact, one rider or another would crash abruptly because he would have no idea when he was crossing the limit of trac-

tion. The crash would be the only feedback that he and the others could learn from. This scenario would be completely absurd! Fast riding among racers would be an unbelievable gamble without displacement of the interface. Varying surfaces, with their sudden, localized differences in traction, are enough trouble as it is.

This point is illustrated even more strikingly by one absolutely top-tier feat: the "power slide." How else, if not with feedback from the motorcycle's tires, could a rider possibly know that the traction was adequate, and without this information, how could a **power slide** work at all? A rider's power slide occurs on the narrow transition between static friction and dynamic (or sliding) friction, with a *visible* **slip angle** at the rear wheel, which is largely regulated with the throttle. This is not just a brief slide but rather one that lasts from the **apex** of a curve just about to its end. Power sliding is anything but a static condition! The rider needs constant feedback about which side of the narrow transition zone he's on at any given time. If he's closer to the inside, then the visible slip angle can stop at any moment; if he's closer to the outside of this transition zone, he risks passing into total sliding friction. He receives this feedback, feels what's happening, and acts on the information. Even if the feedback and his use of it are not completely conscious and could not be precisely put into words, the experienced rider nonetheless feels that some tires are not as communicative as others and that some can operate in a narrower or wider transition zone between static and sliding friction.

We've known for a long time that perceptions of available traction never arrive as conscious thoughts and that the *direct* route from the initial sensing of the physical event to conscious control of action and reaction is much faster and less prone to interference than the indirect path through the rational mind. Once again, this emphasizes why most riders can never say that much about the details of what's happening. Instead, they *feel* what's going on in the contact patches of their tires. This is not so much a matter of the composition or characteristics of the road surface itself that is being communicated; rather, it's about the amount of traction that is still available. Certainly, a rider's experience is also involved, but all immediate real-time reports from racers on the track, such as "softening" of cornering grip (some even describe this as a "crawling away" to the side) or an increasing slip angle, describe a feeling of decreasing directness and precision in the cornering grip. Especially when **drifting** to the outside of a curve in a power slide, a

Bowl and marble: a model

At first glance, it might look strange that Figure 60 shows "braking" to the front (above), "acceleration" to the rear and, still more confusingly, that "right-hander" appears on the *left,* and "left-hander" appears on the *right.* This arrangement of the axes, however, has the inestimable advantage for the non-expert observer of helping to provide a concrete representation of the inherent forces of Kamm's circle. Namely, one can imagine Kamm's circle as a deep, round bowl, in the middle of which (thus at the lowest point) lies a marble (Figure 59). If we pick up this bowl and start to walk with it, the marble will move under acceleration toward the *back* until we have achieved a constant speed. If we stop, the marble goes to the *front.* If we make a right-hander, it climbs up the *left* side of the bowl toward the edge. The opposite occurs if we curve to the left. And if we brake into a left-hand corner, the marble climbs to the right front of the bowl. If we accelerate out of a right-hand corner, the marble climbs to the left rear of the bowl. The direction in which the marble climbs the bowl is determined by the *combination* of lateral turning forces and fore-and-aft (longitudinal) acceleration or deceleration. The combined effect of longitudinal and lateral forces is called the *resultant force.*

Anyone who has spent some time really considering this bowl image can build Kamm's circle in his head at any time and will never forget it.

As is well-known, the transition from static friction into sliding friction does not occur suddenly—that is, the transition zone is not sharp. Instead, it's a matter of a transition zone, such that the experienced rider

Figure 59. A model of Kamm's circle. a marble in a bowl makes visible the acceleration or braking that accompanies fast walking or stopping and direction changes. The bowl is covered with a glass top and is filled with glycerin to slow the movement of the marble.

can clearly feel when he has entered the borderline zone. The more "good-natured" the tire, the broader this zone is. The more a tire has been engineered to achieve the highest possible adhesion (making Kamm's circle larger), the more sudden the loss of traction can be (the smaller the transition zone). The same is true in wet conditions: the transition zone narrows.

Last, Kamm's circle should not be understood as a sharp line, but rather as a narrow band of fluid transition. ■

skilled rider on a potentially slippery surface constantly receives important information through the contact patches about the amount of traction that's available at any particular moment, such as when the first few raindrops start to fall on a dry road. In this amazing feat the rider gathers, or receives, the most subtle information and immediately acts on it!

Kamm's Circle

A wheel has to transmit enormous forces through its contact patch, which is barely the size of one's hand. There are **longitudinal forces** that arise under braking and acceleration, and there are **lateral forces** perpendicular to the direction of the wheel's travel, that arise when the wheel goes through a corner. The wheel balances the longitudinal forces against the tangential forces, and the lateral forces against the cornering forces. Longitudinal forces and lateral forces, resulting from longitudinal and lateral acceleration, are exerted at the center of mass of the vehicle; tangential forces and cornering forces are equal and opposite reactions transmitted through the tire contact patches.

The relationship between these forces is shown in **Kamm's circle,** also known as the "traction circle," the top view of a tire, with arrows representing forces the tire exerts against the pavement (Figure 60). The braking

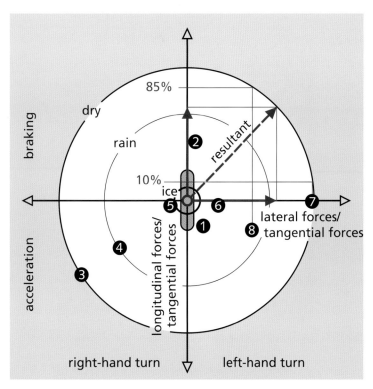

Figure 60. Simplified representation of Kamm's circle.

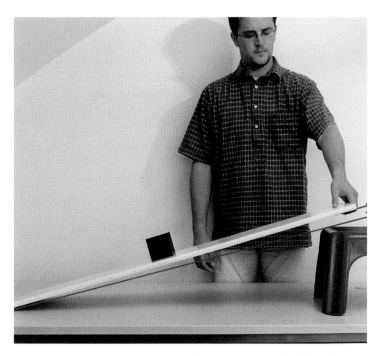

Figure 61. A simple experiment to illustrate static and sliding friction. When it reaches a particular gradient, at which its ability to stick is overcome, the block suddenly begins to move and slides fairly quickly to the end of the board. If, while the block is sliding, one reduces the gradient to a level at which the block had previously been able to stick, the block with still continue to slide. The sliding friction is considerably greater than the static friction.

forces that a tire ❶ has to transmit are represented in an arrow going upward ❷. This arrow would point downward under acceleration. Lateral forces are shown horizontally, either to the right ❻ or left, depending on the direction of the curve. The diagonal arrow (the "resultant" force) represents the equivalent sum (the "vector sum") of the two component forces. The larger the given force, the longer the arrow. If the point of the arrow goes beyond the limit of traction (the outer circumference ❸), then the tire slips—that is, **static friction** becomes **sliding friction,** and, unfortunately, decreases, causing slippage (see Figure 61).

The diameter of Kamm's circle is determined by the amount of available grip at any given moment. In rainy conditions, depending on the surface, the circle might be about 60 to 70% of the usual circle, as shown in Figure 60 ❹. The circle for icy conditions (with friction coefficient of 0.1 or less) is the tiny one ❺ in the center. Because it's so small, even an average motorcycle simply cannot be ridden under these circumstances, not even at a walking pace, and not even if one neither brakes nor attempts to lean the bike. It is simply not possible to keep the operating forces of the rear wheel small enough to stay within the bounds of the tiny circle.

The most useful thing about Kamm's circle is that it clearly shows the interaction of the longitudinal forces (tangential to the tires' circumference) and the perpendicular, lateral forces.

Not even the best tires in the world can ever transfer, simultaneously, the maximum longitudinal force and the maximum lateral force. When these two forces arise at the same time, the resulting force (the "resultant") is greater than either of the two components alone. In Figure 60, the possible lateral forces have in no way been exhausted: the arrow ❻ is still a considerable distance from the limit of traction. However, braking, which increases the longitudinal force, is happening at the same time! Although it's not full braking, the resultant force is already in contact with the circle ❸. With just a touch more on the brakes, the arrow would go beyond the circle, and the possibility of a crash would become very high!

But Kamm's circle also tells us something reassuring: if we maximize use of the available cornering forces, no more tangential forces are available. But, if we use only 99% of the available lateral forces ❼, we still have more than 10% of the tangential forces available to us. And if we only use 50% of the available cornering forces ❽, about 85% of the tangential forces are available for use in braking or acceleration. For everyday riding, one should not use much more than 60% of available cornering forces, not even when riding fast through twisties. Still, this makes for lean angles of about 30 degrees.

Now, two common misunderstandings need to be pointed out:

1. Using 50% of the lateral forces does not mean riding at 50% of the maximally possible speed through a curve. What this actually means is that an 80 km/h curve could be ridden, based on calculations, at 55 km/h, which would be 70% of the possible speed.

2. The resultant force, drawn at a 45-degree angle, hasn't the slightest relationship with a lean angle of 45 degrees. Therefore, do not interpret Figure 60 graphics to mean that, at a lean angle of 45 degrees, one could still brake with 70% of maximal braking! With a 45-degree lean angle, one has already basically exhausted the available lateral forces; with braking on top of that, things would go very wrong.

Today, without too much difficulty, the actual conditions at any given moment can be recorded, or even instantly transmitted by radio. These data produce interesting pictures that say a lot about a rider's capabilities.

The recorded data of an unpracticed new rider (Figure 62) lie almost exclusively along both axes and keep a healthy distance from the limit of traction. Not only does the beginner not exceed the "natural" lean angle of 20 degrees (see Figures 8–11), but he also tries to keep lateral acceleration and longitudinal acceleration tidily separate from each other: *either* by cornering *or* braking. There are occasional outliers, such as (a) and (b) in Figure 62. These are unplanned deviations from the basic rules and are almost always harmless, provided they don't evoke a panicked reaction from the rider.

Figure 63 shows how, with increasing practice and experience, the narrow areas along the axes will gradually broaden. Occasionally in the middle, in the area of the greatest traction, there are already a few instances in which lateral and longitudinal forces are combined— that is, they are being allowed to occur at the same time, and usually more so during acceleration than during braking. In this particular case, the rider seems to feel more confident with right-hand curves than with left-handers.

With more practice and experience, the intersection between the two forces gradually becomes larger (Fig-

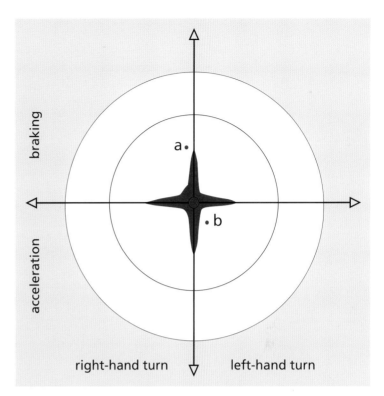

Figure 62. The beginning rider's measured values stay within this range. When he leans at a maximum of 20 degrees, he uses only about one-third of the available static friction.

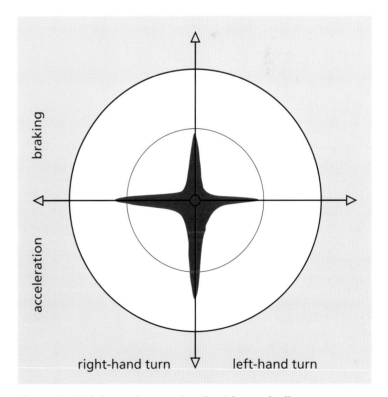

Figure 63. With increasing practice, the rider gradually uses a greater proportion of the available friction.

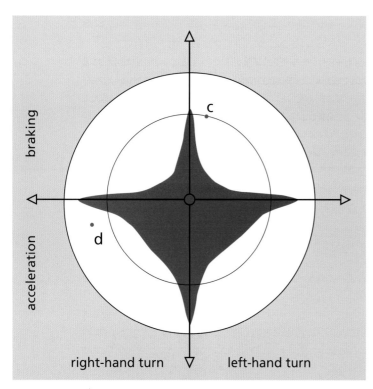

Figure M64. Data for the average experienced motorcycle rider. He already mixes some forward acceleration with lateral acceleration in situations in which there is still plenty of traction.

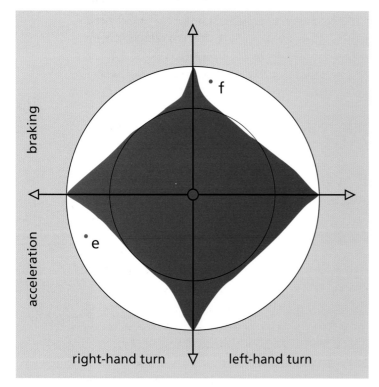

Figure M65. These data show a very good rider, who goes to the edge of where traction is still available. However, he still holds back when mixing forward and lateral acceleration.

ure 64). Lean angles are no longer avoided; instead they are savored with enjoyment. Especially with acceleration, the limit of traction is no longer a limit to be feared. With braking, however, the possibilities are still far from being fully exhausted. And the outliers, such as we see in (c) or (d), are still generally harmless. In the "safe zone" there is much more "mixing" of the two kinds of forces, and this is still much more common with acceleration than with braking. This is basically how most motorcyclists ride. As one can see, there's still plenty of room for improve-ment.

Figure 65 depicts the proficiency of a very experienced rider, who is in a position, under normal road conditions, to reach very close to the limit of traction using lateral acceleration, both to the left and to the right, something he will by now have developed a "feel" for. He has mastered the tangential forces as much as he has mastered the lateral forces and can also get close to the limit of traction with longitudinal acceleration. He already does a considerable amount of mixing of the two forces, but keeps himself well clear of the limit of traction. In terms of the possible circle, compared with the less experienced riders, the image of his data looks more like a square, while the image of the less experienced riders' data looks more like a cross. Outliers such as (e) and (f) can now be dangerous, but they occur far less frequently.

Figure 66, depicts the performance data of a top rider, whose skillfulness reaches into the realm of virtuosity. For every lean angle, he uses the greatest amount longitudinal force possible at the particular moment. He has mastered the power slide when accelerating out of a corner, and, under braking, in accordance with the given lean angle, he exploits all available static friction remarkably well. Basically, outliers no longer occur. This confirms the old rule: form first, then speed—not the other way around.

THE TRANSITION TO INTEGRATION

From cargo to component

"Incorporating the motorcycle into one's own physical self," was discussed above, as were "slipping into" an inanimate object, or into the machine; "becoming one" with the motorcycle; and "prosthesis-like use" of a tool. These ways of looking at things differ from each other only with respect to the point of view, but they all aim at the same nominal condition, namely the use of an instrument, tool, piece of equipment, or machine as an integrated artificial organ. The different ways in which we have explored this same idea have been less concerned with getting the most precise possible grasp of this condition than with becoming familiar with the desired condition. The goal has been to connect you with your own bodily experiences and give you a *feeling* for the phenomenon of interface displacement. The fourth part of the book discusses conceptual aids and exercises and mental training, which facilitate the transition into this special state of motorcycle operation. Once this "slipping in" has been successful, something very remarkable occurs: The rider transitions from "cargo" to "component."

An equestrian example

Practiced horsemen like Karl V usually understand this idea instantly. On the one side is the "cargo-rider" who *sits on* the horse, and whom the horse just carries around like a piece of cargo. This rider gives the horse a few imprecise commands about the desired direction and pace. On the other hand, there is the accomplished equestrian (the "component-rider"), who melds with the horse and is connected to him by means of numerous "control circuits." A horse and rider functioning as a single unit like this can be a pleasure to watch. A stream of information flows continually in both directions, between rider and horse: reports about conditions, processes, possibilities, plans, and commands. To transfer this from horseman to motorcycle rider, and from horse to motorcycle, only a few concepts have to be swapped.

Getting into the ride

There are many facts that support the idea that the terms "cargo" and "component" are more than just jargon. The subjective experiences and expressions common to motorcycle riding and riders, such as "warming to the bike" or "now I'm finally back into it," may not be all that convincing, especially for riders who are not yet familiar with the experience of becoming one with the bike. However, the proof becomes more solid when one hears very experienced riders say that the first lap—whether starting a race, after changing riders, or during training—is never among the fastest, even when one subtracts the additional time required for the start.

It's also relevant that in rallies or endurance races, crashes or disqualifications due to rider error occur disproportionately more frequently after breaks or rider changes. This was especially evident in one of the last

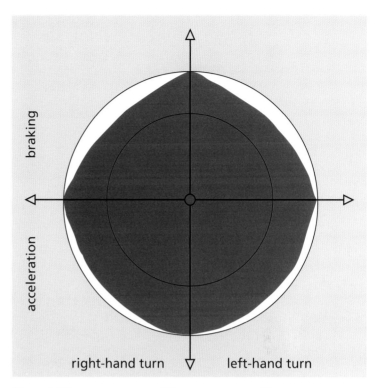

Figure 66. Data of an expert rider—more about this in the text!

(1953) Lüttich–Rome–Lüttich races. It was largely a pure race because the prescribed times were simply not possible to attain on many of the legs of the race. It started to rain at the beginning of the third night, right after the control point Ponte nell' Alpi, and there was a segment that appeared to offer all kinds of grip but, in reality, was as greasy as could be. Many cars with big-name drivers slid off the road; others just managed to save themselves. In the entire rally, which entailed more than 5000 km and 90 hours, there were never as many dropouts as at this particular point. Almost the entire German contingent was out, but what is important in our context is that almost all of the German teams had changed drivers at the control point Ponte nell' Alpi. The Italians had changed drivers earlier, in Ferrara or Padua. They managed the critical stretch much better, even thought it no doubt took a hefty amount of "magic." So it was not the ones who had started out fresh in Ponte nell' Alpi who had better chances; instead, the ones who had been at the wheel longer and already had become deeply integrated "components" of the vehicle.

Similarly, it is also relevant that some airline companies' rules require that on long-distance flights, the pilot must have flown the plane for at least one hour before the landing.

➤ Reaction time in territorial animals

Closely connected with the shortened reaction times that result from increased **integration** into the surroundings is a statement by Konrad Lorenz to the effect that it would hardly be possible to catch territorial animals such as lizards or butterfly fish as long as they stayed in their own territories. Without any slowing in reaction time, these animals, which are highly integrated into their surroundings, would be so fast and unerring that there truly would be no chance to catch them. But once such an animal went beyond its own territory and into a much less familiar environment—and was thus *dis*-integrated with his surroundings, it would be easier to catch (Lorenz 1985, p. 133). ■

The importance of **mental** preparation on reaction time cannot be overstated, especially during something like hillclimbs. During a race there is no chance, with the pressure of the first round, to warm up and get comfortable with the bike. An entire run may last only a few minutes, so the utmost performance has to be produced immediately.

The influence of mental preparation on reaction time

There is much more solid proof, however. Reaction time, which hasn't been determined as precisely as it would appear from reading some textbooks, becomes shorter as soon as a rider becomes a "component." Having become a unit with his machine, the rider achieves a substantially closer, deeper, and more direct connection with the entirety of his surroundings. The reaction times can, in some cases, be considerably below the times measured in laboratories (see Burckhardt 1985).

The deeper connection even relates to physical matters. It is a prerequisite for the more direct connection

that becomes evident with respect to actions and reactions. It is well known that in car racing, especially in Formula 1, a lot of painstaking care goes into the precise fitting of the seating area and the driver controls. On a motorcycle, one should therefore put some time into optimizing the position of levers, handlebar, and other controls, as well as the riding position. Appropriate adaptation, as one can see, is not just a matter of simple comfort; it also helps one attain a more direct connection with the machine and thus fosters unity with it.

One should make use of all the possibilities for a close connection with the motorcycle. A prime example is not just keeping the knees in, but also keeping the feet on the pegs. Many a rider has the habit of letting the foot on which he has been supporting himself while stopped, to hang out a little behind him as he starts accelerating and then placing it on the footpeg at a higher speed, often with fluid agility. This doesn't seem like a big deal, but unfortunately his dangling leg impairs the man-machine connection, and this connection might suddenly be very important. This impairment is often underestimated, but one can immediately get an idea of its significant negative effect with a simple exercise in an empty parking lot. Allow your right foot to hang out behind, and then use your right hand to brake at a moderate intensity to bring the bike to a stop. While braking, plan to make two or three smaller changes in direction, maybe to go to the right or left around a manhole cover or a stain on the asphalt. You'll be surprised how miserable and imprecise your handling of the bike will be. But the following principle applies even when you are riding at very slow speeds: Keep your feet on the pegs as long as possible—a motorcycle does not fall over easily! From the standpoint of riding physics, it is not desirable to have heavy masses, such as the legs, dangling freely and randomly altering the center of gravity.

"Slipping in," all the way to the edges of the vehicle

How much more direct the connection with the vehicle really becomes after the rider or driver has "slipped in" (feels unity with the vehicle) is also evidenced by certain new capabilities that arise within the rider or driver. A new driver clearly has difficulties estimating the shape and extent of his car and keeps far too much distance, especially on the right side, between the car and a wall, for example, when maneuvering and parking. A well-practiced driver doesn't do that much better until he has incorporated the vehicle's size and shape into his conception of his own physical body. Then he will be in a position to drive unhesitatingly through a small gap between a building and a parked car, knowing that "it's just barely enough space." His passengers—generally operating as cargo (and thus not connected to the information system)—are horribly frightened, however.

Another example that may be helpful in understanding "slipping in," or the lack thereof, is the very experienced motorcyclist who, with wide saddlebags on his machine for a longer trip, much more frequently "taps" them here and there than does the rider with less experience. The latter simply get stuck if they try to ride between standing cars because he has only taken the narrow silhouette of the un-laden motorcycle into account in his spatial perception of his body. The accomplished rider commonly rides past stationary objects with minimal clearance, but the saddlebags have not yet been taken into account in his physical perception.

Taking surroundings into account

"Slipping in" is not just a matter of the rider as "component" becoming one with the isolated vehicle. The rider also has to achieve a connection with his entire surroundings (see the sidebar on p. 104). For this reason, it can sometimes be very surprising how especially gifted drivers can "foresee" events that are about to occur but aren't yet recognizable and that aren't at all evident to a passenger: "Watch out, this guy's asleep, he'll crash right into us from behind!" or "Caution, he's about to pull out to the left!" This is nothing more than the result of a high degree of integration of the driver and his surroundings, including his vehicle. It is a capability and feat of the subconscious self. Because there clearly is some sensory information available, the signs of which are only vague, this information is largely inaccessible to acquisition by the conscious self.

◄— The phenomenon of "mysterious message" transmission

The idea that "mysterious messages" of sensory information are actually transmitted without being aware of it sounds rather mystical to the critical, rational reader, yet we encounter this phenomenon often in everyday life—for example, when we tell a close friend, "I could tell right away by looking at you, that . . ." even if the person might have been trying to evoke the opposite impression.

In his short story "Master and Dog," Thomas Mann gives a wonderful description of nonverbal, sensory communication between man and animal. Whatever the master planned to do—as long as it had the slightest bearing on the interests of the dog—the dog knew it right away. When, for example, the master wanted to sneak out of the house because he didn't want the dog along on his walk, he left the room as nonchalantly as possible, acting as if he were just going to get something from another room. But it was to no avail: the dog jumped up with excitement. There was something that revealed his master's plan to the dog.

Another example is a battle between a mongoose and a snake. The lightning-fast, nearly simultaneous head movements of the fighting animals always occur in parallel with each other, so that it's impossible to tell which is attacking and which is defending—a so-called "mirror reaction." This

becomes even more obvious when you observe an encounter in slow-motion films: the only possible conclusion is that both mongoose and snake are picking up on all the signs of an impending action and are not merely reacting to a move by the adversary. ∎

THE EFFECTS OF THE DEEP, SUBCONSCIOUS SELF ON INTEGRATION

A very direct connection

What's interesting about communication that arises from the deep subconscious is that, without any sign or signal having even been recognized as such, not only is there increased watchfulness and preparedness, but there is also a readiness for a lightning fast and, if necessary, very vigorous reaction. The discussion of a "more direct" connection between the driver or rider and the vehicle that exists once he has achieved the condition of being a component, should be understood in a very literal sense. The spontaneous initiations of actions as they emerge from the **movement plan** are directly connected to the centers that control and guide the actions. That is, they do not first undergo any kind of monitoring or "revision" by more conscious aspects of the brain (described earlier as the interplay between the subconscious self and the conscious self). This immediacy leads to several things: reaction times are shorter and the courses of actions are more assured and less disruptable. At the same time, fatigue is minimized (as is the use of energy). But more important, the **coordination** of the individual movements, that is, their interaction, their equilibrium, and their harmonization with each other, become more fluid. A youth in a dance lesson makes his first great progress at the moment in which he no longer thinks about the individual steps, but instead, for example, begins to exchange a few words with his partner.

Training progress and hitting the plateau

Training progress in any pursuit often occurs rather suddenly—and is most readily evident in activities that can be measured with a stopwatch. In spite of dogged practice, there may be no improvement over quite a long period of time. Performance stagnates at a particular level, and the athlete experiences the so-called "plateau." Then, at some point, there is a surprising leap forward, which often occurs after the athlete has achieved an altered attitude toward his performance and his capabilities. This is nothing other than a "direct" course of events: the desired behavior sinks in better, the degree of **automation** of the course of actions increases, or in the case of the rider, an even stronger **integration** of the component (the self) with the motorcycle and the environment occurs.

A different kind of judgment

This direct course of events, in which one can simultaneously see a strengthened involvement of the subconscious self, is also responsible for the disproportionately greater experience base that the person now has access to. These are the contents of the type of **memory** that was previously described as the "procedural memory" (p. 78), and to which our conscious self has no direct access. An example: if a rider, even one of the best in the world, was walking on foot on the edge of a racetrack that he has not ridden before, and he had to say how fast he can ride a certain curve, he not only feels how hard it is to answer that question but also will generally misjudge it by a considerable margin. This situation often occurs at hill climbs. Because the course wouldn't be closed off for training until relatively late, riders would look at it on foot beforehand. But when a rider actually rides the course in training (now with his subconscious self deeply involved), he would approach it—often in the first run—with a speed that would usually be much closer to the optimal speed than the original estimate he made on foot.

Of course, when riding (and not just when walking) the rider also has to make these "estimates," but this estimation occurs in a completely different aspect of his being—the subconscious self—and the result of the estimate goes *directly* into the action. This is something the rider can do successfully only as an *integrated component,* with all the advantages that have already been described. The estimation of maximum speed done on foot was entirely the work of the conscious self. It deliberated, considered, set up comparisons with various other more familiar curves, and in spite of it all, still could not come up with a solid answer—regardless of the fact that the question sought a particular value (speed, thus mph) that later, during the ride, *in this form,* is completely immaterial.

Minimally fatiguing riding

Now it's easier to understand why "riding as a component" is so much less tiring. It is the "direct connection" of the brain centers that control the actions to the subconscious self, and this allows an ever greater number of individual actions to sink in at an **automated** level.

Maybe the reader has already had this experience: he's riding a particular route though the city and suddenly remembers that this is the same stretch of road where, with a learner's permit, he had his first experiences with city traffic. He would probably also remember how strenuous it was at the time, and possibly also, after 45 minutes of it, that he had been completely exhausted. Today, by contrast, riding the same route is perfectly easy and occurs without noticeable fatigue—it's happening "automatically." No one would be able to last through an endurance race or a rally with eternal stages. They wouldn't even be able to last to the first rider change, if it weren't possible for the riding to occur "far beyond" the conscious self. There are different degrees of **automation,** connected to different degrees of "absence," which could be described as a stepping back by the conscious self, resulting in a pronounced narrowing of the field of consciousness.

A skilled endurance rider rides almost as if in a **trance** after a while—that is, he is highly concentrated and entirely focused on the part of his environment that is important to him (riding in a narrowed field of consciousness). He is largely, and more or less directly, governed by this portion of the environment. If one talks to a car driver in this condition while he is driving, it's possible that he won't answer right away, almost as if he were asleep, but it would be an extremely selective sleep. The driver is certainly very close to the **vagotonal economy,** the largely passive state that occurs just before sleep, but this is not true for the focus of his attention. The only trick here is, on the one hand to reach this level quickly (and thereby become fatigued only very slowly), or on the other hand, to keep oneself at this level and keep the focus of attention particularly lucid and concentrated. Distance or endurance riders (and long-distance truck drivers) have mastered this. The danger for the untrained rider (but also for the expert who is overtaxed because of sleep deprivation) lies in the fact that he sinks further and further away and neglects to maintain a lucid focus; thus, the governance by the surroundings that is so important becomes less and less complete, until it finally results in a dangerous dissolution of the surroundings. At this point, it's not yet a matter of the rider's actually falling asleep (which he is fighting the entire time); this phase begins with the eyes still open and quite a bit sooner.

This dangerous dissolution from one's surroundings is described as a reduction of so-called "environment coherence." The environment is certainly still perceived, but the things that are perceived no longer easily break through to the brain centers that control actions, as if they were no longer considered to be sufficiently meaningful. Based on long-distance driving tests, it is fairly well known what happens after that (these are tests that take a lot of time and effort to carry out). If, for example, a truck appears in the right lane ahead while the test driver is in this condition, because of this decreased environment coherence, there are two things that can happen: either the driver moves to the left lane to pass, at first hesitantly, and then with a sudden jerk; *or* (and this shows nicely that the idea of "breaking through," as described above, isn't quite right), the driver manages to initiate the pass in a timely manner but pulls out much too slowly, necessitating a sudden correction of the insufficient steering input. Hopefully, this happens in time.

The ability to recognize the relatively early signs of reduced environment coherence is extremely important, especially for the motorcyclist who often rides in relative isolation. Regardless of whether he's involved in a long-distance tour or an endurance race, he must recognize that the danger is present long before he actually falls asleep. The actual nodding off occurs much more rarely among motorcyclists than among car drivers, but the danger the motorcyclist is subjected to as a result of decreased environment coherence is at least as great as the danger for a car driver. A final cautionary note: one should not forget that decreased environment coherence and nodding off do not happen only at night.

Related to environment coherence is a concept that has been discussed more and more in recent years: the phenomenon of "flow," which some see as the work of the devil, and others praise as a gift from heaven.

Flow, simultaneously helper and enemy

As the holy Niklaus von Flüe mowed a field (the story is sometimes also attributed to the lanky Saint Francis of Assisi, although it's questionable whether anyone would have ever told him to mow an entire field) he was asked: "What would you do if you only had this day left to live?" And he answered without looking up: "Keep mowing."

This is **flow:** one becomes completely absorbed into an activity, feels a strong state of well-being (or happiness), and desires nothing more; uninvolved circumstances in the environment are largely blocked out. For this condition to set in, one very special type of condition has to be fulfilled, one that doesn't occur every day and that some never encounter at all. The demands that

Figure 67. Motorcyclists sometimes experience the sensation of "flow," a condition of floating or being detached that be exhilarating to driders who have mastered their activity.

the activity places on the person doing it must stand in good balance with his capabilities and also with his *motivation* at that moment. Thus, there should be a perfect intermeshing, or a nearly complete match between the demands on the one side and the capabilities and motivation on the other. Then, according to Mihaly Csikszentmihalyi (1993, 1996), the founder of the study of flow, there is the onset of a condition in which a person has characteristically sunken deeply into himself and has a feeling of abandon along with the deep feeling of well-being described above. This feeling of well-being has its biochemical basis in the form of endorphins.

Examples of this condition can be drawn from such different activities as long-distance swimming, mountain climbing, chess, cross-country skiing, playing music, and creating art. All of these activities have at least one common feature, namely an extended temporal dimension such that the performer of the activity can arrive at a "steady state," as Americans descriptively call it in the physiological realm, or a new balance, in which the demands placed on the person are largely compensated.

This condition also applies to motorcycle riding (Rheinberg 1991, 1996)—not, of course for a single short lap on a Grand-Prix course, but absolutely for an endurance race and even for a normal GP distance, at least when there is not a constant battle for position. It also applies to everyday touring. Kenny Roberts has described such a trance-like state (involving limited self-criticism), which can only be interpreted as an experience of flow. This was his experience when, far in front of the field, he rode alone, out in front.

As previously mentioned, the constellation of pre-conditions that must exist in order for flow to occur don't exactly occur on demand. Thus, it is hard to reliably predict when this special activity-related condition is going to set in. In any case, the activity must be flawlessly mastered, and the required capabilities must also be sufficiently challenged by the particular situation. If the challenge is too great (and this may occasionally be required for training), the person's capabilities are likely to be overtaxed, leading to the activity's no longer being flawlessly mastered. Conversely, if there is less of a challenge, it appears that everything is in place for flow to take hold, but from a certain point forward the person's motivation suffers because of insufficient challenge and flow will stop. It's not just the capabilities but also the motivation on which sufficient demands must be placed.

People's descriptions of this condition almost always connote a feeling of flowing, floating, and being detached: "It was as if I were riding a wave;" "there were no dangers, no strain, no fatigue; only an effortless lightness;" "I was gliding along, *as if in a dream.*" The detachment is concentration—the *effortless* concentration on a very specific activity, on a tiny excerpt from the world—which, for that person, is his entire world while he is engaged in the activity. He dominates the activity, oversees it, sees through it, and it is completely subject to him. Concerns and dangers stay on the outside, as do any higher goals, considerations of utility, or payment. It is flow that not only makes long and enduring stress possible but also bearable, keeps it from becoming drudgery, and actually converts the stress into worthwhile goals.

In this way, flow can be a friend and a helper, whereby one should qualify the condition: *controlled flow,* or the flow that is monitored and mastered. Because a state of flow into which one has fallen unnoticed (perhaps because he has no experience with it and may have never heard of it) hides enormous dangers in high-risk sports; it becomes *uncontrolled flow.* The extreme feeling of well-being is a signal that a person is doing the right thing and calls for more of the same. The focus of one's conscious becomes ever tighter, and all warning voices are blocked out. However, in a disastrous way, the willingness to accept risk also grows. With every risk that is successfully survived provides a renewed "kick," the person decides that there's no need to take any breaks because they would only interrupt a condition that could hardly be improved upon.

These are typical flow phenomena, which immediately potentiate themselves and really cannot be reigned in because it has become a situation of absolute disinhibition. Any stripping away of this total disinhibition almost always occurs as a result of the breakdown of negative feedback, that is, of the regulating forces that pull a person "back to Earth." For this reason, flow phenomena, even if considered only in the very limited realm of riding at high speeds (especially at speeds that have not yet been practiced) are really nothing new. Even as early as the 1950s, it became necessary for people to take a closer look at the phenomenon of disinhibition through speed (Spiegel 1953).

"Built-in" parts and self-observation

With our consideration of rider as "component," we again cast light on the controlling and monitoring observation by the person performing an activity. Now, one can see, from yet another point of view, why self-observation can be so detrimental: the component (the self) is disengaged from its usual system connections—in some cases, more so, and in some, less so. It is probably only in very rare cases that self-observation remains entirely without influence. The fourth part of this book discusses the tasks of the conscious self, including self-observation and self-control.

PART 4

What's Left for the Head to Do?

TASKS FOR THE CONSCIOUS SELF

Up to this point, the topic "mind and gut," to put it in everyday language, has come up several times. We've paid particular attention to all the things that are best left to "gut feelings." As described in Part 3, these things all tend to go much better if left to the "gut" than they would if they were subject to conscious management. However, the main recommendation is *not* simply to do as much as possible based on gut feelings and give the gut (subconscious self) free rein to the greatest possible extent. Although it's true that we all tend to apply too much conscious attention to particular actions, especially in training, it's a matter of achieving the *correct interface* between mind and gut, that is, between conscious self and subconscious self.

What, then, should the conscious self be doing? What are the duties of the mind's rationality, reason, and conscious attention? Is there even anything left for the conscious self to do?

A very long list!

If we briefly review what has been discussed in the foregoing sections, we'll find a great many tasks for the conscious self. The first thing that might occur to us is that consideration of the physics of riding can be very useful; it's almost indispensable for top-level riders. However, it's not so much a matter of what one must know, should know, and could know or what the conscious self can do either in preparation for an activity or in a post-activity analysis of what happened. Instead, it's chiefly a matter of the conscious self's duties during the actual riding, and at this point, you may be wondering if it has anything to do? Absolutely . . . more than enough!

Defense against external dangers: forming hypotheses

One of the main tasks for the conscious self is the continuous construction of hypotheses: what might happen now or in the next moment, and what can I do to be prepared? This is the capability of the human cerebrum: to imagine the future—in this case, the very near future.

Our cerebrum gives us the ability to imagine how something might be, even if it doesn't exist or hasn't happened yet (compare p. 52).

This *construction of hypotheses* must truly occur continuously: we must constantly evaluate every perceived situation and its anticipated further development and potential dangers. This might be referred to as "danger anticipation," or the theoretical presumption (and possibly forestalling) of dangers. However, there's more to the **hypothesis construction** than this. It's actually a process, and one that doesn't have to occur very consciously. It is often described as "alongside consciousness." The degree of consciousness of hypothesis construction is constantly changing, but as soon as there is evidence that strengthens the hypothesis into *reasonable suspicion*—"there's a chance that the cyclist at that driveway . . ." or "it looks for all the world like the guy in front of me . . .")—it becomes the object of fully conscious attention.

The consciousness of hypothesis construction

Here's an example: a rider is getting closer to the car in front and plans to pass it; there are a few buildings on either side of the road. The general hypothesis would be that the car could, without signaling, turn left. There are several suspicious signs that immediately raise alarms: the car slows down; the driver turns his head a little to the left; the car pulls a little farther to the left than it had been before, or maybe it's swung a little farther to the *right,* but in any case, it's deviated from its previous line; there's a driveway on the left side of the road; someone's standing there who nods in greeting toward the driver; etc. Thanks to the advance construction of the hypothesis, the rider is adequately sensitive to these hints, which can be very subtle. More precisely: it's the act of constructing hypotheses that puts the rider in a position to perceive the relevant details. The hypothesis allows him to sift these relevant details out of the constant overload of at first meaningless, and to some extent unimportant, events and other situations and information that he faces.

Here are three more aspects of the relevance of **hypothesis construction:**

1. Out of a multitude of stimuli, we will preferentially pick out and see the things that have a bearing on our own *interests and concerns* (see also p. 129). The continuous engagement, our thoughts, with potential events, especially dangers, makes these potential dangers increasingly part of our *interests and concerns.*

2. Events that suddenly happen will be more quickly and more reliably perceived if they are expected (or at least if their occurrence is considered possible). The expected event does not have to be concretely specified at all: it has a beneficial effect even if all that has been mentally prepared is a particular category in which the event belongs. For example: in testing in which groups of letters or numbers are flashed in front of participants for an extremely short time, participants' ability to perceive what they see is made measurably easier if they have been told in advance whether the next image will have letters or numbers. Categories (in this example, numbers or letters) that have been prepared are more quickly and more reliably identified than they are without this kind of general preparation. This general preparation can be compared with an expectation, or hypothesis. As in the example of simple symbols, it's also true of more complex objects of perception: they are not only more quickly identified, but the certainty of interpretation is improved, which also improves the stability of the course of action.

3. A prepared hypothesis robs the element of surprise from a suddenly occurring, threatening situation. This is the basis of an important strategy in desensitization training (see p. 135).

Another good example of this is the children's ball that rolls out from behind an obstacle and, apparently harmlessly, across the street, but there are more subtle examples: Imagine riding through a narrow town lane, with opposing traffic and pedestrians on the right side, one of whom is carrying a long ladder over his shoulder, and you think, "If he turns into the building site, the end of his ladder will close off my lane like a railroad crossing!"—a complicated prediction in a rare situation.

Here, we are reminded of the rider who blasted at full throttle around a blind corner that he was familiar with but could not see into (see page 21). He was riding accord-

Figure 68. What lies just over this hill? A prudent rider must construct hypotheses to anticipate potential hazards

ing to an imagined image rather than the image he was actually perceiving and thus met an unexpected obstacle. No hypothesis construction occurred, although the rider would have been capable of it, unlike the dog who fell into the water along with his sausage (see page 21).

One should be aware of when and under what circumstances hypothesis construction is either absent or impaired. It will obviously be absent when the necessary "equipment" is not present, as in the case of the dog. But often enough, it is also absent in some of our fellow riders who behave recklessly at all times and in all places and, after the fact, are always surprised. Everyone knows riders like this: those who are careless and ride even more carelessly. Thus, they don't build hypotheses except in extreme cases, and unless they improve, it's only a question of time before something goes wrong.

Impaired hypothesis construction

So how well does the average motorcyclist perform in **hypothesis construction**? What about a good rider, a very good rider, or an excellent rider? Even among these kinds of riders, there can be problems with hypothesis construction. For example, with increasing fatigue (maybe on too long of a ride with too few breaks), hypothesis construction is notably diminished, but it can also be impaired by overflowing happiness and other emotions, especially anger. Sensitivity to hidden dangers ebbs away, and the hints and suspicious events are no longer recognized or, at the very least, do not trigger conscious attention as quickly.

Hypothesis construction allows the theoretical (in our thoughts) anticipation of events that might be just about to happen, especially (but not only) dangers. Ideally, it occurs *constantly and continuously,* and usually not on such a highly conscious level, but rather *subconsciously.* Only the more critical or conspicuous situations lead to fully *conscious attention.* For this reason, the reader who is considering his own riding habits will remember only these more critical situations and fear that he's not so good at the "constant and continuous" part, or he eases his qualms by telling himself, "This hypothesis construction is certainly very important, but this thing about the barely conscious hypotheses is just a little too much!"

"Hidden" hypotheses

I would suggest, however, that barely conscious hypothesis construction is extremely common. Here's just a single example: on a country road, a rider approaches a blind entrance on the right side. He usually rides on the right side of the lane, but at a reasonable distance before the entrance, he gradually moves over to the left side, close to the centerline. After passing the entrance, he gradually moves back over to the right. When asked about it afterward, he has no idea ("Really? I did?"). The hypothesis, thus, stayed hidden. It hadn't even been formulated into a thought, but nonetheless it was transformed into an action, and not such a simple one at that. To keep a smooth line, he had to move left *at the right time* and *at a very small angle* yet one large enough so that he could achieve the desired distance from the right side of the road before passing the entrance. And then he had to move back to the right, appropriately.

In hypothesis construction, then, fully conscious awareness is not a mandatory prerequisite. This is something that is not readily apparent when first considering the concept of hypothesis construction, which really does sound like a *rational* activity. Herein lies the irony: because the conscious self is engaged when a rider starts to construct hypotheses, eventually, this happens frequently enough that it starts to happen by itself (becomes **automated**) and thus only requires **conscious attention** in special cases.

Market psychology and buyer perception

One of the most important market psychology concepts is that it's not the *objective* qualities of a product that make up reality in marketing, but rather, and only, its *impression* on the potential buyer. When correspondingly expanded, this statement is valid for any object about which an opinion is possible and for any circumstance that we might experience and in response to which we feel compelled to action (or inaction). ∎

SELF-PERCEPTION

The hidden dangers in self-perception

So much for perception and the processing of *external* dangers. It's an accomplishment that, as we have seen, does not even require fully conscious attention in all cases. However, when it's a matter of dealing with *internal* dangers, we can appropriately talk about *making it conscious.* This is closely related to hypothesis construction. Thus, *perception,* and in this case the perception of a particular *internal* psychological situation, is the key to everything that follows.

The perception of a particular inner-psychic situation is called "self-perception." The capability of self-perception is desirable and it can be trained, but this does not mean that the *accompanying self-observation,* which we have recognized to be disadvantageous, has crept back in (see p. 73). Even if self-perception and accompanying self-observation are neighboring concepts, and there is even some overlap, there is still a clear difference. Self-observation is, especially if it accompanies an action, entirely *intentional,* meaning that it is deliberate and goal-directed; it is supervisory and tense. Self-perception, in contrast, is an expectant openness to qualities of an experience that might come about; it is loose and without direction.

Realistic perception of oneself, required

The sports psychologist Eberspächer (2002) points out emphatically that no one can ride a motorcycle safely over the long term if he does not have a realistic sense of himself, a realistic self-perception. The *objective* view and the *subjective* view (that is, the observation of the rider from the *outside* and his own view, the observation from the *inside)* should be in agreement. At no time in our lives (and not just related to motorcycle riding) do we act in accordance with the way a situation *is.* Instead, we always act in accordance with the way we *believe it appears to be,* that is, with the way we *perceive* it.

Lean angles

Our actions become more appropriate, and thereby safer, the closer our subjective image matches the objective reality. Eberspächer explains this for the motorcyclist, using the example of lean angles in corners. A beginner or someone with little practice has an image of himself riding at enormous lean angles, maybe close to the limits of possibility, when in reality he's still riding quite moder-

The lean angle and its limits

There have been interesting experiments about this: a group of moderately experienced motorcyclists who were all fearful of leaning had to ride through a 90-degree corner on a level parking lot with a "grippy" surface. The corner was marked, but not at the outer edges of the path they were to follow; instead, it was marked only with the line on which the participants were supposed to ride through the corner. This line was represented by white dots on the path, and according to the instructions, the riders only had to *more or less* adhere to the line. It didn't matter if they came out a foot or so the right or left of the line, provided the rider's own track ran roughly parallel to the marked target line.

The participants had to approach the corner along a similarly marked straight line at a prescribed speed (which was checked) and ride through the corner with exactly the same throttle opening. The personal limit of lean of each participant had been previously determined. The prescribed speed determined a particular target lean angle. If this was less lean than the personal limit, then everything went according to the instructions. *But if the lean was more than the personal limit, then the corner was inevitably opened* (or, in a few cases, the riders reduced their speed). This was also true if the targeted lean was only a few degrees more than the personal limit of lean. The only difference in outcome between when a personal limit was slightly exceeded and when it was substantially exceeded was that, with the former, the corner was only slightly opened, and with the latter, the corner was significantly opened. In short, the participants always rode the line that was allowed within their personal limit of lean angle.

In the human mesocosm (see p. 24), the world of median dimensions, in which we can get our bearings immediately and without problems, and in which we can just as well act spontaneously as purposefully, we encountered lean angles in early stages of our evolution, but we also encountered *limits* to our lean angles just as early. The limit is right around 20 degrees!

Lean angles are familiar to us because the human being, as the *runner* that he became, took on considerable lean angles when changing direction,

Figure M69. People feel comfortable at lean angles up to 20 degrees. We instinctively avoid greater lean angles because traction on typical surfaces is unpredictable.

just as do all other fast runners, including horses, dogs, or birds such as ostriches. But just like these animals, the human being also avoids lean angles greater than 20 degrees, because anything more would be risky on natural surfaces, with their widely varying characteristics.

This is why humans can use up the 20 degrees very quickly, whether learning to ride a bicycle or with their first attempts on a motorcycle, but gets stuck at that angle at first. But, as described on page 24, a human being is capable of expanding his personal mesocosm, although this demands a high level of learning effort.

The human being is thus very much *pre-adapted* to the single-track vehicle. That is, he can take adaptations that were in response to entirely different conditions (that existed much earlier) and suddenly put them to use with a two-wheeler. Without this pre-adaptation, at most there would only be a few artists who were capable of managing such a vehicle (Spiegel 1989). ■

⚙ Hanging off

Even **hanging off** (see Figure 70), which is really warranted only on the track and for which one can hear the most bizarre justifications even from absolute experts, can be systematically practiced by means of a gradual increase of the lean angle. A person practicing this will quickly recognize that the crucial—if also most noticeable—element is not so much folding one's knee out, but rather moving one's body far to the inside, pushing the inner thigh *emphatically* forward and downward, and along with the thigh, also the inside shoulder and inside knee (most precisely described in Niemann 1999, p. 33). This shifts the body's center of mass toward the inside and, in turn, allows the motorcycle to lean less (by only a minimal amount).

Now we turn our attention to the knee. It's the same in systematic training of hanging off: the knee is not considered until this point. If it is folded out now (it can't go that far, since the pelvis is now turned toward the *outside*), at a reasonable but not necessarily extreme lean angle, so it will already be very close to the ground. In this position, the knee fulfills two functions: in the milder form of hanging off in which this technique is most commonly used, the tapping down of the knee puck provides very immediate information about the lean angle that has been achieved. In the more extreme form, the knee is actually pressed against the ground; this is *stabilization on a third point,* which for many riders is

Figure 70. Hanging off. The knee is only moderately turned out, but more significantly lowered and moved forward. Correspondingly, the inside hip and shoulders also move forward.

associated with an indescribable feeling of safety. This is easy to imagine using the example of a dirt-track rider: near the limits of traction and without stabilization, the motorcycle will try to wander away laterally by way of its **contact patches,** which will lead to a still-greater lean angle that can no longer be corrected. With support from a third point, the lean angle can, however, be held constant, and the relatively small stabilizing forces that can be applied by the knee are enough to achieve this. ∎

ately and his lean angle could be increased considerably. Result: in a dangerous situation—for example, if he misjudges a corner or an obstacle appears and he has to tighten his line—he can't make use of the *actual* margin available in the lean angle. Conversely, the rider who is leaned to the limit but thinks, based on his self-perception, that he still has sufficient reserves, will someday, maybe even in the next moment, try to increase his lean angle beyond what is actually available in a particular situation.

He who rides in fear of the lean is living dangerously!

Really? Shouldn't it be the other way around? We all know brave, level-headed touring riders, with many years of riding experience, who never go looking for

trouble and are more likely to ride with too much reserve than too little. For this reason, they avoid larger, especially extreme, lean angles. And these people are suddenly at risk? Not necessarily: only if they *fear the lean,* which they probably do.

What is the nature of the risk? Someday, and it's only a matter of time, even the most cautious rider will find himself in a situation in which he suddenly has to take a corner on a much tighter line than he had planned. It might be that he has judged the corner to be more open than it actually is, or that he suddenly has to move to the inside to evade a hazard. Maybe he didn't actually need a tighter radius than planned, but he misjudged his speed and entered the curve at simply too high a speed. In any case, the result is the same: he suddenly needs more lean than expected. When this "more" means that he's leaning to an extent *that he is not familiar with,* it can get hairy (see also p. 36). As if there were rock-solid lock, the rider will usually go as far as his own lean angle limit and, come what may, not go beyond it. The consequences can be extremely grave: in a right-hander, the rider will cross into opposing traffic, and it doesn't look that much better in a left-hander.

In this way, the rider ends up in a life-threatening situation and there's not much he can do about it anymore. However, it's not because he's reached the limit of his tires' traction but rather because he has literally run into his personal lean angle limit and can't go beyond it. This makes for harrowing accident sequences: as if on rails, the motorcycle adheres to a cornering radius that is far too large, and, at a lean angle that's not threatening in the least, heads straight for an oncoming vehicle, and the ride comes to a horrific end . . .

Breaking through the fear: the circle

There's only one solution: *the fear of the lean has to be overcome.* This is possible only if one becomes familiar with lean angles that go beyond his personal limits. Becoming familiar involves practicing systematically. The best and safest way is by slowly increasing the lean while riding in a circle and thus gradually pushing one's personal lean limit farther out.

The circle—a favorite device for motorcycle training classes—can be set up on a level parking lot (without gutters) and has a radius of about 14 or 15 meters. The circle is marked with cones, and riders are to circle their motorcycles around the outside of them. The objective is to make the riders comfortable with larger lean angles in situations in which the risks are manageable, by having them gradually increase their speed with the guidance of an instructor. The proper body position and stance is also practiced: looking far ahead, holding the head out of the lean, pressing the inside knee forward, etc.

Once the fear of greater leans has been removed, the objective of the exercise evolves for the more advanced participant: he can now—much better than he could on a track, to say nothing of the street—systematically become familiar with how his motorcycle behaves close to the limits of traction. This is why even experienced riders in training courses take advantage of the opportunity to ride in circles.

This familiarization with lean angles can be enhanced with **mental** training (see p. 117) if, during training, a rider frequently makes note of his own lean angles and

🏍 Parts and attendant dangers

"Soft" parts such as fairing panels, folding footpegs, spring-mounted centerstands, exhaust pipes that give way, etc., are harmless when scraped, and simultaneously serve as warnings that can't be missed. However, because of the possibility of being levered off one's wheels, dragging parts are more dangerous, and the danger increases the more rigid they are, the closer to the inside they are, and the farther forward they are. The cylinder head of a boxer motor, for example, is certainly rigid but far to the outside of the motorcycle, but with an oil sump that touches down at an extreme lean angle with simultaneously compressed suspension, the part that touches down is not only rigid but also fairly far to the inside and dangerously far forward. ∎

consciously makes it his **objective** to "lean, lean, lean" (see p. 159). This means that in a critical cornering situation, unless there's a more or less risk-free bailout option (*escape offroad*), there's only one possible solution: to increase the lean angle without regard for any kind of limitation, that is, to really *lay* the motorcycle over.

In the majority of cases, experience has shown that the limit of traction is not reached. Modern motorcycles, with today's sticky tires, ridden on a grippy road surface, can basically be leaned until some part or other (footpeg, centerstand, exhaust) touches down, and even this point is still not the limit of traction.

However, even if the traction limit actually is exceeded at some point, what happens is the best possible outcome of the given situation—at least, if one does not consider the dangerous highside that can occur in racing. The rider "*gets off*" on the "lowside," as riders somewhat euphemistically describe this type of crash. This kind of crash is relatively harmless, which is why it is sometimes intentionally used to avoid something worse (see p. 133). For one thing, it's not such a long way to the ground (this is meant absolutely seriously; compare the distance to the ground of falling to the outside, the "highside"), but most important, the motorcycle slides in front, and the rider, who usually slides a little more slowly, follows behind. In addition, the deceleration involved is considerable; it roughly corresponds to the deceleration achieved in well-executed braking.

However, this cannot be compared to the lean-fearing rider who, paralyzed by his fear, stays seated on his bike. With practically no deceleration, he will have crossed the outer edge of the road with lightning speed, at which point the actual crash starts, maybe on the shoulder or, in the worst case, not until the guardrail, which he is thrown over, head first. And it's almost always the case that he "gets off on the highside," which means that he flies out ahead, with the heavy bike behind him. One can only hope that there's no obstacle in the way.

Monitoring the self-image

In both cases, the internal image—or more precisely, the self-image, the image from the inner point of view—is so convincing that a major exertion by the conscious self is needed to critically examine and consider that image and, even though it seems trustworthy, to turn away from it. There are many possible ways to compare the internal image with the external image, to match the subjective self-image to reality, and to examine it again and again. Eberspächer (2002) lists a number of possibilities. When following another rider, one can observe that rider's lean angle and compare it to one's own subjective image. At times, one can also use the tip of his boot to feel how far the footpeg is from the ground. One can draw a chalk line across the tires from rim to rim and look at them later to see how much of the line has been worn off. Finally, one can be photographed or filmed, as occurs in some rider-training courses. Of course, these are ways to get an idea of the lean angle. The image of a motorcyclist has several other facets, although the lean angle is one of the most important.

It's not only the correction of the self-image that's important, however. One must also clearly understand that this internal image, in contrast to the external image, is unstable and can fluctuate. Depending on how the rider feels at a given moment, it might be sometimes more and sometimes less distant from reality. Only an old hand can manage to keep his internal image stable *and* close to re-

ality, and only then does it become reliable. Thus, acute internal perception is required for critical self-monitoring: How do I feel? What am I feeling? And at this moment, in what ways does my self-image deviate from the objective situation, the external image? One can train himself to have a remarkable sensitivity for this, even without external aids, and thus achieve greater certainty about his judgments.

Monitoring the attitude toward risk

The same is true of the **risk composite** (see p. 73), that controls us all. It is not enough for us to *know* about this dangerous error when managing risks. Instead, by constantly maintaining our willingness to critically examine ourselves, we have to be in a position to "listen in" on ourselves to recognize when we are being threatened by this dangerous situation. The risk composite itself is actually an outstanding example of the necessity of bringing things to **conscious attention,** that is, the need for the deployment of monitoring by the conscious self.

Monitoring flow

When it comes to **flow,** the state of consciousness that can be so helpful during long-lasting exertions but can also become a deadly danger, the situation is no different. In risky types of sports, a state of *unregulated flow* occurs because of a lack of monitoring (see p. 107). It leads to an uncritical euphoria, similar to the feeling that can arise at previously unpracticed high speeds.

Up to this point, we have discussed all kinds of duties for the conscious self! For one, we have addressed the proper way to deal with *external* dangers by means of continuous **hypothesis construction** as well as the proper way to deal with *internal* dangers by means of making them part of one's conscious awareness and applying critical self-perception. This allows a person to correct very specific errors in behavior: errors such as trusting in a perhaps misleading self-image; such as our fateful tendency to engage the **risk composite;** such as excessive, uncritical indulgence in the experience of *flow* and the unnoticed disinhibition that occurs with high speeds that have not been practiced or experienced before.

Everything that relates to planning

The conscious self has still other important duties. One that cannot be overlooked is its responsibility for everything that has to do with planning. The cerebrum, the foundation of the conscious self, is involved in planning for the future. Planning is all about what *should* happen. All strategic decisions are part of this planning: geographic orienteering and the selection of the best route, the distribution of breaks, deciding when to stop for gas next, etc. Compared to what has been discussed up to now, these are relatively long-term decisions, but there are also very short-term ones, such as various tactical decisions in racing, without which no racer could ever succeed.

Training, oriented toward the future

We still haven't come to the end of the conscious self's duties. Something that is also related to the future and, in this regard, also requires planning, is *training.* Training has a *future* status as its goal (for example, an achievement, proficiency, or conditioning): something that is to be improved or at least maintained. However, training *success* doesn't happen by itself; it must be systematically developed. The most important prerequisites for this—especially if one does not have a trainer who's always there—are sufficient readiness for self-critical observation and sufficient capability to accurately perceive one's level of competency.

Training as correction

In all considerations of training and practice, one should be clear about the following: training is usually not simply a matter of an improvement in skills in the sense of building new programs or refining existing **programs.** It is much more often the case that there are certain erroneous behaviors, or "bad habits," as they are sometimes described, which would be harmless if it weren't for the fact that they've long since become **automated.** Thus, it is not enough to just tell the trainee (or oneself) that this or that is detrimental and he shouldn't do it anymore. Instead, it's a matter of replacing an existing program (or part of one) with a new one, and this is disproportionately more difficult and tedious. This is the case in all kinds of sports (and also other kinds of activities) in which actual training usually doesn't occur until the person has already achieved a certain skill level.

In extreme situations, the level of achievement can already be extraordinarily high, for example, among competitive athletes who want to convert to the use of new methods or techniques. Relatively sudden conversions have been fairly frequent in recent decades, such as in the high jump, alpine skiing, cross-country skiing, and ski-

jumping. The old programs, which have now become limiting, are so deeply entrenched that they can't just be suspended from one day to the next. This is why some athletes, usually against their trainers' better judgment, have to deny themselves the learning of a new method or technique.

The danger of relapse

Once conversion through training has finally succeeded, the old program still exists but is dormant. In critical situations, especially if they cause panic or fear, the old program may, however, catch a person unaware and take over, and the athlete reverts. This is a clear sign that the old program is not overwritten, deleted, or thrown out; instead, the new program is just *superimposed* over the old.

After a change in behavior that has been brought about by laborious and painstaking practice, maintaining the change is often the hardest. The following is a statement that has been attributed to Konrad Lorenz, who made clear in few words how difficult it is to bring about an enduring change in behavior: "Said is not heard, heard is not understood, understood is not agreement, agreed is not application, applied is not retained."

The more deeply a program has sunken in (i.e., the more automated), the less susceptible to disruption it is. However, in contrast to the old one, which isn't even supposed to be "valid" anymore, the new program hasn't yet achieved equivalent stability.

In any case, in practice and training related to motorcycle riding, it's not just a matter of building onto existing behaviors, but most often also a matter of *changes* or corrections in behavior. This means that there are previously acquired, and unfortunately suboptimal, programs to be pasted over and thus are just not that easy to get rid of.

Training intent

Anyone who boasts of having ridden for 20 years (accident-free, of course) hasn't really said that much about his degree of perfection as a rider. It's true that he's lived though a great many situations and has thus collected *experience,* but the extent to which he has translated these experiences into improvements in his riding behavior remains an open question. He has most certainly had spontaneous gains in his capabilities, especially at the beginning, but without any *intent to train* (or to learn) he would have soon stagnated at some more or less modest level, depending on how talented he was. The fact is that there are young riders, obsessed with perfection, who, after only two seasons, can already ride better than these 20-year veterans.

Improvement requires a constant *intent* to improve. A passive openness to learning is not enough. An active desire to learn—the *intent to train mentioned above*—is necessary. The implementation and maintenance of this intent is a task that requires the utmost in rational control, which is a *duty—a "leadership duty"—of the conscious self.* The application of the training processes and training aids that are useful in the implementation of the training intent is a job for the conscious self.

Subsequent sections discuss training aids and processes that one can use by himself, without a trainer.

Monitoring of hypothesis construction

Along with hypothesis construction, which hurries ahead in anticipation of events, comes *monitoring,* which hurries along after the fact and evaluates what has just happened. In other words, while hypothesis construction is directed at the not-yet-happened, monitoring is directed at the what-just-happened. Monitoring is not directed at what *is happening* at the very moment, but instead, afterward, it's directed at what happened just a moment ago. Otherwise, we'd be letting self-observation in through the back door, and self-observation *during* the course of action is definitely something we want to avoid, as we learned earlier (see p. 74). The observation of what's happening at the moment can absolutely be distinguished from the observation of what has just happened a moment ago. While the *accompanying* self-observation is more likely to disrupt the course of action and always has a tendency to meddle in the control of the activity, *retrospective monitoring* waits until the activity is over. The conscious self registers and evaluates the activity after it has occurred and modifies it only if an error has occurred and the execution of an action has proved itself to be in need of improvement.

Objective self-criticism and object criticism

The conscious self doesn't ordinarily perform objective self-criticism by itself. This is something that has to be systematically trained. Usually only truly profound mistakes—events that leave a lasting impression or that could have been avoided simply through the proper behavior or actions—break through as errors and lead to conscious attention to the problem. Most small errors, even if they were readily evident, are not noticed; even if they are conspicuous enough to push their way into our consciousness, it is still possible that they will be dispatched as "meaningless" or as "unavoidable" and ascribed to the circumstances—blamed on the behavior of a third party, for example—which is *object criticism,* not objective self-criticism.

We all have a tendency toward object criticism. What this means is that if we make a mistake, we usually don't look for its cause in ourselves but instead seek to blame it on some object that was closely involved in the activity, or maybe even on another person ("*self-serving bias*"). Problems in setting an alarm clock might be ascribed to the writing on it that's impossible to read; a collapsed cake might be blamed on a bad oven; or a computer that does something other than what the user expects might be called "a piece of junk."

There's a lot of animosity lurking in this, and once the subconscious self has identified an object as the suspected cause and spoiler of what would have been a good outcome, it sees that object as an adversary. This can actually go as far as physical attack. In earlier times—although it supposedly still happens today—these unfortunate objects have been viewed as bewitched, cursed, or subject to some other mysterious influence ("ever since he came to my mill, it just hasn't run right!")

Without a doubt, to look for fault in an object (and to also find it there and become convinced of its fault) is very "practical" for one's self-esteem, and swearing (or throwing the tool at the wall) serves to release animosity and aggression. However, object criticism also has its disadvantages: it is *one of the biggest impediments to learning.*

➤ The farmer's swim trunks

Our tendency toward object criticism is illustrated by the old saying: "If the farmer can't swim, it's the fault of his swim trunks." ∎

If we start to watch for object criticism, we notice it first in the behavior of others. This is a good way to improve our ability to identify object criticism, but if we want to benefit from this ability, we have to direct it mostly at ourselves. Because there is no human being with the slightest bit of regard for himself who is free of object criticism (and this is true of all normal people), object self-criticism requires training, beginning with the question, Do I persist with the object criticism, which sets in automatically to relieve me of the burden (do I effectively get stuck), or do I manage to break through this mechanism and identify the actual causes of the error, even if they are to be found within myself?

Object criticism is usually strongest when one has reached the limits of his personal ability, that is, when the challenge threatens to become too great. In fact, increased object criticism is a reliable indicator that a person has been challenged beyond the limits of his abilities. In motorcycling—for example, in rider training or group rides—participants whose abilities have been exceeded will express various criticisms remarkably often. Their criticisms have no objective justification: "Behind him, it's impossible to stay on the right line!" "I keep losing the rear wheel." "The bike is just bouncing and hopping . . . I can hardly hang on!" "My tires are completely worthless; they have no grip at all!" etc.

Becoming able to be self-critical

It goes without saying that this constant downplaying of self-criticism certainly soothes the ego of the rider; however, it throws away every opportunity to stamp out error. This is one of the main reasons why there are so many riders with a tremendous amount of experience ("20 years without an accident!") who still constantly make the same errors. The only thing that they've *gradually* learned is to deal better with their mistakes. As we discussed, what is lacking is the intent to learn (**learning intent**) and thereby also the *readiness to criticize* one's own actions.

How does one arrive at this higher ability to be critical of oneself? To take it one step back: how does one achieve a level of self-perception that is sufficiently sensitive not to let errors simply go ignored, allowing them to become objects of self-critical consideration? This is a matter of motivation, and one can influence motivation exquisitely using particular techniques for setting **objectives,** as used in **mental** training. However, precisely in this situation, there's a much simpler way: the error counter.

Figure 71. The error counter. The simple test question: Would I do it exactly that way again?

TRAINING AIDS

The error counter

This is nothing other than a simple tally counter—each time the button is pressed, the counting mechanism jumps one number further. It is sometimes used in endurance racing to count laps (see Figure 71) and is mounted somewhere near the left grip. The "rules of the game" are extremely simple. One merely has to count *each* mistake he makes by pressing the counter button. The type of mistake is not taken into consideration because the usual classification into *traffic errors* (for example: violating a traffic signal), *operating errors* (for example: missing a shift), and *riding errors* (for example: misjudging a corner) would be too complicated. Likewise, it's completely irrelevant whether it is a serious error that could easily have dire consequences or just a harmless "cosmetic" error. There's also no place for any kind of consideration of where the blame for the error lies, and it's meaningless whether the error was the result of blind chance or one brought it upon himself. A mistake is a mistake. Every mistake that a rider notices is treated in the same way: with a single press of the counter button.

There's only one instance in which an error is not counted, and this is when the error is committed with deliberate intent. This does happen: for example, if one thinks that a speed limit is overzealous and believes he should exceed it a little bit or if one thinks he needs to start a passing maneuver a few yards before the passing zone starts. The error counter is meant only to capture the errors that one *accidentally* commits, not the "errors" that he intends to make.

When one tries to count errors when riding in a group, a very small error is likely to unleash a great debate about whether it really should be counted as an error: for example, a bit of a jerk during an upshift, or even barely touching an invisible centerline while exiting a right-hander. There's a very simple rule to determine errors, however. One must only answer the following question: If I were to ride through the same stretch under the same circumstances, would I do it exactly the same the next time? If one's response is that he would leave out the small irregularity, then it is an error. Every questionable case is easily determined using this method, and after a short time, one finds that whenever he has to consider whether some small irregularity really was an error or not, he might as well go ahead and push the button because it was most certainly an error as we have defined it. Here's another example: one is wearing heavy and somewhat stiff winter gloves and, after hitting the turn-signal button, accidentally catches the button for the horn, which briefly sounds. This is a tiny mistake (the rider wasn't truly "at fault") and it has no consequences, but it is still an error! Why? Because it's clear that the next time he signals, he'll take a little more care when moving among the controls so that he doesn't hit the horn again.

At the beginning, the recording of errors doesn't always work out so well. One certainly sets out to consciously record each error but soon forgets. It's true: there are more important things to do, but then, at some point, a more serious error occurs, which reminds the rider of the error-counting plan, and it works again for a little while.

The noting of an error by means of a push of a button on the error counter is experienced by most riders as an *unburdening*. It's almost as if the error, which one has admitted to oneself, is thereby to some extent "forgiven" and forgotten. This is extremely important, since one should not dwell on an error that one has just made during a continuing sequence of actions, and should never get angry at oneself about it, because that would have a negative effect on the next procedure! Every sophisticated orator, every pianist, every actor knows this. Because of the unburdening function that it has, the error counter takes on much more friendly characteristics in terms of the **mental** state of the rider, who is surprised that he so frequently forgot to use it at first. The error counter is forgotten less and less frequently because, of course, the counter is always there and will require some attention as soon as the next error occurs that's obvious enough to be consciously recognized.

The reader should now understand that, at first, after a short period of using the counter, the registered errors become *more common*. Years ago, in the first experiments with the error counter, this finding was surprising. One of the best skiers in the world almost began to doubt her abilities because of this. It is important to emphasize that the number of errors does not increase because the rider is suddenly riding worse, but rather because he has become much more aware and critical of his own riding. One can also say that the reason is that the conscious self has improved in its role of reminder and teacher, which means that it notices even small errors and irregularities—more precisely, because the smaller errors are no longer being suppressed. Finally, the rider practically starts to hunt for his own mistakes and is pleased when even the tiniest errors cannot escape his notice.

The error rate

What is the real usefulness of the error counter? Actually, its usefulness is multifaceted; otherwise, all this discussion about a simple device would be unnecessary. The first thing one thinks about is, of course, the *counting* of the errors. If not this, then what else could the device be good for? Use of an error counter isn't primarily about the counting but rather about the creation of a more purposeful *measurement*: determining the number of errors within a given stretch of road or a given period of riding time—determining the *error rate,* that is, the number of errors made every 50 miles or every hour.

In coming up with error rates, one finds enormous differences not only among riders but also within individual riders, in whom daily swings in performance level are unexpectedly large. There are days on which the errors trickle in, and others on which they practically pour in. Thus, the error counter, even when one doesn't always evaluate the numbers with precision, is a useful instrument that provides information about how one is doing on a particular day. It's even useful on long, possibly strenuous trips. If the distance was too great or if there weren't enough breaks from riding (these often go hand in hand), at some point in the afternoon the error rate either climbs or falls to zero because the rider just doesn't have any more synapses available for the error counter.

Either way, it's a reliable sign that it really is time for a break or that the training should stop for the day. Usually it is completely ineffective if one then strictly commands himself to pay attention or wake up, and the farther the fatigue or even exhaustion progresses, the less effective any attempts at "pulling together" become.

Errors counted and accidents

To be very clear: the number of errors and the error rate are closely related to accidents and the risk for accidents. Every error is potentially the seed of an accident. Whether an accident actually develops from this seed is largely dependent on circumstantial factors upon which the rider has no influence.

There is one other aspect that is useful about the counting of errors. There are some riders who are convinced that they ride without errors or almost without errors. But when an error counter is put to use, it becomes obvious that the rider who commits no errors simply does not exist. That is a very substantial insight, because it actually contributes to our safety! An excellent rider stands out because, thanks to his well-developed ability for self-perception,he knows that even he is always making mistakes. And probably he has become such a good rider only because he has noticed his errors and because, the better a rider he became, the more perceptive he became for even the tiniest errors.

What follows from this is that, as useful as the counting of errors can be, the actual recording of errors (by pressing the button) is more important. By means of this technique, the rider is forced to increase his sensitivity to his errors, and this keeps his critical observation skills finely tuned. In this sense, it really doesn't matter whether the final error count is ever read. For this reason, the whole thing still works pretty well if, in the absence of an error counter, one only "symbolically" presses on the head of a screw or something similar within easy reach of the left handgrip. Consistency is crucial, however!

MENTAL TRAINING

What is it?

Among the duties that the conscious self has to manage is **mental training,** one of the most important aids in approaching perfection: influencing a specific future action or a general way of behaving by means of conscious implementation of certain ideas or images, conceived by and stemming from the conscious self. Unfortunately,

A caveat

It must be acknowledged that thinking about an upcoming task or competition now and then is certainly a first step in the right direction toward preparing for it mentally. The worst thing that can happen is to not think about it at all—or more precisely, to prohibit any thoughts about it ("Oh God, I don't even want to think about it! I'm already getting heart palpitations and sweaty palms!"). Thinking about it is a first attempt at processing the idea.

Certain techniques in psychotherapy, namely confrontational techniques, take up this processing principle and involve an encounter with the situation. In therapy, the encounter is usually only an imaginary encounter (see p. 122). However, "imaginary" does not mean that such encounters are going to turn out to be less intense and thereby less striking than an actual encounter would be. The opposite can be true: using different imagination techniques, situations that are considerably more intense (even nightmarish) than the real situation can be created. Thus, for example, a person who is always paralyzed by stage fright would repeatedly be mentally confronted with an exaggerated version of a situation that triggers his stage fright in order to desensitize him to its effects.

Precisely because of the use of exaggerated trigger situations, this method soon found its way from the realm of psychotherapy into sports psychology, especially as it was applied in the intense sports competitions that took place in the former Eastern bloc countries. In sports, these techniques can be used for relief when the pressure to perform is too high; or for desensitization to the effects of overpowering triggers of fear that perhaps arise and take over regularly in the night before a competition; or to moderate an abnormally high level of excitement that sets in before the start of a competition and threatens performance; or finally to dismantle an overly fearful disposition (see also p. 134). ■

"Mental" in the context of motorcycle training

The word **"mental"** is used in remarkably inconsistent ways, and this leads to a certain degree of imprecision. In psychology, in which the term has its origin, the word is used in many ways ("mental disorder," "mental experiment," "mental health," "mental hospital," "mental hygiene," "mental set," "mental test," "mental work," etc.)

To understand "mental" only in the sense of intellectual or thought-based would be too one-sided—that is, it would be too rational. According to modern understanding, "pertinent to thinking" is too narrow for a description of mental processes and does not signify enough of what is actually happening (or should be happening) during mental training, which is the incorporation of the entire person. It's true that the process has its basis in very conscious and intentional conception by the conscious self, but it has the goal of an enduring influence on the subconscious self (perhaps in the emotional-affective region) and also on the **procedural memory** (p. 78), where **automated processes** are stored.

"Mental training takes place in the mind, but the entire body thinks along with it." This saying, or at least the thought it expresses, is much loved by trainers. In the pragmatically broad formulation "takes place in the mind" lies a crucial hint about what exactly mental training is: training that isn't actually real but occurs in the head, in thoughts, as a conception—that is, *mentally.* The psychic entities that are affected by this training don't even have to be determined, and they are widely diverse, given all the individual types of training that are included in the collective term "mental training." In any case, the effects on the entities that are responsible for thinking are only minimal.

In the context of motorcycling, the most interesting form of mental training is the learning and the refinement of particular **action programs.** Under the broad super-ordinate concept "mental training," this kind of training can advantageously be further specified as *ideomotor training* (see "Thoughts are forces," p. 70).

these days all manner of things are hawked as mental training, so it's important to define more precisely what we actually mean by "mental training."

Someone who, at times, thinks about an upcoming task or competition and considers how everything might work out is still a long way from mental training. This person is no more performing mental training than a person having a pleasant doze could be said to be meditating.

Mental training is much older than its name. When a student silently recites a poem in order to see whether he's really got it down or to improve uncertain passages, or when an actor does the same as he memorizes his role (when he silently speaks his lines, while also intensively and concretely imagining his steps and movements on the stage), then both are engaging in "mental training," with all of its associated characteristics. The systematic development of mental training techniques didn't really take hold until after World War II, when their use with elite athletes and in preparation for space flight became common. These are two realms that have at least one thing in common—namely, at the time they were seen as important national pursuits, especially in light of the

Cold War. As such, they were both objects of research and, in some instances, heavy involvement by the state and even some degree of secrecy of the sort that is otherwise seen only in military technologies.

The mental training that is relevant in the context of this book was only a part of the development of mental training techniques. A whole complex of concepts called "Psychotraining" and "Supertraining" was developed (Porter and Foster 1987, Syer and Connolly 1987, Eberspächer 1990). The goal was not only to train a person physically for his activity but also to put him **mentally** into the best possible condition for that activity.

Basic goals of mental training

The training methods of psychotraining and supertraining go far beyond the basic *motor* completion of the necessary actions and beyond *becoming familiar with a particular situation.* There's more to it:

- *Mental stabilization, so that the trainee gains the psychological ability to handle everything associated with his task.* For an athlete, this would include the competition with its particular burdens, such as the pressure to perform and succeed, noise, spotlights, television cameras, influences of spectators, provocations from competitors, etc.

- *Developing a high level of certainty about the course of events and certainty about the trainee's concentration*—that is, attaining a level of certainty that the trainee or athlete will not be easily distracted and can rely on his own ability to concentrate.

- *Developing an effective means of self-support, to break down any self-doubt and build up self-confidence* (positive and stable self-esteem).

- *Developing the right motivation and the right attitude* (which are absolutely not the same).

- *Achieving the appropriate degree of relaxation* (not just before a coming competition or mission but more generally, because all of these training approaches only result in success when the trainee remains in a condition of comfortable, tension-free relaxation).

The training measures required of the trainer are entirely dependent on the psychic condition of the trainee. It's not just about strengthening or increasing insufficient self-confidence, or about re-establishing lost self-confidence, or about stabilizing a wavering self-confidence. It can also be about curbing excessive self-esteem, which can easily lead to a dangerous overestimation of one's own capabilities (compare also the realistic self-assessment described by Eberspächer, p. 112).

Excessive self-esteem is less likely to occur among top athletes than among less accomplished athletes. It usually rears "its ugly head" at a time when the acquisition of a particular capability occurred a relatively short time in the past, regardless of one's level of general competency. Studies of the relationship between self-assessment and achieved performance level in different phases of military flight training showed this, and the results can be transferred directly to motorcycle riding. It is basically irrelevant whether we consider instruction for beginners, later skill-improvement courses, or even the systematic development of a young racer.

Thus, it's a matter of *subjective perception*—self-assessment and self-confidence, closely connected to feelings of security—and of *objective reality,* accurately reflecting the achieved level of training and education and the level of security. One might imagine it as two side-by-side columns in a diagram. Immediately before the start of training or education, the subjective column is larger than the objective column; otherwise the candidate probably wouldn't start the training at all. At this point, there's a healthy portion of self-confidence along with more meager helpings of knowledge and capabilities.

At the beginning of training, then, support is quickly available to ward off the first signs of downward pressure on the subjective column (self-assessment, self-confidence, and a feeling of security), while the ability to perform is already beginning to grow. Already at this point, the teacher, instructor, or trainer, whether in a beginners' class, an advanced course, or in race training, must attend to the relationship between the two columns. It might be satisfying if, suddenly, more realistic relationships take over in a rider who initially was cocky or loud-mouthed, but to allow good progress, it's not bad if the subjective column lags somewhat behind. As long as the trainee doesn't get out of control, it can even be good if the subjective column gets taller from time to time. Occasional damping by the instructor, and especially by the myriad difficult situations in which the learner will find himself and which he will have to recognize as such, will ensure that the subjective column doesn't reach "into the sky" and doesn't get dangerously taller than the objective column (the rider's actual performance level).

In the case of new rider training, gradual recovery of self-confidence and self-esteem as a rider should be the stage of development that the rider has reached when the course has ended. The level of performance, the objective column, is still a long way from those tip-top heights at which further climbing is only slow, minimal, and difficult. At the point, as long as one puts in just a bit of effort, this column can still grow taller relatively quickly. However, if there is a break in the training (for example, a vacation or the end of rider training without an immediate opportunity to apply the new knowledge and skills), the objective column gradually sinks again. Conversely, the subjective column will "blast skyward," now undeterred by reality, and possibly further spurred on by others' stories of experiences that get better in the telling. However, when training resumes, this unbalanced relationship is a considerable danger, as has been thoroughly demonstrated in studies of military aviation. The performance level can be increased again but usually not before a few scary moments that bring self assessment and self-confidence more or less back into alignment with reality.

"Over-relaxation": a case in point

It is known that, in the extremely successful support and management of top athletes in the former East Germany, the greatest problems cropped up with the introduction of relaxation training, especially for self-relaxation.

Because the relaxation instructors, all of whom were renowned sports psychologists, had perfect mastery of the technique, the degree of relaxation among the athletes was very deep. The result was that the athletes, because they felt extremely good and at ease, lost part of their motivation, their drive. One could also say that they had something of a pleasant afterglow and did not do as well in competition. ∎

Things go rather differently, however, when the training is immediately followed (under one's own management) by continued practice. This is the rule among motorcyclists. Alois Weidele, who made a name for himself in research as a suspension specialist, was apparently also not bad at pithy pronouncements. He hit the nail on the head with the following statement: "The license is permission to continue to practice without supervision."

The performance level of the newly licensed rider, although it can certainly still improve, is really not so bad. But the new licensee, when first riding unaccompanied, usually rides very conservatively at first. The subjective

Relaxation "chains"

These days, in a top-tier sport, the athlete no longer gives himself individual relaxation or loosening commands (which have previously been practiced) during the execution of the actions. Instead, there is currently a tendency for the athlete to call up entire "chains" for relaxation, which have been firmly connected together in previous training. "Calling up" these chains happens by means of a single command, such as drop the shoulders, which can occasionally be seen among ski jumpers immediately before the jump. At the same moment, the other links in the established chain that has been practiced, such as loosening the abdominal wall and dropping the chin, are activated, as is confident calmness that has also been practiced along with the other components of the technique. This chain also includes maintaining the original degree of attention that existed *before* the chain was called up. ∎

column is usually suppressed at first, and since the rider starts out with corresponding timidity, errors in operation and inappropriate reactions to situations he encounters are likely to have less serious consequences and to occur less often. Klebelsberg (1982, p. 181) in particular has studied this extensively. As more accurate self-assessment and self-confidence grow, the subjective column will certainly grow taller, and it will grow much faster than the objective column, which can't possibly keep up. Setbacks in self-confidence become rarer, not because true perfection has already been achieved but because the rider learns to compensate for the particular deficits that he still has. Thus, Klebelsberg correctly sees the actual danger in the fact that the new rider soon *no longer feels like a beginner,* although there has not yet been much improvement on the objective side.

Motivation and attitude

We talk about the "right" motivation because—and this is especially true in motorsports—there are also states of "over-motivation," which the responsible trainer, coach, or psychologist must recognize. A similar situation is true with respect to attitude. There isn't simply one right and one wrong attitude, but often there is clearly a strategic momentum that plays into it.

Just as there's such a thing as "overmotivation," there's also such a thing as "over-relaxation," which is why there was discussion earlier about the goals of some types of training that involve the determination of the *proper* level of relaxation.

The danger of over-relaxation exists in principle for motorcycle training, although it must be conceded that this extreme degree of relaxation is hardly likely to be achieved under the usual conditions: carried out in a large group, sitting on the motorcycle, often being led by a professional motorcycle instructor. Still, instructors always have to be prepared for participants who respond especially well to such prompting toward looseness and relaxation. Every release of tension, such as relaxing the abdominal wall or letting the shoulders drop, or lightly opening the mouth and letting the lower lip hang loosely, leads to an amplification in the focus of attention. It is helpful to use the analogy of a headlight beam that is adjusted to be wider, so the illuminated area becomes larger, but consequently, the concentration of the light (that is, the focus of attention) is reduced. At moderate levels of relaxation, the effect is only small and often actually desirable, because initially there's a tendency to ride with too tightly focused attention anyway. However, in states of deep relaxation, the amplification is very pronounced (this can be seen in electroencephalograms [EEGs]), and there is hardly any focusing of attention.

Of course, no human has ever ridden a motorcycle in such an extreme state of relaxation. Also, with the relaxation exercises commonly practiced sitting on the motorcycle before riding, people do not even get close to such a state, but even a much lesser degree of relaxation *during the ride* can be too much if a rider is *already* well-practiced and "gifted" in relaxation. Such a rider might, in his carefree disengagement, suddenly start to look away from road, which is relatively harmless if he notices it right away thanks to sufficient capability to be critical.

Vagotonal economy and the parasympathetic system

The more relaxed a person is during mental training, the more he attains the so-called **vagotonal economy.** That is a condition that is characterized by a change in mood or attitude of the entire organism and that is most pronounced during sleep. It is a time when the sympathetic nervous system, which is largely in control during waking, steps back and lets its counterpart, the parasympathetic system, take more control. It is no longer the *sympathetic nerve*, but instead the *vagus nerve* that is now responsible, hence the description "vagotonal economy." This leads to a significant general loosening (not just muscularly), leading to a decrease in control by the more reasoning and rational parts of the brain, thus allowing deep relaxation.

The deeper the relaxation, the more of an increase in **integration** a person will experience. This can be proved in all kinds of objective tests and experiments, but self-observation is much more convincing: everyone who has done some kind of training by himself and finds himself in a deeply relaxed state will also feel more like a unified system than usual. It's not only that the most varied aspects contained within the subconscious self can arise much more easily, but also the opposite: contents of the conscious self (for example, particular behavioral goals or attitudes), even if they initially have only to do with rational insights, will more easily sink into the subconscious self because the *permeability* increases and the inner psychic walls become less solid.

Obviously, this is not how one should explain everything to the elite athlete, or at least this should not be the only explanation. He should not only come to an under-

standing of relaxation and its consequences but should also try to truly live in accordance with these concepts. Thus, the explanation of how to reach a deepened understanding should more closely resemble that which follows (it's best if it's delivered during a deep relaxation exercise):

If you are completely relaxed, then you are completely open. You are also open on the inside. No longer encapsulated and closed off from the outside and compartmentalized on the inside. You are like a big, complicated building with many levels and long hallways, with elevators and stairways. The more relaxed you are, the more widely all these inner doors and passages will open.

When you came into the world, you moved into this building. At the beginning, you lived and spent all your time at the bottom, in the basement and then on the ground floor. It took a long time before you moved and spread beyond these lower levels of the subconscious self and gradually, in several phases of increasing consciousness, finally arrived at the very top, the "executive suite," of this large and complicated building. The executive suite is the office of reason and understanding; all the upper levels are those of consciousness, in which the "I" resides. It sees most everything but is still not omnipotent with respect to the entire system below, and this is something you forget all too easily.

However, if, through relaxation, all the doors are opened, then you will suddenly feel that there's a lot more there. In silence, it can still be heard and felt even more. It may not be entirely clear, but it is certainly there, belongs to the whole system, and belongs to you. And now it's much easier for various impressions and mysterious dream images, symbols, or feelings to climb up from deep below into the ever more lucid levels of consciousness. Earlier, when everything was closed off, and you were wakeful and full of tension, all of these thoughts and feelings were locked and blocked out. The opposite is also true: your plans no longer remain as "lonely executive decisions" handed down by the conscious self up above, and more or less non-binding for the lower levels. They will not be decisions that, over the long term, no one heeds. Instead, they will gradually sink in more and more deeply, from floor to floor, until the entire self sees and acts according to the same image and is oriented toward the same goal. Thus, a resolution to do something in a certain way becomes binding for all aspects of the person, not because these aspects fall in line and obey the executive decision, but because they have made these resolutions their own. In this way, attitudes become internalized and motives become binding, and cooperation and harmony in the entire self is achieved. This is ultimately how even activities— ever more strongly and ever more deeply rooted— are controlled by automatic programs that, although they are acquired programs, can run their course without much involvement by the conscious self. (V. Bregaglia)

Mental simulation: "dry run" training

It's possible even in aerobatics training to conduct "dry run" training. The aspiring pilot sits in a chair with his legs moderately bent, his feet on the rudder pedals that aren't actually there, with part of a broomstick between his legs that he holds in his right hand as a control column, and his left hand on his knee, ready to operate the gas (power lever), which, if it were there, would be to the left of his knee. If he has no aerobatics experience, he can at least practice certain movement processes. Since the movements required for some maneuvers will sharply contradict his previous experiences, mainly because certain rudder combinations otherwise never occur, this kind of prior practice makes subsequent training in the plane easier to a certain extent, but nothing more.

This example makes clear why Eberspächer (1990) stipulates that sufficient actual experience must be present for mental training to be successful. Without this actual experience, if and when the aspiring pilot moved on to the first attempts in actual practice, he would not only be surprised and highly distracted at first by the pressure at the rudders, but also and especially by the different acceleration forces (which are substantial) and by the optic and acoustic pressures. In short, "dry run" training can bring about worthwhile progress only after sufficient practical orientation. At this point, the achievements from "dry run" training can be considerable. ■

It should now be clear that mental training is not simply thinking through a course of action (or a whole chain of actions and events, more precisely), even when done together with a trainer. This thinking, alone, is not a worthless activity, but in a state of systematically created relaxation, the training effect is incomparably greater. *Systematic* relaxation refers to the strict application of appropriate relaxation techniques such as self-training, particular breathing exercises and meditation techniques, yoga, progressive muscular relaxation, special imagination techniques, etc. A very good overview of the variety of relaxation methods can be found in Vaitl and Petermann (1993).

Let's take a closer look at what actually happens in mental training. Many things will become clearer, including why *proper* relaxation is crucial.

It's an amazing phenomenon that we are even in a position to take an impending action, and even the whole event in which our action is going to take place, and view it concretely like a film "on an internal screen;" we can, like a director, jump in and change the course of events; and we can then repeat the whole thing in the same way or under new circumstances. Here, we are reminded of the special capabilities of the cerebrum, with which we can literally reach into the future (see p. 52).

In the same way in which man, with the help of his cerebrum, can take equipment that doesn't even exist yet and "try it out in his head," he is also able, without actually doing anything, to allow **action programs** to run "in his head." This works even with action programs that he hasn't yet tried out in reality. The "preview" will make it easier for him to manage the situation in reality when this subsequently occurs.

A disinterested spectator or an actively involved participant

Mental training is a pure and deliberate act of the conscious self that has its effects on the subconscious self. It's the subconscious self that will be controlling all the actions when the activity is carried out in reality. Only the subconscious self can take the program for this particular course of action, along with all the sub-programs and alternative helping programs, and run them with each other at the expected level of **automation.** For this reason, simply "playing through the action film," as a conscious act, doesn't actually achieve that much—it is really only a non-binding and uninvolved spectating by the conscious self. At some point, the entire self, and thus also the body, has to be present and involved. The individual **muscle innervations** that are demanded by the program will literally *touch* the body, even if the program itself does not carry out the individual movements, at least not visibly (see "Thoughts are forces," p. 70).

In order to fulfill the requirement of involving the whole self, including the body, a state of deep relaxation must be attained. The relaxation should get as close as possible to the state of **vagotonal economy,** as mentioned above. This is what a person experiences when he is about to fall asleep or is completely lost in a daydream. Only then is the necessary degree of permeability achieved for conscious thoughts and processes to sink deeply into the subconscious.

SPECIFIC ACTS OF MENTAL TRAINING

Track visualization

The most well-known application of mental training in motorsports is track visualization. This is something one cannot afford to neglect on long and challenging tracks such as the Nordschleife of the Nürburgring, the TT, or, in earlier days, the Targa Florio. It's not just that the rider memorizes the track and recites its corners. It goes beyond that: he reviews the entire route as if he were playing back a film on an imagined, internal screen. Among the true experts, this even happens at the same time as the actual event—it really does! The lap times in the visualized "race" are nearly in agreement with the actual lap times (there are only a few seconds of variation).

Interface displacement

It doesn't always have to be such concrete courses of events as track visualization. It can also be a matter of general "operational conditions" that one first has to mentally work himself into and fully adopt and adjust to. This is an excellent way to mentally support the all-important "slipping into" the motorcycle, as discussed so frequently in Part 3 (p. 84): the *displacement of the experienced interface* to a point deep within the motorcycle (p. 88) so that the rider goes from being a strapped-on piece of cargo to an *integrated component* (p. 102) of the bike. With mental training and relaxation, this can happen in preparation for the ride, before the key is even turned.

In contrast to the usual relaxation exercises that are often performed in rider training classes (the main goal of which is to loosen tight and tensed muscles and which are often done with the bike on a stand), the rider who is mentally preparing to slip into the motorcycle, with the help of relaxation, sits on his *unsupported* bike. This is best done with the guidance of a person knowledgeable about this kind of training (see also Vaitl and Petermann 1993). The head falls to the chest; shoulders and arms drop; the face loosens; the chin falls; the abdominal wall is released; everything sinks and becomes heavier and heavier. The rider should feel as though he is "pouring into" the motorcycle. The feet are resting on the ground, and are either pushed forward a bit or as far backward as possible. This latter position is most likely to occur if the rider allows his upper body to sink down onto the tank, which can be extremely beneficial. Each person must discover for himself the position that brings him the greatest possible relaxation.

Once complete relaxation has been achieved, then one tries to "think himself into" the **contact patches**; although this really involves more feeling than thinking. One will not succeed right away. First, one concentrates on the front wheel and makes a slight change in the lean angle, back and forth, to the left and right, thus rolling the motorcycle around the tires crossways. It is helpful if one has some idea of what the contact patches actually look like, how they move when the tires are rolled from side to side, and how they change shape under braking and acceleration (Figures 72 and 73).

If, by coincidence, there is some sand or gravel under the tires and one feels the crunching more than he hears it, he's pretty much home free. All of a sudden, he feels all the way into the tires, all the way to the road, and experiences first hand exactly what *interface displacement* is all about. A personal anecdote comes to mind: Under a southern night sky in Le Castellet, we tried first using, under our tires, crushed sugar cubes and then croutons from the kitchen of Jean Phillipp's motorhome. Suddenly no one said a word. It became very quiet, and for several minutes, one could only hear a quiet crackling and crunching and feel the texture under the tires. Complete disbelief—it was like magic!

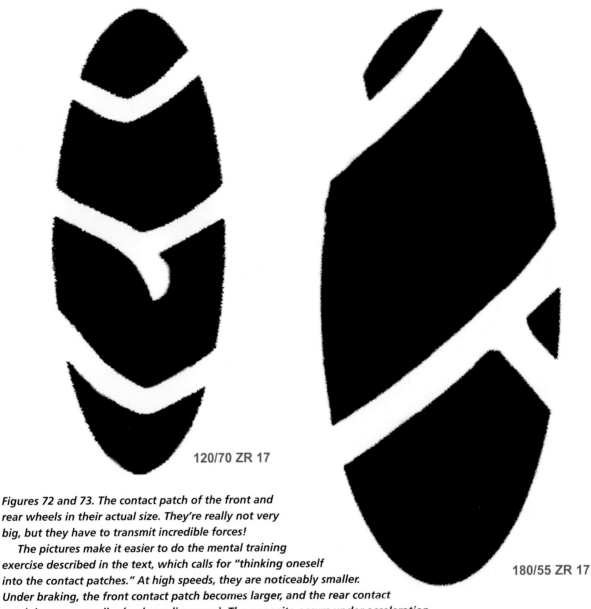

120/70 ZR 17

180/55 ZR 17

Figures 72 and 73. The contact patch of the front and rear wheels in their actual size. They're really not very big, but they have to transmit incredible forces!

The pictures make it easier to do the mental training exercise described in the text, which calls for "thinking oneself into the contact patches." At high speeds, they are noticeably smaller. Under braking, the front contact patch becomes larger, and the rear contact patch becomes smaller (and can disappear). The opposite occurs under acceleration. Beyond that, the change in shape under braking and acceleration, and also when cornering, occurs in a pear-like fashion. Particularly under high lateral acceleration, this leads to a change in the shape of the print. (Metzeler's Sportec M-1)

Mental preparation of complete action programs

As impressive as mentally achieved track visualization and interface displacement can be, there's even more to the concept of mental training. It's not just about activities or processes that we know we will have to carry out (as is so evident with track visualization). It can also be about preparing complete **action programs** to have ready for rare special situations that may or may not occur. These are mainly the kinds of situations in which, when they do arise, there's absolutely no more time available for any kind of consideration, however brief, of what to do.

Actions about which lightning-fast decisions have to be made and that have to be carried out with lightning speed can be safely managed only if they have been practiced. However, in many instances, to actually practice the actions would be far too dangerous. For such situations, one can definitely benefit from mental preparation for the real emergency. Here are some practical examples that should be of interest to all readers. In general, the individual reader must recognize his own personal deficits so he can address them with the help of mentally trained action programs, but the action tips listed, starting on page 144, might be useful in the search for areas in need of improvement.

The topic of the *escape* route is an apt example of the practical application of mental training. If a rider suddenly is left with a choice between a hard collision and riding down a steep embankment (this would be the escape route), it's clear, at least from a purely logical and rational viewpoint, that he has to make a decision. There are *alternatives* and there is *uncertainty*—that is, there is no obvious preferred action. To resolve this situation, a few things need to happen. Assuming that all present alternatives have been recognized (and this is certainly not necessarily the case), then the consequences of each alternative have to be considered, and the probabilities of their occurrence have to be evaluated and weighed against each other. But there isn't the remotest chance that any of this will happen because of the lack of time. This is why the notion that this kind of situation isn't a "true" decision situation can't be rejected out of hand. Although the baseline conditions (existing alternatives and prevailing uncertainty) are clearly those of a situation requiring a decision, the act of deciding, according to the objection, still has to be a part of a true decision. But nothing was decided; nothing *could* be decided. The controversy is tiresome in the sense that it ends in a question of definitions, namely, what is understood under the term "decision": the visible act or the inner psychological process.

With his formulation "Chess with no time to think," (title of a 1958 book about motorsports), Richard von Frankenberg distilled the problem down to a nutshell. It is truly a matter of *spontaneous actions,* without any rational involvement to speak of and thus also without any real consideration. It's not even certain that the rider has a full understanding of the situation and has really registered all possible alternatives. It's possible that he will be aware of only a single option as "THE escape."

In any case, the assumption is that when the danger presents itself, the escape route is *immediately* evident and available. It can't be something that has to be sought out; it has to simply be there. In addition, this works only if one has more or less trained, or *conditioned* (as the experts would say), himself to recognize escape routes.

Sensitization

When certain objects repeatedly *catch one's eye* spontaneously (that is, they sift themselves out of the incredible multitude of stimuli that constantly have to be processed), this is a clear indication that a *sensitization* has been developed for that kind of object. Particular objects of perception have acquired the *characteristics of a challenge:* they suddenly touch the *interests and concerns* of the affected person.

An example is the fastest way to explain what sensitization is on the basis of altered interests and concerns. The head of a large American advertising agency once told me, although he was well aware of what was actually going on: "It's just strange how all the magazines are suddenly full of ads for baby food, baby blankets, baby care, and baby toys now that my wife is pregnant."

Here, because of an external situation, the alteration of interests and the establishment of a new sensitization were initiated. In the case of escape routes, the same thing happened by means of an actively induced systematic change in *conditioning,* with the help of a training prompt that had been followed for a sufficiently long period of time.

It can also be a dire emergency or fear of an enemy that creates enduring sensitization: while driving, for example, former fighter pilots, even decades after battle, still immediately spot even the smallest flying objects in the sky even if it is tiny, close to the horizon, and deep in the periphery of their field of vision. For others unaware of the situation, this is an incomprehensible ability, especially if it happens repeatedly, but for former pilots, it is easy because it was once a necessity for survival that has remained intact.

Similar perceptive abilities can also be found in more harmless aspects of life, such as with children who specialize in finding four-leaf clovers, or, for example, with hunters who clearly see a deer, while their companion, who is not visually impaired, in spite of all the whispered hints about where the deer is, can't see the deer at all. ■

Watching for possible escape routes

The formula for this is simple, but it requires persistence: one simply makes it his practice to always be looking for the best (or least disadvantageous) escape route in all possible everyday traffic situations. Especially when riding along "with nothing to do" in places with low speed limits and long no-passing zones, when creeping along in heavy traffic, and whenever it gets boring, it's really not such a bad habit! And it's absolutely correct to see a mild form of mental training in this practice.

One constantly asks himself: What would I do if the car ahead suddenly stopped? If he slid out and ended up sideways? Where would I go if the oncoming delivery truck suddenly turned left in front of me into a driveway? If I came upon a tree down in the road? If the oncoming truck loses his load in the corner? There are many uncomfortable situations in which an escape route would be useful.

One will notice how quickly he becomes adept at spotting possible escapes. Sometimes, one will even notice an escape route even when he hadn't been looking for one. That's a good sign.

To become adept at spotting possible escape routes, one has to stick with it: this is difficult only until the constant search for escape routes has become a habit, and then, it almost happens by itself. Initially, to get used to the idea, the error counter described on page 119 can be useful: one can record each escape route and be pleased to read a sizeable number on the counter at the end of a ride (or be unhappy to find that he forgot about it completely after only a few times).

It's true, however, that there are places in which, despite the best of intentions, there simply is no escape. And it's precisely in these places that this mental training becomes most important. It's a matter of sharpening one's eye to find the least of all evils in a bad situation so that one can recognize it immediately in an emergency: "Better there through the fence than into the wall," "Better there into the bushes than into the side of the car ahead," "Better into the thickest forest than head-on into oncoming traffic." One learns to "play the best card" when "dealt a bad hand" instead of being paralyzed by fear and doing nothing at all.

The escape route doesn't always have to take you off the road. Like the choice between the fence and the wall beside the road, there is sometimes a choice between obstacles on the road that present different levels of danger. The "hard" obstacles aren't nearly as dangerous as those with substantial bulk, even if they appear, externally, to be "soft." A stack of straw bales, maybe a yard high, which can occasionally be seen at the edges of the road during harvest times, may be "soft," but it is more dangerous than a "hard," but very light bicycle trailer or an empty crate. One learns these differences by means of constant mental occupation with escape routes, and it is one of the objectives of mental escape-route training. Even more important is that the location of obstacles often leave various holes open, at least for a motorcycle.

Yes, the sentence sounds trivial—everyone knows that! Well, they may well *know* this, but we've already seen instances of how far apart knowledge and action can be. It's no different here.

Figure 74 is a cross-section of a highway with two lanes in each direction, the so-called *regulation cross-section 29* of the Autobahn. Beside each 3.75-meter lane, there is another 0.5-meter strip of pavement to the left, then the grassy median where the railing stands. To the right, there's a 2.0-meter shoulder, then a 1.5-meter drainage strip that may be grassy but is often partially paved.

Finding the gaps!

Figure 75 shows a car in the right lane, but the size of the car in the picture is only the size we imagine it to be. This is not entirely unimportant, because our perception of things strongly affects our behavior. The tiny little cars in Figure 76 shows them in their actual size. As enormously large as the remaining gaps are—and this is what the tail end of a back-up that might be hiding just around a corner or over a rise would look like—it never fails that one car after the next, hard on the brakes, crashes squarely into the car ahead. The police could tell many a tale about this. The involved drivers always say the same thing: "I was driving along—pretty fast, I admit—and all of a sudden there was *nowhere to go!* Both lanes were *blocked!*"

So let's take a look at just what is meant by "nowhere to go" and "blocked." A whole 30% of the paved road was occupied; 70% of the road—*seventy percent!*—was still open! And if we add the grassy strips, then three-quarters of the road were available. The edges are, of course, only to be used in an emergency, and the surface might even be soft, but they're still far better than a certain, solid collision.

Thus, this kind of driving behavior is very peculiar, but there is an explanation for it. Starting with our very first driving experiences, we have been accustomed, when following another vehicle, to more or less follow that vehicle's path. We've practically been "trained" to do this. Only if we want to move a bit faster and decide to pass do we break out of that path; otherwise we follow behind. If the driver ahead brakes, so do we; if he brakes hard, we brake harder, staring fixedly at his bumper; and if he brakes still harder, such that we can't slow down fast enough, we brake as hard as we can but continue to stay exactly in the same path, as if we were aiming for the car ahead. The greater the fear, the less likely we are to swerve.

Let's continue the series of pictures. Figure 77 shows how many cars could fit side by side, still leaving an escape to the right and left! In Figure 78, which depicts a pretty major accident and, about which, one could say "everything was blocked," there are still escape routes, provided the driver is not seized with terror.

It's not even necessary for there to be a traffic jam in the first place to unleash such a fateful course of events, which reminds one of lemmings that jump to their death one after the other. In the case of a traffic jam, the repetition of the process is even more spectacular; all it takes is a single car being followed by a second car—or motorcycle—with not quite enough following distance (see "When two people do the same thing," p. 20). If the car in front brakes hard enough to make the braking distance for the second vehicle too small, *it's highly likely that it will crash into the car in front*, even if there is room to go around on either side. The more frightened the driver, the more likely it is that he'll crash into the car ahead. Braking comes first; the thought of swerving comes second, if at all. As stated above, we have simply been "trained" to drive nicely in lines behind each other.

Mentally preparing to evade an accident

The search for escape routes goes further. There's the question, *"Where and how can I get off the road?"* One should always have an answer to this. However, when following other traffic, one also should always be considering this question: "Which side am I going to go around on if it suddenly comes down to it?"

While "training" this avoidance plan, one should tell himself every few seconds: *right – right – right – right – okay, now left – left – back to the right – right – right – still to the right – back to the left – left, etc.* Corresponding to the direction one has decided upon at any given moment, he would then also move in that direction by just a tire's width, especially when riding in a group of motorcycles. This, too, is a mild form of mental training. It's not about—or it's not *merely* about—preparing a *current* escape route, but it's at least as important in the constant familiarization with the idea of riding around and past something. Just as described above in the discussion of actual escape routes, it's important for increasing one's general *readiness* and *willingness* to use an escape route. It doesn't matter whether one goes to the right or left, provided he doesn't crash right into a braking car in front of him.

Figure 74. Highway cross-section with two lanes in each direction (dimensions given in meters for a German Autobahn).

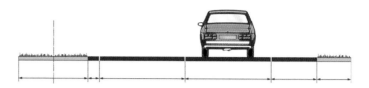

Figure 75. One car occupies the right lane, but it's actually only this big in our imagination.

Figure 76. Representation of the end of a traffic jam, with realistic size relationships. More than two-thirds of the road is still open!

Figure 77. Six cars of this size would be able to fit side by side—and still there are escape routes to the left and right!

Figure 78. Even in this kind of accident situation, there are plenty of escape routes for the motorcyclist.

There's no big difference between mentally training oneself to ask, *"Where is the escape route?"* or *"Where is my gap?"* The use of a gap in the road leads to an escape route, and conversely, when using an escape route beside the road, one certainly also looks for gaps and tries to avoid obstacles, especially if they are large and solid.

Figure-ground reversible images

Eberspächer correctly points out that encountering stalled traffic is a matter of a so-called "figure-ground problem." This plays an important role in the theory of perception and becomes clear in so-called "figure-ground reversible images": the picture of a figure on a background can *reverse* so that suddenly the background becomes the object (usually with a different "sense"), and the figure becomes the background. *Only the perception of whatever happens to be the figure at the time, and not the background, consciously registers in the mind of the perceiver.*

When there's a risk of a rear-ender, the obstacle (the braking or the already stopped vehicle ahead) is the figure and thus the consciously registered object, and it becomes ever more so the more the horrified follower stares at the back of the vehicle ahead. But the object that should register in one's mind is the gap, which would then be transformed from background to *figure*. Remember the old training admonition: "You'll go where you look!" Thus, when meeting oncoming traffic on a very narrow but just wide-enough street, one should not look at the oncoming vehicle, especially not at its threatening left side. Instead, one should look unerringly into the open gap. ■

Keeping action programs at the ready: escapes offroad

Remember, with the escape route and gap searching training discussed here, it's only about building up *the search skills* and increasing *preparedness;* it's not yet about taking action. When an escape route requires one to ride off the road, a solid automated course of action should be available, and mental training is particularly well-suited for the preparation of ready-made programs that can simply be called up when needed. This course of action is called "escape offroad" in some rider training courses. In terms of the search for escape routes, besides asking the questions *when* (that is, under what circum-

stances) and *where to* only, it's a question of *how:* the best way to carry out the escape.

The process is not complicated, but the individual stages follow each other very closely (much more quickly than can be described in words), and the rider is under considerable pressure, even when he's only practicing the ESCAPE OFF PAVEMENT. The individual parts of the chain of action are as follows:

1. With the gaze focused on a fixed object on the edge of the road, ride toward it with as little lean angle as possible. While doing this, use the remaining amount of roadway, with some traction for maximal deceleration—that is, brake hard with the clutch in. (Once the decision has been made to escape off the road, never change course in attempt to see if there isn't enough room after all. It's all too easy to get stuck in the middle and fail at both solutions.)

2. At the edge of the road, before the start of the loose surface beyond, release both brakes. This has to happen to leave enough time for the front suspension to recover from the hard braking before encountering bumps when leaving the road.

3. At the same time, stand on the pegs and grip the tank with the knees, moving your body weight toward the rear of the bike, and *keep the clutch in!*

4. Once off the road, carefully come to a final stop. The front brake should be applied with extreme caution—wet grass can be amazingly slick! If the front wheel locks, *immediately* release the front brake for a moment before cautiously reapplying it and continuing to brake. If there are obstacles in the path that cannot be surmounted or ridden around, emphatically overbrake with the rear brake, while lightly steering in one direction or the other, and slide it to a stop just before the obstacle.

"Brake hard;" "stand up and release the brakes, but keep the clutch in;" and "cautiously brake to a stop"—there's not much there to do wrong. Nonetheless, one would not believe how commonly it happens in training that when the rider stands up, he not only releases the brakes (which is correct) but also the clutch lever—it's the same action with the right and left hands— or how frequently the hard braking is skipped altogether, as if the decision to ride off the road meant that all problems were already solved. In fact, there's absolutely nothing more important than first scrubbing off as much speed as possible, provided it's possible to do so!

The only thing that can help is practice: we can do some "dry runs" with the help of mental training, at best on a motorcycle on its centerstand, activating and releasing all the various levers as needed, but still muscularly as relaxed as possible. Once the actions are somewhat mastered, it should be done a few more times with the eyes closed. If the same thing is then practiced with real actions, as in a rider training class, then the course of action is already much more stable and everything works much better than it does when riders try the whole action program right away, after only brief spoken instructions. The stabilization of the course of action is also urgently necessary because in the event of a threatening situation, it will be carried out as an *emergency* maneuver, and this means that there will be an enormous amount of additional pressure.

For safety reasons, the actual practice is not done at high speeds. Anyone who really braked as hard as he might in an actual emergency would probably have already come to a stop by the time he reached the edge of the road and this have learned nothing. For this reason, the braking in training courses is fairly minimal. However, in mental training, higher speeds should be attempted—that is, shorter processes with rapid succession of the individual stages should be practiced (and with harder bumps after leaving the road).

Mentally preparing to increase the lean angle

Sometimes an offroad escape is initiated too early, before all other means of escape are far from exhausted. One of the most important means of escape when the emergency situation involves cornering is to fully engage all lean-angle reserves (see "He who rides in fear of the lean is living dangerously!", p. 114). For example, if a corner unexpectedly tightens, or one has misjudged it and has entered too fast and thus braking in the corner (which could use some practice) isn't enough, one should just lean the motorcycle farther—that is, increase the lean angle rather than trying to un-tighten the curve while riding without control. An exceedingly inviting ideal escape route would have to present itself if we weren't better off to first fully exhaust everything that was possible on the road. Therein lies the rationale for the mantra, *"Lean, lean, lean!"* It's a useful incantation for all those who cannot really ride at their maximum lean angle without difficulty, and we'll encounter it again when we discuss goal-setting (p. 157). However, in an emergency, increasing the lean will work only if the goal has truly been *in-*

ternalized (automated). Perhaps it will be available spontaneously, without the slightest thought, thanks to mental training, and might actually almost impose itself on the situation.

The limitations of training in real situations

The escape offroad and the "lean, lean, lean" can be safely practiced in reality, at least with relatively slow speeds. But what about situations for which real-life practice is simply not an option? For these, only mental training remains. The alternative is absolutely no preparation at all for an emergency! Examples of this are *mental crash training* and *mental collision training.*

No one would ever want to really practice crashing (unless he were a stunt rider, and even he would only do this with several safety measures in place). However, especially for a motorcycle crash at higher speeds, there are certainly some things that could be trained mentally. One of these is how one should behave when an actual crash, which can occur in a multitude of ways, has just happened—namely:

1. *Let go of the motorcycle* (many hold on to it as if for dear life!).

2. *Spread out your arms and legs slightly* (when rolling has stopped and you are simply continuing to slide).

3. *Stay loose* (obviously easier said than done, but this can be successfully trained).

4. *Before standing up, be sure that you are no longer sliding* (a recommendation that seems superfluous only on paper).

5. *Do not run blindly from the road or track.* (Any following traffic will have a much better chance of avoiding an obstacle—you—if it does not suddenly move in an unexpected direction, possibly straight into the path upon which he was going to ride around you.)

Another example of a situation that cannot be practiced is a collision with a car. In its most common form, the collision of the motorcycle will be into the side of a car that has failed to yield the right of way to the motorcycle. (May all readers be spared this experience, but that is no reason not to talk about it!) For this, too, there are useful rules of behavior (which remain completely ineffective if the rider is simply aware of them but has not mentally practiced them to the point of automation): immediately before the collision, stand on the pegs; better still: jump up. The goals here are to get one's head above the roof of the vehicle—this is well-known to be a particularly stiff part of a car's body—and to create better conditions for being thrown over the car. Please don't believe that this is only an issue at higher collision speeds; there is a good chance of being thrown at speeds as low as 40 km/h! This is certainly bad enough, but it's still incomparably better than a flat-out collision.

As previously stated several times, in an emergency there is no guarantee that any particular intended action really will run its course as planned. This can be the case even with implementation of our internal "action film" (p. 127), which at some particular point simply does not lend itself to being carried out perfectly in reality; or, as we saw in the escape off pavement (p. 132), when, despite good intentions and better knowledge, the clutch lever was released at the same time as the brake lever; or, in a crash (p. 132), in which the rider still tries to stand up even though he's still sliding.

Combating the enemy: fear

This warning is not necessary simply because, in an emergency, *one doesn't think of these things* or because one *forgets* everything that he has learned. The warning is necessary because of the pressure of the situation, and in extreme cases, fear. Specifically with motorcycling, fear has a significance that is much greater than is generally assumed. Fear is the true enemy, and it must be fought more than anything else.

Frequently, a crash or an accident is not at all the *direct* consequence of some triggering disruption that could not be managed; rather, the disruption has done nothing more than trigger the fear of the rider, who *only then* commits the error that actually causes the crash or accident. Usually it's not just one single error that follows fear, but a whole number of errors in rapid succession—a downright **cascade of errors,** that has been ignited by fear (Spiegel 2004).

The triggering event can be almost anything. It can come upon us from external sources or we can bring it upon ourselves: a loud clap of thunder; a car spinning out of control; an unexpected left-turner; a big patch of oil that suddenly shows up in front of us in a curve; even the sudden, if possibly erroneous, realization that we're going too fast for a corner; or maybe a bad wobble when braking before a corner because of too much braking on one wheel. There are, in fact, infinite possible reasons to be fearful. Certainly, there are some accidents that are simply unavoidable, but among the avoidable ones, most are accidents in which fear is a connecting link that plays a *decisive role* in the subsequent course of events; otherwise, the rider would have been able to manage the triggering event—*the fear*—just fine.

The important questions are twofold: What happens when the rider is frightened? What can one do to prevent it?

The consequences of fear

Only a relatively good rider has an extremely close relationship with his motorcycle. There are numerous control circuits that involve both vehicle and rider together, although the rider doesn't necessarily feel much of this. The regulation itself occurs with extreme sensitivity by means of **automated** behaviors and behavior **programs** that have been acquired through painstaking training. We've encountered these programs several times already. The better trained the rider, the more finely interwoven the rider and motorcycle will be, and the higher the level of **integration.** Or to use a pair of key words: the less like "cargo," the more like a "component" the rider will be, as previously discussed. The programs of automated behaviors are constantly being further refined and becoming more and more automated. In other words, this means that they become more and more independent of external stimuli, and thereby less subject to disruption, the more automated they become.

When the rider is frightened, he abruptly steps out of this finely woven system whether he wants to or not, and far worse things happen than what one can observe from the outside at first glance. The physical changes affect mainly the vital physiological functions: the heart rate goes up dramatically, and breathing immediately becomes shallower and tighter. Simultaneously, the rider tenses up in broad regions of his musculature: his hands tightly grasp the handlebars, his teeth and lips press together, and his buttock muscles tighten. In addition, his gaze drops and becomes far too short. Thus, in an exaggerated manner, the rider does the opposite of everything he should be doing if he wants to ride well.

Just as suddenly, the close connections between rider and vehicle are cut, and the integration falls apart: there can be no more talk of the rider as component. If he is experiencing extreme fear, the rider just sits helplessly on the seat. It's as if he were isolated from the motorcycle, and because of his tenseness, he can no longer perceive the subtle information that the motorcycle is transmit-

👈 "Tension release in seconds" method

A proven method is to use the trick of "tension release in seconds." This would be done *immediately* after encountering a major fright, and before even applying the described relaxation measures (for which one may not even have time). A sudden, short interjection, such as "hepp!," is pressed out forcibly *out loud* three or four times in intervals of a few seconds. This is done with a tensed diaphragm and simultaneous tensing of the entire musculature of the lower abdomen, although this extreme tension should be exerted only *at the moment at which the word is "released."* In similar cases in the car, the same thing can be done by the driver to produce immediately palpable results, provided he doesn't frighten his passengers in this way. (I have to admit that this might at least seem strange to the boss, who may happen to be along at the time.) ∎

ting. In the same way, the rider is in no state to influence the motorcycle with sufficient precision, even if it weren't for the fact that most automated behaviors have broken down or have at least been disrupted. The above-mentioned cascade of errors runs its course, and the outcome is uncertain.

Countermeasures

Now let's consider the second question: What can one do to prevent this? Let's start with what one can do *after the fact,* when one has just suffered a frightening experience but has survived without consequences: *take a deep breath* (we have a tendency to do this anyway), *and, while exhaling, systematically release muscle tension, muscle group by muscle group.* One can feel very easily how cramped he has been sitting, especially once one has had a little practice with muscle relaxation and thus knows what a tense group of muscles feels like and, conversely, what an *un*tensed group of muscles feels like. So . . . let the head drop for a moment, loosen the mouth, separate the upper and lower teeth slightly, consciously let the shoulders and abdominal wall drop, lay the hands loosely on the grips . . . and if this doesn't help (maybe because the fright was too intense), one should stop to allow better relaxation.

But what can one do to keep the fear from coming in the first place, or at least to keep it from being so intense?

One can't select the events that are going to elicit fear, but by practicing similar situations, one can familiarize himself *with certain frightening situations.* We'll have a better understanding of how this can be helpful once we've spent a moment considering what fear actually is.

Sudden, surprising, and threatening: the three characteristics of fear

Fear is a negative effect that arises as a reaction to an event that occurs suddenly and unexpectedly and is experienced as threatening (but must not necessarily also be an objective threat). That fear is an *effect* means that it can be counteracted only through extreme will power and rational thinking, if at all. The three characteristics of the triggering event of fear—*sudden, surprising, threatening*—are, in combination, very important. Suddenness alone is not enough, no matter how sudden; there are thousands of events that occur suddenly each day and we are not frightened in the least. All three characteristics, or conditions, must be exist to trigger fear in a person. Herein lies the key to coping better with the danger of fear: if it's possible to "turn off" these conditions, the danger is averted. The first (suddenness) is not something we can control, but we can influence the other two conditions, at least to a certain extent. A frightening event can't be quite so *surprising* if we are prepared for its possible occurrence. It's true that it may arise just as suddenly, *but it won't be as unexpected* and thus it can no longer frighten us. Likewise, a frightening experience that we have already successfully managed several times is familiar enough that we no longer find it as *threatening* as something completely unknown. This means that someone with good training will be frightened disproportionately less often because he experiences a much smaller number of events as threatening.

This is the reason that including the systematic practice of very specific situations in rider training classes is so important. In everyday life, one has too little opportunity, and even less desire, to perform these exercises, which include, for example, hard braking under different circumstances, even from very high speeds; intentional overbraking in the rear to the point of lock; short "grabbing" of the front brake to the point of lock; braking in a curve; unaccustomed lean angles in a circle to the point of dragging parts; and swerving around obstacles with and without prior braking, all the way to the escape offroad.

If these exercises are performed under the guidance of a knowledgeable instructor, the objective risk is minimal. The experienced risk, however, is high, but only at first. With repetition, it rapidly decreases, and this is precisely the goal: to neutralize the situation's *threatening* nature.

Breaking down the surprise effect and the threat

The importance of breaking down the element of surprise has already been explained; it's the same principle as that underlying the importance of breaking down the perception of threat. Basically, the more we confront ourselves with certain experiences by deliberately bringing about these situations under controlled circumstances, the more familiar they will become to us and *the less surprised we will be when they arise.*

We have previously become acquainted with events and situations that are far too dangerous to be brought about intentionally for the purpose of becoming familiar with them, but even with these, there is a way in which we can improve our chances from the beginning. With mental training (p. 121), through the intensive imagining and planning in as relaxed a state as possible, we can repeatedly confront ourselves with these kinds of frightening situations and **mentally** practice the optimal course of action. This is the great potential of **mental** training!

With mental training, as we have already seen in a few examples, one does not have to stop as one does with actual training, when the training would otherwise become too dangerous or because fate may have already stepped in. A mental training exercise might be a "hairy" situation such as oil or gravel in a corner with opposing traffic. *(For this, the mentally trainable reaction is, once again, lean, lean, lean, even if the limit of traction is exceeded. In no case should the curve radius be increased!)* Or one might think of an obstacle that suddenly appears, and there's no more time to swerve and not enough room to brake. *(Here, the answer would be to immediately "dismount," and "get off" to the inside—that is, initiate a mild curve while simultaneously braking fully with the rear brake.)* Or, we might think of a crash at a high speed or a collision that cannot be avoided.

These are indeed ugly situations that we would prefer not to think about at all. Nevertheless, we should always and repeatedly play through these situations, and not just the ones named here. Not only does this allow us to acquire, in advance, certain action programs for use in an emergency (see p. 127), but—and still more important—*we gain control over the fear by breaking down the element of surprise.*

If the event does actually occur at some point, then it doesn't catch us nearly as unprepared and naive as it would if we had never thought of it before.

CONCEPTUAL AIDS

Their purpose: eliciting certain feelings

Closely connected with mental training are the so-called **conceptual aids,** which can be used to influence our own behavior by means of the conscious implementation of particular concepts or images. While mental training involves a realistic conception of the *execution* of an action, conceptual aids are, in contrast, usually oddly unrealistic and, in terms of their content, are frequently completely *foreign* to the particular action. They don't necessarily have to be connected with relaxation or deep relaxation (which is not true of mental training per se), but a condition of relaxation is usually conducive, especially when conceptual aids are used not as *accompanying* aids (that is, during the execution of the action), but rather when they are implemented *in preparation* for an action. The goal in using conceptual aids is the clarification of particular feelings in the body and the **habituation** of the corresponding movement experiences. Therefore, it's once again a matter of making an activity that was originally the domain of the conscious self to "sink in" deeply, to the subconscious self: it's making the transition from the conscious realm to the subconscious.

For our purposes, conceptual aids can be defined as conceptions of feelings in the body that make the actions easier or improve them. The conceptions are not only foreign to the topic but also are often factually unfounded and can even be nonsensical. In addition, the user can be completely aware of this without diminishing the effect of the conceptual aids. For example, a tickle in the throat can occur at the worst possible moment; singers and actors are therefore taught to "breathe past it" in such a situation. Objectively speaking, that's not even possible. Still, the conception is only superficially nonsensical. In truth, it's a fairly reliable method because it redirects the anxious attention of the afflicted from the tickled spot (the obstacle, the disruption itself) to the act of getting around the obstacle and resolving the disruption.

Singing and diction lessons, in particular, are full of conceptual aids, especially those related to breathing and things that influence resonance, but accomplished sports coaches also have long used conceptual aids ("You have to pretend like you're . . ."). The success of the conceptual aid depends on its quality.

Preparatory and accompanying conceptual aids

Whenever conceptual aids are in use, one can make the distinction, described above, between *preparatory* aids and *accompanying* aids. The latter are implemented *during* the execution of the action. A few examples of this from the world of motorcycling are described below.

Examples of conceptual aids

It is important to first point out that a particular form of mental training, as described on p. 127, in which the rider, while not moving, tries to imagine himself "flowing" into the motorcycle ever more deeply, all the way down into the contact patches of the tires, is, in fact, a conceptual aid, with all of the associated characteristics. This is an example of the *preparatory* application of a conceptual aid, and in this case, not so much an application directed at a particular course of action but rather more one directed at a particular kind of *physical feeling* that should set in.

Because a conceptual aid is used in *preparation* for an action does not mean, however, that this physical feeling can't be reactivated later during the ride and then, perhaps when riding in circles to explore traction limits,

Plateaus and leaps forward

A conceptual aid that precisely hits the training difficulty at a particular moment of disruption can lead to an immediate and *substantial improvement.* Training advances don't occur continually, over time, as a gradual increase in performance. Instead, there are intermittent performance plateaus during training. These are especially easy to recognize by performance measurements in the "higher-faster-farther" sports. However, a precisely aimed conceptual aid, often nothing more than a few words, can lead to a jump to a new plateau, even after long periods of training that seem to have done nothing to improve performance.

The existence of performance plateaus points up the reality that an instructor (teacher or trainer) doesn't instill every last detail of a movement process, step by step, in his trainees and that he doesn't *shape* them through and through like a sculptor shapes his pieces. Instead, the instructor gives the trainee individual hints or little tips that are appropriate to the trainee's current performance level and that may really only have to do with a single aspect of his performance. Nevertheless, the instructor can be hopeful that, along the path to complete and total **self-optimization,** all the other possible segments of actions or details of behavior that are connected to that single aspect, will likewise be modified and incorporated into the new order at a higher level. The legendary American golf teacher Harvey Penick, who instructed a whole host of famous golfing greats, was a master in recognizing the momentary training difficulties of his students. Central to his preferred teaching method was the use of comparisons, images, and parables— in other words, conceptual aids (Penick & Shrake 1997). ∎

suddenly provide a surprisingly large amount of information about the contact patches.

But even the simple recommendation "sit deep inside!" or "don't sit *on* the bike, sit *in* it!" has the character of a conceptual aid. Again, this is a preparatory aid that first has to be implemented while standing still but then should be preserved to the greatest possible extent during the ride. Whenever the rider loses this feeling, usually because of too much tension, he should immediately try to re-establish it. After all, he's familiar with this condition and knows what it "feels like." If he's sufficiently well-practiced, then after a particularly difficult or critical situation, he only has to remind himself of the feeling for a moment, and he's back to normal. Sitting "deep inside" is then already his "normal" position, and he quickly finds his way back to it. The more a rider has perfected his skills, the less often he will have to resort to conscious use of a conceptual aid, because the desired behaviors will have long since become habit. But even a well-practiced rider is not immune to reversions to old behaviors or habits (see p. 117).

Sitting deep inside the motorcycle—which, in the ideal situation, is taken all the way to "flowing" all the way to the contact patches—is part of relaxation exercises. It only works with good muscular relaxation. Conversely, when performing relaxation exercises, the command to let oneself sink deep into the motorcycle aids in relaxation. For relaxation training itself, Eberspächer has an outstanding conceptual aid: after releasing the tension from the shoulders and the arms, imagine that one's hanging arms are full of sand, and then feel how the tension slowly, *like the sand in an hourglass,* sifts out. That is not just a general training aid such as those used in rider training; it is also a quickly effective means for the professional who needs to do something to immediately release tension before the start of a race, provided that the method has been sufficiently trained in advance in less stressful situations.

A few more examples of conceptual aids: in racing, there are alternating corners, and every inch of straight-line riding between them is one too many. The high and extremely sudden muscular exertion that is required in this situation often goes against the grain of the more sensitive rider, because a sequence of movements is abruptly required of him that otherwise does not exist in this form. The tried and true conceptual aid for this situation is: "Imagine that, at exactly this point, you had to *forcibly throw the motorcycle over*" (meaning: *throw it to the other side*); then this *sharp* change in lean angle suddenly works. The sport rider can learn from this, too. It's nothing more than a very intense steering input, and one that, in ending the first corner, simultaneously initiates the next.

In the example just described, the conceptual aid is a *conception of movement,* just as in this example, in which the goal, in a braking drill for inexperienced riders, is to practice an appropriately steep increase in braking pressure: "It's as if you're holding a wet sponge that you want to wring out all at once but you must *gradually* squeeze tighter."

The next example identifies an especially important conceptual aid, and probably one that is not used nearly enough: "In a certain corner or series of corners, you have to imagine that *you yourself are already there, at the point where you are looking.* Your body and the motorcycle will come by themselves, behind you—you are pulling them along." One can see immediately what is supposed to be achieved with this conceptual aid. It not only encourages looking far ahead while riding, which has already been amply discussed, but incorporates the essence of **integration,** the ultimate goal: the conscious self plans the activity but is then more or less sent on ahead and is thus sent away from the actual execution of the plan, leaving the subconscious self undisturbed to take care of the details and the individual actions.

Even when surrounding conditions have deteriorated, an appropriate conceptual aid can suddenly change everything for the better. Example: while riding on a paved country road, one suddenly comes upon a thick layer of gravel that covers the entire lane. One slows down but still feels extremely uneasy. The motorcycle feels unsettled and floats to some extent, and it's tough going. But this can change from one moment to the next, when one uses the following (imaginary) conceptual aid: it's not a paved road with loose material on top, but rather an unpaved road consisting of nothing but gravel. Absolutely nothing else has changed, but from then on, everything is much more fluid and much less arduous, and it's an especially noticeable difference if one had tensed up when first encountering the situation.

Developing your own conceptual aids

The above examples weren't really meant to provide the reader with a "stockpile" of conceptual aids. Instead, they were mainly intended to clarify what conceptual aids actually are, and to show that one can absolutely trust them, even if they may sound a little absurd. *Above all, the examples were meant to encourage readers to develop and use their own conceptual aids.*

TRAINING OBJECTIVES

Setting objectives and supporting them

Finally, there's one other highly important task that the conscious self performs: forming training intent, which means creating the most concrete possible conceptions of one's goals, that is, objectives. There's hardly any other means by which one can consciously do more to contribute to rapid training progress than by setting **objectives.** Setting objectives is nothing other than a conscious recognition of how a certain behavior, and sometimes also the *outcome* of a behavior, should look. We have already discussed how little there is to be gained from "just rid-

Improving Riding Behavior Through Supported Objectives

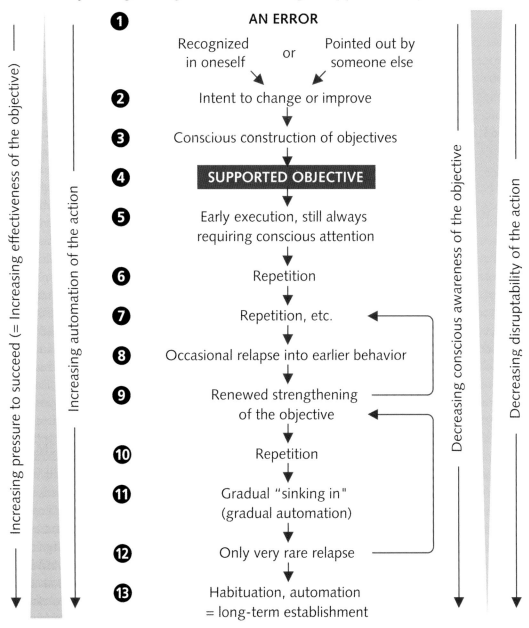

Increasing pressure to succeed (= Increasing effectiveness of the objective)

Increasing automation of the action

1 AN ERROR

Recognized in oneself   or   Pointed out by someone else

2 Intent to change or improve

3 Conscious construction of objectives

4 SUPPORTED OBJECTIVE

5 Early execution, still always requiring conscious attention

6 Repetition

7 Repetition, etc.

8 Occasional relapse into earlier behavior

9 Renewed strengthening of the objective

10 Repetition

11 Gradual "sinking in" (gradual automation)

12 Only very rare relapse

13 Habituation, automation = long-term establishment

Decreasing conscious awareness of the objective

Decreasing disruptability of the action

Figure 79

ing around," with no intent to learn (**learning intent**) and no training goal in mind (p. 117).

When one is seeking to change his behavior, objectives, or even resolutions, are an important prerequisite, and man, alone among species, is capable of coming up with them, but all too often, simply setting objectives is not enough. People have known this for a long time; as they say, "The road to hell is paved with good intentions." There's even an old Arabian saying: "The good intention is a horse that's often saddled up, but seldom ridden."

To undertake something, or *to come up with an objective,* is much easier than to actually realize the objective, especially if the objective is related to a long-term behavior change, rather than being directed at a one-time activity. Not only is this true for athletic training but also for all tasks that arise from the *management of one's own person,* which is precisely the problem. George Bernard Shaw hit the nail on the head when asked if it was hard to quit smoking. His answer: "Oh, there's nothing easier! I've done it a thousand times."

Use of reminder stickers in training courses

A good quarter of the participants in Perfection Training courses (run by *Motorrad* magazine) start using reminder stickers during the training. Those who don't want to reveal themselves hide the stickers under their tankbags. In the group, these participants still feel too uncertain to essentially publicly proclaim their weaknesses as riders, and they may also be afraid of being picked on. However, more than half of all participants report having later used the stickers, and there are even instructors and racers who use stickers from time to time to monitor their riding. ■

Keeping objectives at the forefront

What we need is a way to *support* our objectives. Even the teacher, whose constant repetitions and reminders might seem irritating to us, is clearly trying (perhaps not always effectively) to *support certain objectives that we hopefully have set up for ourselves.* An objective is not "supported" when it is just a "single executive decision" by the conscious self that, over the long term, remains more or less non-binding, but rather when supporting techniques are implemented with the goal of creating a *constant presence and currentness* for the objective until it has been enduringly established (see Figure 79).

A reminder: motorcycle training consists in large part of taking certain activities of the conscious self—insights, rules, the advice of others, all things that have been taken on as intentions affecting actions and behaviors—and making them into activities of the subconscious self—that is, turning them into *automatically managed* **action programs.** In other words, actions that require **conscious attention,** which are almost always inadequately coordinated, become **automated** actions and thereby simultaneously gain a greater degree of **coordination.** Accepted recommendations (such as those of a trainer) or even one's own insights into what would be correct action (action- and behavior-related intentions) are transformed into processes that run their course automatically. As the intended change sinks in, the conscious self is increasingly unburdened and the susceptibility to disruption of the action or behavior is continually diminished (see "Programs that control actions," pp. 28 and Figure 79).

Objectives in the form of preemptive corrections: reminder stickers

There are different methods of supporting intentions. In a certain sense, even the error counter (p. 119) has something to do with the support of intentions. In sports, briefly stated action- or behavior-related objectives written on small stickers have proved their merit. The stickers, or *labels,* should do nothing more than serve as a reminder to adhere to certain objectives. The objectives themselves must already be familiar to the person (usually they've already been comprehensively explained by the trainer), and they should actually be formulated as solid training objectives.

Reminder stickers appear to have been used first in aerobatics. This was a natural development, because stunt pilots already had a related method: using so-called Aresti-pictograms (after the Spanish flyer J. L. Aresti), they listed their entire flight program on a small piece of paper, which they then affixed to something in their field of vision. Great experts often limited themselves to individual hints. In this sense, they were really just *anticipated corrections* that were relevant to particular figures that still needed some work, and in which perhaps one particular error that needed to be avoided and eradicated kept recurring. This is quite clearly an *objective* as we have discussed them, and it is much stronger than an entire aerobatics program, with all the figures that are to be flown in the program. It is an *anticipated criticism* and precisely corresponds to modern *reminder stickers.* A Swiss master aerobatic pilot, Francis Liardon, once told me, "It's just like magic! I can't even read the objective in the cockpit, but whenever I don't have the sticker there, my old mistake comes right back!"

Later, the use of tiny memos appeared in tennis, as the American aces trained with labels on the backs of their hands. Alpine skiers also showed up for training with stickers on the tips of their skis. The application of a sticker on a ski isn't about giving the trainee an opportunity to "cheat": the athlete already knows what it says on the sticker, and he's known it for a long time; these are the particular objectives, the "anticipated corrections," as described above. The sticker is put on the ski just as a constant reminder. This has much more in common with a string around the finger than with a cheat sheet.

Still later, the pharmaceutical industry and physicians recognized that even a patient's intention to take his medication regularly could use this kind of support.

They are well aware of how poorly many patients follow dosing instructions. Lately, medication prescriptions requiring regular and consistent dosing have been accompanied by ready-made stickers printed with the dose to take before bed, for example, with the suggestion—and not a bad one—to put the sticker on one's toothbrush or alarm clock.

So where is the best place on a motorcycle for reminder stickers? Most commonly, they should be applied to the tank or tankbag (Figure 80); the fork yoke is also a possibility. The stickers should focus the rider's attention on his main problems, for example, that he has a tendency to clench his teeth or to lock his elbows—both of which are signs of too much tension—and they should state appropriate objectives: "Loosen mouth!" "Loosen chin!" "Don't lock elbows!" Multiple objectives can be stated, and this works best if they are interrelated, *but with any more than three objectives at one time, the effect is diluted.*

As already mentioned above, the rider shouldn't be checking during the ride to see what he's supposed to pay attention to; the mechanism of the sticker effect is more indirect. The *selection* and *application* of the reminder sticker for the objective is the first reinforcement of the intention. Much later, maybe at a stop, the rider's glance may catch the sticker, and he realizes that he's forgotten about the objective because of all the other distractions. He undertakes to pay attention to that behavior, starting at that point. He'll probably forget it again, but each time he's reminded of it by the sticker, and his drive to achieve the objective grows again, and he consciously exerts effort to do so. Even if there are still many parts of the ride during which the execution of the objective is forgotten, the rider's drive to achieve the objective will keep being renewed. The more profoundly a rider feels an immediate improvement when he follows this kind of behavior prompt (many riders have this kind of experience with the recommendation "Push the inside knee forward"), the more rapidly the objective will establish itself. However, there are behavior prompts for objectives whose long-term implementation are met with fundamental resistance, such as "look far ahead" (see p. 150). These objectives have to be trained with special intensity until they become more or less permanently acquired and are halfway panic-proof.

After a certain amount of training, something strange occurs: the rider spontaneously follows the sticker prompt without even having thought of the objective.

Figure 80. Supporting objectives with reminder stickers.

When this happens, the action or behavior is usually still a conscious one because it hasn't yet been fully **automated,** but the objective on the sticker doesn't occur to him until *after* he's already fulfilled it. The sequence has thus reversed itself. *This is the start of the development of an automated act,* that is, the action or behavior begins to no longer require conscious attention. This is a good sign, but it's still necessary to continue to support the objective for a little while longer with the reminder sticker.

The rider himself is the best judge of when a reminder sticker is no longer needed and has truly become superfluous. When this happens, it's time to tackle the next objective.

This method of supporting one's intentions, using reminder stickers, is not suitable for beginners because there are *so many* individual steps and actions an instructor has to teach someone who is completely new to motorcycling. For beginners, focusing on individual aspects of behaviors or actions is more likely to disrupt than to aid the learning process. Picking out particular objectives means that the other aspects are ignored, and there is too much that still requires conscious attention. Once a solid foundation of skills has become adequately automated, the individual can turn his attention to the most important parts of each action, such as **looking where one wants to go.** What this shows is that the technique for supporting the objective is chiefly about *changing* behavior: the fundamental objective is change, and the specific objectives are recommendations for improvements.

Refreshing one's objectives

Occasionally, for example after a winter break, it is time for a rider to "freshen up" his objectives. All the behavior and action goals previously selected as objectives should be **mentally** inventoried by the rider, along with the corresponding physical aspects. In so doing, he can feel fairly sure whether or not these objectives are still in his automatic **programs.** If the rider has the slightest doubts, then he must again take up these objectives, with the help of reminder stickers during actual riding.

A periodic mental inventory serves as a review of what requires updating—that is, it serves to detect objectives that were previously set and achieved but have since become insufficiently manifested by the rider. ∎

Overcoming ingrained behaviors and actions that are undesirable

The longer a suboptimal or erroneous behavior or action has been in use, the harder it is to stamp out because it is that much more deeply ingrained (automated). This is not news to a riding instructor, especially if he frequently deals with students who come to the class with significant previous experience (because this means they come in with erroneous behaviors that have already been practiced and become habitual).

Some fundamental skills, such as *shifting,* remain at a miserably low level for a long time after the initial learning period. If one wants to improve his shifting after years of what has been at least somewhat successful riding, the processes surrounding it are so well established that they can be lastingly changed only with great difficulty. For this reason, shifting is a *prime example* for the implementation of supported objectives.

The right way to shift, an example

Even among otherwise good motorcyclists, shifting skills can "get stuck" at a very rudimentary level. Why should the skill improve itself? It's entirely adequate; therefore, aside from the occasional clatter, there's really no impetus to optimize it. Also, it's not something that can be *gradually* improved simply with increasing practice, as is the case with so many other aspects of riding. Instead, it happens all at once: either wrong or right—and as long as it's wrong *and noisy,* the transmission gets the blame.

With lighter motorcycles—the kind that people usually ride when they are learning and in their first few years—one can usually get away with careless shifting, but by the time one moves on to a heavier machine, he should take a cleaner approach to shifting. Of course, it can't be denied that some motorcycles require more care in shifting than others.

When a rider shifts into first gear (before he even rides off), one can see what kind of relationship he has with his transmission. First gear might not be *engaged* with the toe or the ball of the foot, but instead, after pulling in the clutch, the unwitting rider might quickly stomp his entire foot down on the shift lever—crack!—as if it were a recalcitrant kickstarter. It's painful just to watch!

Pulling in the clutch and shifting into gear are closely related and occur almost simultaneously (just as when downshifting, in which squeezing the clutch, adding a bit of throttle to match rpm, and operating the shift lever occur *simultaneously,* and the clutch is let back out again, also without the slightest pause). Specifically when shifting into first gear on an idling bike, the gears, which have a very short spin-down time, should not be allowed to come to a stop. The more disengagement the clutch provides, the more important this is.

The rider with rudimentary shifting skills will continue to shift into subsequent gears using the same method as he used for first gear: he'll first pull the clutch in and then shift, just as he learned to do on a lighter motorcycle or with a particularly patient transmission. He'll probably still be doing it this way five years later and complain about noisiness and false neutrals, about the transmission popping out of gear at first once in a while and then more and more frequently, and maybe even about an expensive transmission repair.

It's possible, though, that at some point he might actually find out how it's properly done—that is, as we've said, to pull in the clutch and, essentially simultaneously, engage the gear, and then to *continue to hold the shift lever just a moment longer, until the clutch lever is out again.* When one gets the clutch in and out fast enough, the delayed release of the shift lever is not even noticeable to an outside observer.

However, the rider might try this proper technique out once or twice without remarkably better results than he otherwise usually has and thus will probably soon fall back into his old shifting habits. Over the long run, though, if he had continued to use proper shifting technique, he would have noticed that his trouble with gears popping out and mysterious false neutrals ceased.

The loud "clack" when shifting up, which occurs especially at high rpm, can also be avoided when the rider slightly "preloads" the shifter *just before squeezing the clutch.* When he does this, at the moment the clutch lever is pulled in, and at the same time as the throttle is rolled off, the gear engages as if by itself. It's not the shift lever that selects the gear, but rather the clutch that determines when the shift occurs. Besides its superiority as a shifting technique, this is a good lesson in what minimal forces are needed to complete a shift.

Once this technique works, the rider is just steps away from shifting without using the clutch at all, because in using the preload method, he might have noticed that it wasn't just the disengagement of the clutch, but also the unloading of the drivetrain caused by getting off the gas, that brought about the shift. This is a lightning fast and, for reasonable engine speed, even more transmission-friendly way to shift. It quickly becomes clear that the unloading of the drivetrain only has to be slight and momentary to allow the next gear to quietly slip in. Changing gears this way used to be fairly common in racing, but it stresses the transmission considerably at higher RPM because the transmission gears don't have time to come to a complete stop. For everyday riding, every rider has to learn by experience how much the engine can be revved without producing undue noise when shifting.

However, because there are more rules to follow, this does make shifting more complicated. Shifting up without the clutch only works when, before the rider briefly lets up on the gas, *there is already a load on the drivetrain:* the engine is pushing the bike forward under acceleration. Thus, anyone who wants to try this should be warned: if, after acceleration, a rider out touring is just rolling along at a constant speed on flat land, then there is only a minimal load on the drivetrain and this can easily lead to a reverse in the load (that is, it changes from pushing the bike along to pulling it back, as occurs in engine braking). At this moment, if the rider were to try shifting without the clutch, as described above, it would probably result in horrible noises—after which many riders, given such negative reinforcement, never try it again.

The bottom line is that one has to practice and internalize a few more **automated** behaviors to complete the required arsenal of acquired **programs** for addressing the different situations for shifting up and down.

Otherwise, the rider will have to think about "when to" and "when not to" each and every time he shifts gears.

Proper shifting, as just described, is a prime example of a change in behavior that can be accomplished with the help of reminder stickers, a method of supporting objectives. Using the method of supported objectives immediately before a ride, the rider affixes the appropriate sticker to his bike; this can transform even an everyday ride into a special training ride. To support the objective of achieving proper shifting technique, the following two reminder stickers would be needed:

> **"HOLD THE SHIFT LEVER!"**
> **(UNTIL THE CLUTCH IS BACK OUT)**

> **"CLUTCH AND SHIFT**
> **ALMOST SIMULTANEOUSLY!"**

Calling up a complicated objective using keywords

One should try using reminder stickers early on to become familiar with this method of supporting objectives. The rider will easily see that the stickers do not need to contain every detail one needs to know to perform the action: *when* to hold the lever and *for how long,* for example, need not be stated at all. The rider has to know more about the action than what is written on the sticker. *The sticker is always just a brief reminder, or an abbreviation of the objective;* it is related to a more complicated action.

With the specific objectives related to shifting supported by reminder stickers, the rider's shifting proficiency will improve. A rider who has already mastered shifting can add a third sticker that focuses on a third objective ("Lightly preload the shifter!") and might even try his upshifts without the clutch, as long as it is done under acceleration (and not just two or three times, but during the entire ride, without exception). Only then will the rider truly be able to understand what deeply ingrained (automated) action programs are, how challenging it is to achieve this high level of integration, and what backsliding is like! To repeat: this section has only superficially been about certain refinements in the shifting process. The fundamental goal was to familiarize the reader with the principle of the supported objective.

So what if, after successful "retraining," one still catches himself doing it the old, improper way? This sounds like a job for the error counter!

PART 5

Objectives: Give Them a Try

This chapter summarizes general objectives for improving riding behavior. What follows is a series of specific tried and true recommendations to put into practice. They can be used for everyday riding and for sport riding. Without exception, they arise from the concepts and principles described in previous parts of this book. This fifth part is thus to some extent a summary, not of the entire book, but certainly of its practical recommendations for rider training. This is why it also contains cross references for the reader who wants to take another, closer look at a topic.

The recommendations are formulated as objectives so that they can easily be used with the reminder-sticker technique described in detail in the final segment of Part 4. This allows the reader to implement the *method of the supported objective.* One can use regular stickers available in stores, then write the objectives on them and apply them to his motorcycle.

Sometimes a recommendation contains the entire action command (such as "Hands loose on the grips!") that should become a concrete objective and eventually an **automated** behavior; sometimes a recommendation is only an abbreviated *reminder* of a more complicated process that needs to be practiced and acquired, and the reminder sticker is the first step. Most objectives and processes cannot possibly be contained in their entirety on a tiny sticker, but the objectives can generally be summed up with a few key words.

The recommended objectives are organized into five groups. The first group is related to the *looseness* that is desirable for motorcycle riding; it is the cornerstone of good riding. The looseness and relaxation objectives are not useful for the novice alone. Even racers, in certain pressure situations, have to struggle to stay loose, and there are some who use precisely the objectives described here to loosen up.

The second group of objectives, *rider and road,* is about the behavior of the rider in relationship to the road, and this, of course, is mainly related to curves and cornering.

The third group is about how the *rider* carries his body on the motorcycle. This isn't about whether he looks good or doesn't look good, but rather whether a certain position or posture is beneficial for physical reasons (such as "Balance head and chest with wind pressure") as well as from a psychological-functional standpoint (such as "Arms slightly bent" or "On the balls of the feet").

The fourth group provides examples of *practice objectives.* These aren't so much exercises that one can do during a ride "on the side" but rather exercises for which one should undertake special practice rides, even if they are only very short.

The fifth group contains a few *general objectives.* Most are related to emergencies and aren't actions that one can physically practice. For this reason, one should always let them run through his head whenever possible, especially while riding.

Remember that these are only examples. Each person can replace these with his own personal corrective objectives and use the same methods. Therefore, the reader should not just *think about* his own personal objectives while reading the following sections; he should *write each on a sticker* (using evocative keywords) and then, of course, actually use them!

The number of possible objectives is enormous. I trust that these examples are among the most important.

LOOSENESS

Let's begin with what may be the most important general objective for motorcyclists: being relaxed, tension-free, and loose. What follows is a group of seemingly varied looseness objectives, but they *differ* only with respect to *where they originate:* hands, mouth, abdominal wall, or lungs. The objectives themselves all have the same goal: when one of these objectives for relaxation and loosening is followed, it leads to a conscious and deliberate change that initially alters only a *symptom.* With this change, however, the rider's entire system changes—that is, the rider's entire bearing becomes different, and in this way, his other symptoms of tension are also alleviated, even if they weren't specifically "called on" to change. This works even better the more one has trained himself to undertake this loosening of the individual parts together, in a connected way: the place in the body where the relaxation originates thereby causes a sort of chain reaction, loosening up the other parts of the body. Each person must determine for himself which starting point works best for him. If there's enough time, it is definitely worth not just calling on an individual area to loosen up, but instead going through each one and thereby exploiting their mutual amplification.

The basic issue is the same in all instances: the greater the pressure and the longer it lasts, the more the general level of muscular tension increases, especially for a novice. The muscular tension can progress all the way to the point of cramping. If the tension is effectively interrupted, even if only in selected places, the entire system will loosen itself, physically and psychologically.

One can try an experiment (as described in the sidebar on p. 76) to see for himself that it really is a matter of his entire system being either tensed or relaxed. One also can see in other ways that the subsystems influence each other: for example, if, while playing tennis, one makes a fist with his free hand, his entire system immediately loses its ability to carry out its movement processes with the sufficient degree of fine tuning.

Relaxation, or looseness, is one of the most important prerequisites for making good progress in training.

HOLD THE GRIPS LOOSELY

When we ride a motorcycle, cramped hands (which occur quite frequently) detract from both our sensory and motor capabilities—input and output. The subtle feedback that the motorcycle transmits to the rider simply doesn't get through (see p. 95), and **steering inputs** are no longer transferred to the motorcycle with the necessary degree of refinement. Furthermore, even our *ability to learn,* and with that our success in training, is substantially diminished if our hands are cramped. It's not because our hands are cramped per se but because this is a sign of a general state of excessive tension. This kind of tension is beneficial only in an emergency, in which managing the current critical situation is all that matters. Learning, or preparation for a recurrence of this event, is not on the agenda.

DROP YOUR SHOULDERS

Some people are quite proficient at riding—even over long periods of time—with their hands loosely on the grips but eventually realize that they do not have quite the same amount of control over their shoulders. Even when one is sitting calmly reading these lines, he should—now, at this very moment!—check to see whether he can loosen his shoulders just a little more and drop them just a bit farther. It's almost always the case that even if one is only somewhat awake and attentive, the musculature of the shoulders has already achieved a degree of tension that is slightly greater than the at-rest tension (**resting tone**). One can feel this as soon as he has the right loosening objective and "checks himself." If, in addition to this regular tension that accompanies attention, we have a certain degree of vigilance for some kind of danger (certainly not uncommon when riding a motorcycle), muscular tension will only increase. It's no wonder that when it starts to rain, the average rider's shoulders become higher, his neck becomes shorter, and his head tilts farther forward.

This is true even in everyday situations: tight shoulders are not limited to physical exertion and enduring strain. They are the expression of a persistent vigilance for some kind of threat, which may not even be clearly recognized but is presumed to exist somewhere, perhaps at school or at work, maybe emanating from a dreaded person: "Things are still going okay, but who knows what might happen in the very next moment!"

The shoulder area, together with the mouth and even the voice, is one of the most reliable indicators of the degree of strain—more precisely, strain that has not been adequately offset. Thus, tight shoulders are a sign of impending stress.

LET YOUR HEAD FALL TOWARD YOUR CHEST

One can effectively support the dropping of the shoulders by briefly letting the head fall to the chest. Really let it fall: *let it* fall *down,* and don't try to catch it at the end! If done very briefly, this can even be done while riding, as can dropping of the shoulders.

LOOSEN YOUR ABDOMINAL MUSCLES

Loosening the abdominal muscles is closely connected with letting the head and shoulders drop. Similar to letting the shoulders drop, this is especially suited to being *"called up"* in which a certain basic bearing, such as expectant placidity or relaxed calm, is first constantly practiced in a state of relaxation, in close connection with the loosening intentions described here (hands, abdominals, mouth, chin, breathing). Then, this basic bearing can later be called up, while sitting on the bike at the starting line or even while riding, whereby one only has to pick out the specially planned intentions (such as dropping the shoulders or loosening the abdominals) to activate the entire chain of loosening exercises.

"SIT DEEPLY INTO" THE MOTORCYCLE

Once a rider has achieved a high level of looseness, he will almost automatically "sit deeply into" the motorcycle. What does "sitting deeply into" mean though? It means completely loosening one's "seat" and riding posture to allow him to *flow into* the motorcycle. Imagining doing this is an example of the use of a **conceptual aid.**

KEEP YOUR MOUTH LOOSE

The mouth also is well-suited as a trigger for calling-up the entire chain of loosening exercises. This is why, in so many sports, monitoring the looseness of the mouth is of such primary importance to the experts. One merely has to look at the photographs of the faces of world-class track athletes, especially the women, during the high jump, the long jump, and hurdles. It's true that one occasionally sees, especially in running events close to the finish line, very tense faces, some grimacingly distorted,

➤ The "play face"

What is interesting in the context of relaxing one's face is that in animal behavior research, the so-called "play-face" is exactly this relaxed face, with slightly parted lips, that signals un-purposeful absorption in play. It is an expression of the mood at the moment and is thus simultaneously a physical signal to a playmate that a behavior that might appear aggressive isn't intended as such and certainly isn't meant to hurt the "adversary."

There was once a participant in a Perfection Training course, who despite knowing better and wishing it were otherwise, kept finding himself in a state of highly aggressive tension. As an educated animal keeper, he fortunately knew a lot about primates and beasts of prey, so my hint to him about using the play face was an instantly effective training aid for him. All the systematic loosening in the world had been of no help for him, but when he started mimicking the play face of tussling young animals, he was able to achieve and maintain looseness. ■

but one also sees wonderfully relaxed faces—for example, in the women's jumping events, after the take-off, many of the athletes, with their mouths slightly open, will sort of wait expectantly, looking to see whether the jump is going to be high or far enough. If one saw only the face, it might appear that the athlete was relaxing during a rest period after an easy practice.

The most important rule for all objectives related to looseness and relaxation is: *all muscle groups that are not required for the execution of the current action should be relaxed.*

KEEP YOUR CHIN LOOSE

To make things easy, whenever one starts to loosen the mouth, he should always also check whether his chin and lower jaw are relaxed. There are people who manage, even with a nicely loosened mouth, to still keep the teeth firmly clenched together; some even do this with the lips slightly apart. Keeping the chin loose is really not that easy when riding on a challenging road or track, especially if there's pressure from competing riders. One will constantly catch himself with his teeth clenched, especially during and after difficult braking maneuvers, when braking is done a little bit late in a downhill curve. There's almost literal truth in the saying "Don't brake with your teeth."

DON'T BRAKE WITH YOUR TEETH

Teeth clenching is especially easy to observe during braking exercises. Unfortunately, the objective usually doesn't help much, even if it's supported, because one doesn't notice violations very easily and can't remember the situation very well after the fact (at most, one might later feel that the entire lower jaw aches). For this reason, an effective training method for keeping the chin loose is to hold a bean between the back teeth. When one bites it, he notices it right away. Experts use coffee beans because they have little elasticity and break apart with even minimal impact. Top-level fencers often use a pea, fresh or canned, between the teeth.

CONSCIOUSLY PAUSE BETWEEN BREATHS

Proper breathing also is essential for a rider's achieving looseness. All of the relaxation objectives should be supported by appropriate breathing, which further enhances one's ability to loosen up. Proper breathing techniques, once one has mastered them, can be *called* up just like the other relaxation methods. Obviously, a comprehensive discussion of breathing methods is not possible here (the information about proper breathing could fill an entire library), but it's easy enough to pass on a suggestion as an isolated objective—and it works wonders. It's true that, depending on the application, proper breathing must first be learned, but there's one rule to follow if one wants to relax: pause between each breath.

One of the most widespread misconceptions about breathing is that it consists of two stages, breathing in and breathing out. However, this is wrong; there are actually *three stages:* breathing in, breathing out, pausing. This is something one can observe in a healthy infant, and sometimes the breathing pause is so noticeable that inexperienced parents become alarmed. There's nothing to worry about, however; the pause does not lead to an insufficient supply of oxygen. Instead, this pausing leads to a reduced frequency of breathing, which automatically makes the amplitude greater so that each breath, both in and out, becomes *deeper.* Proper *breathing out* is particularly important. We relax when breathing out (and when we finally fall asleep, it happens as we breathe out). By contrast, when startled, we inhale suddenly, forcibly, and audibly. When our terror subsides, we exhale in relief, and it often comes out as a deep sigh.

AVOID A FEARFUL POSTURE

All of the tensions that have to be broken down are nothing more than an expression of mistrust, suspicion, or even fear in reaction to some threatening danger. This is something we have already seen, especially in respect to carriage of the shoulders. Thus, the objective of avoiding the fearful posture can be viewed as a collective objective, covering all the individual objectives discussed above, once one has sufficiently internalized them as a group and has a precise enough idea of what a fearful posture is. Fortunately, this is easily explained.

Imagine a patient at the dentist, especially if the dentist does not try to help the patient loosen up: the patient quickly assumes a classic fearful posture when the drilling starts, if not sooner. Even though the patient may feel no pain at all, he still cowers because it *might* hurt. Thus, his entire body tenses up: the toes curl or the big toes point straight up, the leg muscles tighten, the knees lock, the buttocks tighten, and the abdominal wall muscles tense up. In addition, breathing becomes shallow, the breathing frequency increases, and there's no trace of a pause in breathing. (In extreme cases, the patient's fear

and anxiety can develop into *hyperventilation.*) Furthermore, the elbows firmly press into the sides, the hands ball up into fists, the shoulders pull up slightly and tense, and the neck tightens up. If it were possible, the patient's jaw also would clench. The poor patient's body does the very opposite of what that of a motorcyclist, or an athlete in general, does in order to perform well.

It's a good idea to try to get a rudimentary idea of what a fearful posture *feels* like physically and what the opposite, *confident poise, feels* like. Poise is that feeling we always lose when we're under pressure and that we constantly try to re-establish, while at the dentist, while riding, and in many everyday situations. The main difference between a sports ace and his less successful competitors is that the former has the ability to maintain his poise under higher pressure than the latter. Another crucial difference between an ace and his less successful competitors is that if he loses his poise (which occurs frequently in risky sports), he has the ability to re-establish it immediately. Even though it was mostly in the realm of elite athletic competition that these differences were first recognized, they are applicable to *every* situation of increased pressure, especially pressure that comes from an increased experience of risk. This is something that constantly arises in motorcycling and is practically unavoidable, for example, when it starts to rain. The topic of rain is so important and so neglected that it deserves its own section and fits nowhere better than here, in connection with looseness.

When it rains: rules for wet, slippery conditions

It never ceases to amaze the observer how well and how confidently the British ride in rain—even completely unremarkable touring riders with no special ambitions. While riders in other places avoid riding in the rain if at all possible, the English have no choice but to consider rainy rides the norm: *typical English weather!* It's not just that they get much more practice with riding in the rain; it's that they go about it with much more confidence, as if it were a matter of course. English riders, compared to fair-weather riders elsewhere, are simply *not intimidated by rain.*

I remember a conversation with English motorcycle friends. Our group could simply not keep up with their pace in the rain. Linguistically and culturally, we were challenged to make clear to them just what we meant by "intimidated" in this context. We arrived at the idea that they, the English riders, simply didn't allow the rain to *rob them of their gutsiness,* but this was met with real bewilderment by the English. They claimed that there really isn't any particular gutsiness needed for riding in the rain, and that, in fact, being especially gutsy in the rain was likely to be dangerous. This captures a truism: it's hard to discuss things that are a matter of course, and riding in the rain is a matter of course for the English.

Within the foregoing anecdote also lies a very important tip: if a person dreads rain, he'll obviously behave differently in rain than at other times. Even at first glance, one can see signs of this, especially when the rain is just starting and the rider assumes the "rain posture." Compared with his pre-rain riding posture, the following changes occur: the head sinks a little and is pulled in, the shoulders rise higher, the back becomes slightly rounded, and the arms are straightened, with elbows locked.

If one observes himself carefully, he'll notice much more: all it takes is a few tiny drops on his face shield to put a stop to any chance of looking far down the road. His gaze falls and only reaches as far as the rear wheel of the bike in front. He watches anxiously to see if the tire leaves a track in the wet. Once he can barely make out such a track, he begins to make all of the errors related to becoming stiff and tense: he grips the handlebars tighter and tighter, tightens his abdominal wall and buttock muscles, sets his mouth in a grimace, and starts to clench his teeth. If, on top of this, a critical situation arises or he fears that the current situation might become critical (for example, because he's riding into a curve that he would rather have taken a bit more slowly), his entire body tenses and his breathing becomes shallow. He's now in the classic fearful posture, as described above. He is no longer sitting *in* the bike, but rather *on top of it,* and he's really not doing the riding himself anymore but is simply along for the ride, being carried along by the motorcycle.

At some time, when riding in the rain, every rider has asked himself—to no avail, of course—how fast he might be able to take this or that curve. The answer is actually simple: he can take it at exactly the speed at which he can still remain entirely loose. This is the confident poise described above. It doesn't mean that no muscle group at all can be tensed, but all muscle groups that are *not involved* in the given activity should remain loose. Additionally, every muscle group that is constantly switching between tensing and relaxing, between activation and rest, should immediately return to the relaxed condition when not in use.

If a rider has gotten stuck in the fearful posture, he has to make a conscious effort to break out of it. It's usually not enough to just ride somewhat more slowly for a little while. The general loosening measures previously described should be initiated: add a conscious pause between breaths for four or five breaths and let the shoulders drop; lay the hands loosely—almost exaggeratedly so—on the grips, and ride almost as if you were not holding on at all; let the head fall to the chest two or three times (*really let it fall!*); loosen the abdominal wall (this makes it much easier to "sit deeply into" the bike); and especially, emphasize looking far ahead, and keep looking farther.

If none of this helps to re-establish the necessary looseness, then the recommendation is to stop and release the tension while standing still.

Some statements express things that seem to go without saying, and one can agree with them immediately. When training in the rain, Hans Heinz Dilthey once said in passing, "The physics are the same." His statement certainly didn't express any novel idea, but nonetheless, it captured a key concept for me, precisely because, in its simplicity, it made so clear that the problem in learning to ride well in the rain lies not in physics but rather in *psychology.* The only physics factor involved is one coefficient: the coefficient of friction (or adhesion factor), which may change. In terms of **longitudinal forces** and **lateral forces,** this means that Kamm's circle may become smaller. On some surfaces, it becomes very small—and "that's it"!

It's true that some grippy surfaces don't lose much traction at all, while others that may have been bad enough in dry conditions are substantially worse in the wet—and then Kamm's circle becomes especially small. Once one has grasped these relationships, the technical consequences for riding in the rain are almost self-evident. They don't merely tell us to avoid higher lateral and longitudinal forces and thus to set a lower overall speed; they also tell us to avoid sudden spikes in acceleration, which is just as important. In this regard, all the recommendations and requirements for good motorcycle riding are still in effect, in some cases just more pointedly. A few special recommendations follow.

The line

The line should be as soft and fluid as possible, which means that the **movement plan** should be wide-ranging and include looking far ahead. The line should be without kinks, and if braking is required, it should be initiated gently and early. Along with this, one needs clean shifting, especially when downshifting, and the rpm needs to be matched before the clutch lever is let back out. A proven rule of thumb is to ride everything one gear higher than usual. And, of course, another rule that belongs in this discussion is this: when getting off the gas before a curve, immediately take back up the play in the throttle cable ("apply the gas") because the support with the throttle has to be dead-on and, especially in the rain, precisely modulated. It's also not a bad idea to apply the front brake once in a while, *very briefly* but fairly firmly. This fosters confidence in the situation. The rider can feel how much braking force can still be transmitted and also notices exactly when the wheel has stood still for just an instant; thus, he can create a "picture" for himself of how much traction remains.

Although, overall, the physics are the same, there are a few new rain-specific problems that arise: reduced visibility, hydroplaning, substantial reduction in tire abrasion, and sudden slipperiness.

Reduced visibility

It's a trivial assertion that visibility can become very bad during rain, but it's not just because of the reduction in sight distance and contrast but also and especially because of the diminished vision by one's face shield. As long as the wetness stays only on the outside of the face shield, things continue to more or less work, but if it fogs up on the inside, or one's glasses fog up because of insufficient ventilation, visibility becomes a problem. In response to this, the shield should be opened a tiny bit, but in heavy rain, even if this is done, it won't be long before the inside of the shield (and also the rider's glasses if he wears glasses) is covered with drops of water. In recent years, there have been substantial improvements in helmets and face shields, but this problem still hasn't been solved, especially not for those who wear glasses—so choose styles with small lenses!

Hydroplaning

Hydroplaning seldom occurs with motorcycles but has catastrophic results when it does. While the car driver, if he's lucky, can get away with a bit of a slide (maybe a collision and a major scare), the motorcyclist almost always goes down because the motorcycle needs the **lateral forces** not just to control direction and tracking—as is the case for a car—but also to maintain its dynamic stability, that is, to keep from falling over.

In order to get a concrete idea of what lateral forces are, one must use a special tire-testing stand to experience the enormous forces that have to be applied to push a rolling wheel just a few millimeters to the side. However, in wet conditions, when the amount of water increases and the tire starts to float (as in hydroplaning), suddenly, two fingers are all that's needed to move the wheel.

It is worthwhile to keep one's eyes peeled for places where hydroplaning might be a problem: this is *anyplace* where water can't drain away and *everywhere* that the water flows together from different directions. However, it's better to train one's eyes in the opposite way: to look for places where hydroplaning-conducive puddles are unlikely to occur. This will work better and better (similar to the **habituated** search for escape routes discussed on p. 129) by means of constant mental monitoring. The rules are simple: on inclined stretches, up or down, even in fairly hard rain, puddles that are enough to cause hydroplaning rarely develop, unless there are torrents of water rushing across the road. This is also true of banked segments, such as those often found in corners, but if a right-hander is transitioning to a left-hander, or vice versa, and a banking goes from a rightward to a leftward bank, then there is no banking in the transition zone. If the road builders didn't pay sufficient attention and thus did not place the transition zone in a segment with a parallel incline, then this will be a classic hydroplane area if it rains hard enough.

Substantial reduction in tire abrasion

This phrase sounds rather meaningless but becomes important when one is forced to "scrub in" a new tire in the rain, because at this time it is anything but grippy. This is most likely to happen on a motorcycle trip when a tire puncture or other failure occurs and the rider is forced to continue his travels on the new tire in spite of constant rain. And it's exactly at this time, in the rain, when a tire that has already been scrubbed in (if possible, over the entire width of the tread) is needed because, in rainy conditions, scrubbing in takes an especially long time, since tire abrasion is minimal. (By the way, this is entirely the opposite of the situation in racing, in which the greater slippage due to wet conditions can actually increase the abrasion on the rear tire.)

This is why some oldtimers carry a bit of sandpaper (or better still, emery cloth) along on a trip: so that they can use it to roughen the surface of a new tire. (This is

Hard-packed snow slipperiness

In the Alps, and in high mountains everywhere, it can even happen in the summer that, immediately after a curve, one will go from a dry road to one with hard-packed snow cover that has been perfectly preserved in shaded areas. This, of course, has nothing to do with rain per se but rather with sheer slipperiness, and in a situation like this, there are a few rules to apply that one should at least have practiced **mentally**:

1. In slippery snow, there is no more front brake! Pay close attention to the right hand, which will otherwise brake "by itself!"

2. Concentrate exclusively on the rear brake! Brief locking while braking is harmless but does extend the braking distance.

3. If, on a downhill and in spite of braking, the speed increases (and there's no real reduction in the grade to be expected and no comfortable escape route evident), then act *immediately:* put the motorcycle *down*—that is, with an energetically over-braked rear wheel, initiate a mild curve so that the slightly sideways bike slides out in the rear (see p. 133). However, don't be paralyzed by fear and wait (while gathering speed) until the next hairpin!

easily accomplished if the bike is on the centerstand, with the rear wheel turning; it's complete drudgery on the front. For this reason, the use of a solvent such as brake cleaner, to rub off the tires is widespread. However, this isn't exactly good for the tires and is thus not recommended.)

Sudden slipperiness

Especially in thunderstorms, one can ride around a curve and *abruptly* find himself on a wet and correspondingly slippery stretch of road. Thus, when riding in certain weather conditions, one must simply take this possibility into account, especially if there are storm clouds up ahead.

Okay, so once again, briefly, what are we supposed to do when it starts to rain and we feel like nothing is working anymore so we sit there, getting more and more anxious? Remember to:

1. Loosen the mouth, abdominals, and "seat" (buttocks).

2. Consciously place the hands very lightly on the grips.

3. Take a pause between breaths and "sit deeply into" the bike.

4. Look far ahead and let the shoulders drop; stretch out the neck; sit tall.

5. Choose a line that is more gentle and fluid than otherwise, and avoid sudden spikes in acceleration by planning (and looking) ahead.

6. Once in a while, apply the front brake briefly, but rather firmly, as a test of the available traction and as a confidence-building measure.

RIDER AND ROAD

The following recommendations pertain to the behavior of the rider in relationship to the road. This is, of course, chiefly about the rider's behavior in relationship to curves and cornering too, as stated on p. 144. First and foremost is the objective of **looking where you want to go**—we have already discussed this several times. Learning to "look" properly is the foundation of motorcycle training. Without a doubt, the most important objective in this group of recommendations is looking far ahead down the road.

LOOK FAR AHEAD

The coaster experiment showed what happens when the rider does not look far enough ahead, and how this makes it impossible to ride a motorcycle well. Anyone who has problems with looking far ahead should probably review the experiment (see p. 68).

Actually, every rider has this problem. There's the beginner who almost never looks far enough ahead and thus has not yet experienced how wonderful it is to ride with a **movement plan** based on the long view. There's the experienced sport rider who's already mastered looking far ahead but has problems with it when he loses his cool, whether because he feels forced to ride faster than he can or because he's tired or even exhausted. And finally even the world-class rider: in a critical enough situation, he, too, will allow his gaze to fall and will have to give himself a kick to reinstate the long view as quickly as possible. It bears repeating that there is no objective that, when **automated,** leads to such a pronounced improvement in skills as looking far ahead. However, it is one of the objectives that are very difficult to achieve at the beginning, even if the rider truly wants to follow it. He stubbornly resists its becoming **automatic,** even though it seems like it should be easy to carry out. There are deep-seated reasons for this, which lie in behaviors developed in the course of human evolutionary history, and it's especially difficult to do things that go against these kinds of behaviors.

Obviously, when the rider is looking far ahead, he should also be doing what is referred to as "reading the road": constantly monitoring the status of the road and its surface. Despite the inborn programmed behavior in conflict with doing this, learning to read the road is just a matter of the proper approach and emphasis. The rule of thumb is to watch the close-range view as often as possible but to focus on glancing farther ahead. Especially after a corner or curve, when a new view opens up, the rider should extend his view that much farther. This is the *baseline,* or starting point, even if it's constantly changing. Starting at this baseline, the rider can quickly jump to the mid-range view, maybe to quickly fix on a turn-in point, or to the short-range, maybe to get a quick look at the road surface, but just as quickly (and this is the hard part), the baseline condition, looking far ahead, should be re-established. In proficient riders, these changes in focus arise from an **automated** behavior that happens without **conscious attention,** as long as what they see in these brief glances is unremarkable.

Looking far ahead and **looking where you want to go** are more difficult if you are following another rider. It's all too easy to fix one's sights on the rider in front, when you should really be "looking through" him. Eberspächer (2002, p. 117) uses the example of a fly on a television screen: one doesn't stare fixedly at the fly but instead looks past it to watch the action.

It's true that following another rider can be tremendously helpful, because in the ideal situation, the follower can immediately imitate all of the movements of the rider in front (which is why following an uncertain rider can be a problem for many). This is called "shadowing." It happens almost by itself in a group ski lesson, when a line forms behind the instructor. It is a form of **imitative learning** that occurs simultaneously rather than after the fact; this is something we know not just from motorcycling classes but also from racing. An up-and-coming racer who can imitate, or "latch onto," a more experienced racer on the track will suddenly ride as though he belonged in the next class up. Training that includes simultaneous imitative learning as a component, can, of course, lead to substantial temporary im-

The inborn hindrance to looking far ahead

It may be surprising to learn that looking far ahead has been hindered in the course of human evolution, since humans' early way of life certainly required them to be *able* to look far into the distance. In contrast to most dryland creatures (to say nothing of those that inhabited the waters), humans have very good eyes—much better eyes, in some respects, than the big cats and most other mammals. As human beings became walkers over short and long distances, they monitored their area as far as the horizon (which might have been a day's march away); thus, they monitored things as far as their *interests and concerns* reached. Try to get a dog, even a well-trained and obedient one, to to carry out this kind of distant perception! But why do we humans now have this difficulty with looking far ahead?

All too often, looking far ahead goes against a deep-rooted behavior: the greater the amount of tension, the stronger the feeling of danger, and the sharper the experience of threat, the more restricted the view will be to the immediate area. This is an ancient human behavior for the management of dangers. It is completely beneficial as long as no high speeds are achieved. In a state of feeling threatened by external dangers, it is indeed highly inappropriate, and could even be life-threatening, to look off into the distance or even just to look beyond the immediate area of action. Humans have retained this behavior. As soon as a danger pops up (or even just the fear of the danger), our view is limited to the nearby surroundings. Thus, constantly renewed objectives have to be used to counteract this old pattern of behavior, and it takes considerable time before the proper behavior sinks in enduringly. The more confident the rider begins to feel, and thus the less danger he experiences, the more likely he is to be successful in implementing the objective, maintaining it over the long term, and ultimately avoiding relapse in a difficult high-stress situation. ■

provement, but if the trainee is left alone—for example, if he has to ride in front of the instructor—he will regress. The individual actions have been firmly mastered, but when it comes to vision and a **movement plan,** the trainee still has a long way to go.

LOOK UP WHILE BRAKING

Instruction on keeping the gaze up during braking belongs in any training to teach a rider to look in the right place. Another appropriate instructional topic is how the right place to look changes through the course of a corner or a curve.

It's a fact that braking causes one's gaze to fall, almost automatically. The kind of braking discussed here is not light deceleration as a result of minimal braking; instead, it's forceful braking in a corner or braking to manage a dangerous situation. The cause of this bad habit of letting one's gaze fall is the sudden distress in which the rider finds himself. However, the tension that develops even during normal braking drills in a training course is enough to elicit this response, despite the fact that there's no actual threat. As if on command, the rider trains his eyes on the spot right in front of his front wheel, often so much that an observer can see the movement in his helmet. This habit is anything but useful, especially if one considers the importance of finding an escape route and exploiting the gaps (see p. 129).

LOOK DEEP INTO CORNERS AND CURVES

Looking deep into corners and curves is a useful corollary to looking far ahead. Even after the rider has more or less mastered looking far ahead, before a corner or curve there's always a danger that his sights will get "snagged" somewhere around the entrance, no matter how well he's been looking far ahead up to that point. As mentioned previously, riding then literally turns into "piecework": consequently, the rider must "claw" his way from point to point, and his overall smooth flow is entirely lost.

LOOK BEYOND THE NEXT CORNER OR CURVE

Once one is able to ride in accordance with his mental image rather than the perceived image (see p. 73), it doesn't cause him any trouble in the least to not only look far into a corner but also to look into the next stretch of road, which at the moment isn't even visible. If he really wants to ride according to his movement plan, then he can't wait until the last minute to create the plan. This is especially important because the corners that are still hidden and the subsequent part of the road can absolutely have an influence on his line in the part of the corner that he can already see (p. 58 and Figure 25). This is not something that's valid only for a memorized racetrack. Even on the street, a rider can have some idea of how a series of corners will continue, even if he can't see all of it, and he can construct his movement plan in accordance with that idea (whereby he would also plan to include some reserves for unforeseen circumstances).

The great value of the objective of looking deep into the corners is that it supports the rider as he strives to constantly construct hypotheses about what is coming next (**hypotheses construction**). The most important of these hypotheses are those related to the dangers that might be hidden in a concealed part of the lane or a stretch of road that the rider can't see.

The next three objectives are related to riding the proper line (**ideal line**). They speak for themselves and need no further explanation. *Why* this is the case was explained in detail on page 58.

LINGER ON THE OUTSIDE

USE A LATE TURN-IN

USE A LATE APEX

These three objectives for cornering are closely related to each other. Lingering on the outside and using a late turn-in are really two sides of the same coin; a rider might prefer one or the other way of thinking about it. Both lead to the same result: a late **apex,** which some jokingly refer to as an extra life insurance policy. In principle, the objective "late apex" could stand alone for all three, but it doesn't express concretely enough exactly *how* a rider can "move" the apex in the direction of the corner's exit. These kinds of objectives can never be formulated simply and clearly enough!

The next two objectives are a little more complicated and have more to do with sporty riding.

THINK ABOUT CORNER EXIT SPEED

The reminder "corner exit speed" can be used to accomplish two things. First, in sporty riding, for example, one should not take the individual corners in a series of corners as fast as humanly possible; instead, one should pay special attention to riding such that he will be going fast *out of the last corner of the series,* even if this is at the expense of his speed in one of the earlier corners (see Figure 25). The basic rule is to take a fast corner and make it faster at the expense of a slower one, but not the other way around. To put it another way, don't worry about letting a slower corner become even slower if it allows you to take a faster one even faster.

Second, the key words "corner exit speed" should also activate the objective to set up the line through a corner such that, relatively early in the curve, its radius can be made a little larger. This not only leads to a faster exit speed but also makes for greater safety reserves at the exit. The fundamental way in which one achieves this is by using the late **apex,** as mentioned above. A "special" line used in racing (**racing line**), with which early acceleration can be even further enhanced, versus the **ideal line,** was discussed on page 64.

GET ON THE GAS EARLY

Naturally, getting back on the gas early is also an important part of achieving optimal corner exit speed. It's not enough to plan a line that allows early acceleration. One must also then actually *open the throttle!* In the second part of a corner, many an infamous late-braker gives up the advantage hard-won in the beginning of the corner. Obviously, any early acceleration done while the bike is still leaned over will have to be executed with extreme *sensitivity.* (This is why the objective that follows, "Apply the gas," is also important in connection with early acceleration.) Delivering a sudden burst of power ("whacking" the throttle) might have a spectacular effect but, for an expert rider, is more a sign that the acceleration got started too late. Otherwise, the power surge would not have been possible to apply so abruptly. When early acceleration is absolutely not possible, this is a sign that the line could probably have been improved.

KEEP YOUR HEAD LEVEL IN THE LEAN

Finally, in connection with looking deep into corners, we have to talk about the carriage of the head. If the rider holds his head at the same leaned angle as his torso or of the motorcycle itself, especially with greater lean angles, it is no longer possible to look far enough ahead into the corners (p. 68). Riders sense this most profoundly on uphill corners of mountain roads.

APPLY THE GAS

This means that after the throttle is closed, the twistgrip should immediately be re-opened until the play in the throttle cable is taken up, so that even the slightest additional twist will produce instant results. One can feel this point very distinctly, and riders should make it a habit, after each time they close the throttle, to immediately turn the grip just as much as needed to take up the slack in the cable. It's true that one might need the gas only in certain situations, but when it is needed, then it's right there, right away. For example, if a rider is approaching a

corner, still going way too fast for it, and is already braking hard (and maybe also has a few jitters about taking the corner), then it will require quite an effort for him to re-open the throttle on top of everything else. And if applying the gas hasn't become a habit—been made **automatic**—then it is an activity that requires **conscious thought** and will therefore be most likely forgotten in such a situation.

Once applying the gas is sufficiently automated (thanks to objectives that have been set up and followed often enough), one has a wonderful maneuver (**action plan**) at his disposal: in the middle of a corner, he can apply the power, suddenly, with the finest modulation and at precisely the right moment. In this way, when power is needed, one doesn't first have to wait a moment while getting through the play in the throttle cable to get to the point at which the gas actually comes on—and then perhaps give it too much gas because he is lagging about a tenth of a second behind (see also p. 47).

Applying the gas can be used every time a finely gauged, precise infusion of power is needed: (1) in the early acceleration out of a corner, when the bike is still leaning (see also "Get on the gas early" above); (2) also and especially if the bike is leaning on a wet road and even more urgently if one wants to test how much **traction** is still available; (3) on extremely slippery surfaces (see the circle corresponding to ice in Kamm's circle (p. 99); (4) for extremely slow riding, especially in turns with the handlebars at lock, when, at the moment forward movement is really needed, there is absolutely no time to get to the gas and the slightest over-throttle will be far too much; and (5) for so-called stabilization gas, the next objective discussed.

GIVE IT GAS FOR STABILITY

The so-called **roll movement** that happens around the longitudinal axis, which is the movement that the motorcycle makes as it initiates a corner, has to be stopped when the right lean angle has been achieved (see p. 38). There are two possible ways to do this: (1) one can use steering at the right moment to make the corner's radius a bit smaller (which increases the centrifugal force that helps keep the bike up), or (2) one can leave the steering unchanged, but give it gas for stability, that is, become a tiny bit faster (which also increases the centrifugal force that helps keep the bike up). In practice, a mixture of both is commonly used. In slow corners or even hairpins, decreasing the radius can be disconcerting to

Rolling resistance and stabilization gas

In longer curves and with larger lean angles, a certain baseline amount of gas is needed simply to maintain the initial speed. Rolling resistance is considerably greater when the bike is leaning. One can test this out in a circle, by starting with a certain speed with a large lean, pulling in the clutch, and then letting the motorcycle continue to roll, keeping the same lean (that is, with ever smaller circles) to the greatest possible extent. After this, one can try the same thing in a straight line and compare the distance that the motorcycle rolls after the clutch is pulled in. ∎

the rider, so giving it gas for stability is more likely to be used.

The situation is completely different when there are very fast roll movements, such as those used in races through quick chicanes. The different roll movements follow so fast on each other's heels that it's not possible to use gas or steering to stop them. Instead, they are stopped when the next one, in the opposite direction, is initiated. This can be achieved only with very pronounced steering inputs (see p. 138).

Using gas for stability not only makes it possible to keep the steering steady but also simultaneously causes a slight shift in the load toward the rear wheel, which is almost always an advantage.

Figure 81. The feet in the long-distance position, almost like lean-angle feelers.

It's not at all a bad habit to get lightly on the throttle to stabilize the bike once the necessary lean angle has been reached. This starts, of course, with "applying" gas, as described above, because gas for stabilization has to be deployed at precisely the right moment with exact modulation. The **habituation** of using gas for stability is a prerequisite for the gradual acquisition of early acceleration, which facilitates a higher corner exit speed (see "Get on the gas early" above).

RIDING POSTURE

The most important objectives for attaining and maintaining a beneficial riding position and posture for riding are described below.

TOES IN

Let's start with something that seems to be nothing more than a formality. It is not uncommon to approach riders from behind who have an otherwise entirely tidy silhouette except that their boots are sticking out diagonally to the lower right and left like two paddles (Figure 81). This is not only aesthetically displeasing, but in certain situations, it's also somewhat risky and a sure sign that the rider is violating the next rule.

ON THE BALLS OF THE FEET

There are two possible positions for the foot on the peg: the ball-of-foot position, in which only the toe-end of the boot hangs over the peg to the front (maybe by 8 to 10 centimeters; Figure 82), and the "hooked-heel" position (Figure 83). In the latter position, the foot peg is right in front of the heel, and the larger part of the foot thus hangs over the peg to the front (Figure 83). On motorcycles with even a slightly sporty riding position, the foot (obviously somewhat dependent on the rider's size and stature) will more or less point diagonally downward.

Figure 82. The ball of the foot resting on the footpeg.

If one really wants to ride with a good sense of (a feel for) the bike in order to form a single unified system (**integration**) with it, this is much easier to achieve with the balls of the feet on the pegs. This has more to do with loosely setting the hands on the grips (p. 145) than one might assume at first glance. Thus, one will do himself a favor if he makes a habit of riding with the balls of his feet on the pegs, either overall or at least when it's time to get down to business and he wants to have fun on demanding roads that require precision riding.

However, two objections to the ball-of-foot position are always raised. The first is that it tightens the angle of the knee. This is a disadvantage because it makes long rides uncomfortable. For this reason, one's riding gear should be cut such that it doesn't dig into the backs of the knees and impede circulation. If the necessary external circumstances are present (appropriate seating position, sufficient circulation), then how long one can or wants to sit uninterruptedly in the ball-of-foot position is a question of the degree of conditioning. Certainly on a long ride, at some point the rider simply *needs* to set his feet a little farther forward (putting them in the hooked-heel position). There's nothing wrong with this, but at this point, it is usually a better idea for the rider to take a break to completely stretch his knees out and walk around a bit.

The second objection is only half valid. The opinion voiced in this objection is that, for shifting and especially braking (in which under some circumstances every fraction of a second is important), one would have to first slide the foot a little farther forward to reach the lever if he uses the ball-of-foot position. This is true: one must indeed move the foot slightly forward (which is why it's not much fun to try this position for the first time wearing boots with deep tread—one might just give up).

However, it's wrong to think that one can get to the brake lever faster from the hooked-heel position than from the ball-of-foot position. Although for shifting or braking, one does have to move the foot forward from the latter position (and admittedly this might become irritating to some after a while), from the hooked-heel position, one has to lift the front of the foot to reach the necessary lever, which requires first moving it sideways around *the shift- or brake-lever*. Thus, one can't access either lever immediately, neither from the ball position nor from the hooked-heel position. In both instances, one first has to bring the foot into position, and this takes the same amount of time, within hundredths of a second! If there's any difference at all, this minimal time difference is absorbed in the disproportionately greater amount of time that makes up the stopping distance, in the day-to-day variation in the performance of the individual rider, and in the still greater differences that exist among different riders. Only on touring motorcycles, with their comfortable seating positions and footpegs relatively far forward, do the toes stay high enough in the hooked-heel position

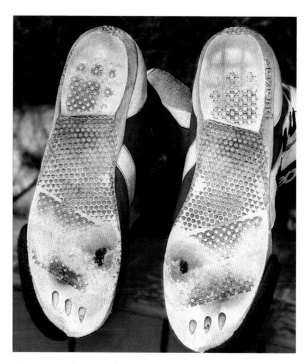

Figure 84. *These rather worn-out racing boots were almost never used in the hooked-heel position, as is evident from the tread pattern in the area of the soles, which is still recognizable. By comparison, the soles under the balls of the feet have been almost completely worn through by the footpegs. (*Security Evo *made by Daytona)*

Figure 83. *The foot in the hooked-heel position.*

that they don't first have to be lifted around the lever before shifting or braking.

In any case, the advantages of the ball-of-foot position are great enough that it's worthwhile for all motorcyclists who enjoy sporty riding to carefully consider the position of their feet on the pegs. Always stick with the ball-of-foot position? Or routinely use the ball-of-foot position and use the hooked-heel position only when fatigued on a long tour and the legs start to ache? Or use the ball position only for really blasting through the twisties? (See Figure 84.) Whatever an individual decides, his personal objectives then have to be formulated in accordance with his decision.

ELBOWS SLIGHTLY BENT

Many motorcyclists have a tendency to lock their elbows when they get tired. Some always ride this way. However, even when one wants to sit up straighter than the position dictated by the type of motorcycle, the arms should remain slightly bent. This, once again, is related to riding at a high level of **integration.** Riding with locked elbows diminishes sensitivity for the feedback from the bike and the road, not only in sensory but also in motor aspects. Try riding extremely slowly with your elbows locked and you will experience the decreased sensitivity!

Even if one has ridden with his elbows in the correct position for years, once in a while he can still catch himself riding with stiff, straight arms, usually on a long trip when it's getting late in the day. If this happens, it's time to resurrect the supported objective, that is, to use the appropriate reminder sticker and work on correcting the problem.

HEAD HIGH, NECK EXTENDED

The above description of how objectives should be formulated includes the requirement that they be briefly and simply stated. Another factor to consider is that, if at all possible, *avoidance objectives* should not be used. Avoidance objectives are ones that are negatively stated—that is, they state what *not to do*—and since they first have to be "translated" into what one *should be doing,* they have less persuasive power. The avoidance-objective corollary of "head high, neck extended," might state something like "Don't roll yourself into a ball, don't hunch your shoulders and pull your neck in" (see the description of the typical fearful posture on p. 147).

CHEST OUT

If a physical therapist tells a patient "push the chest out," he means the same thing as "head high, neck extended," and this is what happens if these prompts are followed. An individual rider might be more likely to feel and realize what to do if he uses the former "command" as his objective, while the latter "command" may work better for another rider. However, both riders will notice, in the same way, that their ability to look ahead improves (because it's no longer limited by the helmet at the browline). More important, both will assume a position that counters the fearful posture, thus negating the physical preconditions necessary for fear to take hold.

BALANCE THE HEAD AND CHEST WITH WIND PRESSURE

Speaking of physical therapists, so-called *static hold* (simply holding a particular position against an influencing force), which demands a constant muscular exertion, is entirely unwelcome in physical therapy. However, motorcyclists experience static hold at higher speeds, especially on highways and certainly in racing, even if the rider makes himself "really small behind the ignition key."

The rider should try to lean his upper body far enough forward to bring it into balance with the wind pressure—that is, he should more or less try to lie on the air cushion. If he alternately leans forward and then back a few times, he will feel it when he reaches the position that requires the least amount of muscular exertion to keep himself up. Then he needs to do the same thing with his head. Because of the turbulence that affects the head more than anything else, it's true that some exertion will still be needed to keep it still, but the right position will relieve the rider of considerable physical exertion. This can make even long highway rides bearable—and not so boring, since one can ride considerably faster.

Once one has practiced this balancing a few times—and for this, a supported objective can be very useful—the technique will become **automated** and the optimal position will happen all by itself, even with changing speeds. If the rider is sitting loosely enough and intends to preserve this looseness, he'll do it right without much additional effort.

Now, there are just three more objectives for posture while cornering. A few have already been discussed in connection with looseness and looking far ahead, such as "keep your head level in the lean."

INSIDE KNEE FORWARD

The rider should start taking a corner by moving the inside knee forward by just 2 or 3 centimeters. He will definitely feel clearly that the forward movement of the knee is actually a movement forward and *downward.* Frequently, this simple movement can lead to an instant and substantial improvement in cornering within the first few attempts, especially if the rider is still a little uncomfortable taking corners and thus had a tendency to *push* the bike away. By "pushing away" I mean that the rider pushes the bike down into the lean and puts it at a more extreme angle than required on the basis of the weight and centrifugal force, and in so doing, the less experienced rider's upper body doesn't need to lean at quite so much of an angle. (Pushing, quickly and aggressively, is only useful for a quick swerve.)

The next step, along with the forward movement of the knee, is to bring the inside shoulder forward. This further increases the movement of the knee until it becomes necessary not only to turn the pelvis but also to slide one's seat toward the inside. In spite of what unfolds in this step, it is not meant as a warm-up for **hanging off,** although one could certainly start out this way (see p. 114). Instead, it primarily facilitates something else: it makes it *impossible* for the rider to push the bike away and lean without him. The posture achieved is more likely to lead to the opposite: because the center of mass of his body has been shifted toward the *inside,* the rider keeps the bike more upright and leans it at *less* of an angle than would otherwise be required on the basis of the weight and centrifugal force.

PUSH WITH THE INSIDE HAND; KEEP OUTSIDE HAND LOOSE

On a normal motorcycle, as the lean angle increases, there is an increasing force on the handlebars toward falling to the inside. If the handlebars were to be let go, the radius of the curve would shrink and the motorcycle would immediately stand up. The rider has to put some pressure on the handlebars to counteract this tendency toward **standing up.** Most riders have become so well **adapted** to this tendency that they don't usually notice the force they exert on the handlebars to counteract it until they pay **conscious attention** to it. They are most likely to notice it spontaneously if they frequently switch among motorcycles that have different degrees of this tendency to stand up. However, most riders can't give

any information about how they initiate the force on the handlebars: by pulling with the outside hand, by *pushing* with the inside hand, or some *combination of both.* Measurements of the forces exerted by the rider have shown that all three forms occur. For this reason, this objective is somewhat controversial. But I don't think it's so bad, especially since the **steering moment** that initiates the corner, the so-called **steering input** (see "Physics of riding 1," p. 37), also happens by *pushing with the same hand* that then becomes the inside hand. But with this objective, as is the case with several of the recommended objectives discussed here, the main point has to do with another effect: the point is to prevent riders from simultaneously exerting too much force on both the right and left side of the handlebars, resulting in two forces that mutually cancel each other out almost entirely, except for the tiny desired difference that is needed to keep the bike from falling in. If the rider does simultaneously exert the same amount of force on both the right and left sides, he pays a penalty in sensory and motor sensitivity, and the habit can lead to tension and cramping. However, this can't happen if, from the outset, one of the two hands rests loosely on the handlebar grip. Once the objective has been firmly established, then a useful little **action program** will have been developed, and the effect is that, even when the rider is under high pressure, he'll automatically ride every corner with one hand loose on the grip. Of course, the more challenging the road (that is, the more corners it has), the more often this will happen.

KEEP KNEES ON THE TANK

Keeping the knees firmly on the tank, or even squeezing the tank with the knees, has long since lost the meaning it once had in earlier motorcycling times. However, it is wrong to see the position of the knees as entirely meaningless and especially to ride with the knees slightly spread. It's not for nothing that there were actual knee cushions on the sides of some tanks. *The greater the amount of physical contact with the motorcycle, the better the sensory connection.* In critical situations, such as the escape offroad (p. 132), knees that are not just kept against the tank but even briefly pressed into it, definitely provide an advantage. (Compare also dangling legs, the bad habit of letting the feet hang back for a moment when riding off, p. 104.)

Applying the front brake hard and briefly until the wheel locks (maximum: 0.1 second)

Be absolutely certain to ride in a straight line, at about 40 to 50 km/h, and pull the front brake abruptly, so hard that the front wheel locks. *But don't wait until the front wheel is still and then decide to let go of the brake—with a locked wheel, that could already be too long!* Instead, plan in advance to apply the brake only very briefly (maximum of 0.1 seconds) but very forcefully and to let the brake lever go again practically at the same moment! If the effort is initially too weak—this is usually the case in the first attempt—the exercise should be repeated as often as necessary until the rider hears the sound of a locked wheel on the pavement. After a short time, it becomes so much fun that many riders, even if they approached the exercise with some trepidation, don't want to stop making short, black streaks on the pavement, even at the expense of the lifespan of their front tire.

Everyone who tries this exercise for the first time is surprised by the strength of the short, sharp jerk. In the brief instant that it takes to lock the wheel, the rider is still a long way from using the full braking power! The extremely steep increase in braking pressure—intentionally brought about in this exercise—creates a situation that can be fateful for the fearful braker: "dynamic overbraking" (Weidele 1994, p. 36). The dynamic shift in wheel load (that is, the additional load on the front wheel and the reduction of load at the rear wheel) has just begun, and consequently the front wheel has not yet achieved the full amount of additional tire load (which would substantially increase the transferable braking forces) by the time it has already locked up. Motorcycles with fork designs that minimize brake dive offer slightly better conditions.

This exercise is extremely beneficial because it familiarizes the rider with the idea of a locked front wheel so that he isn't terrified if this happens under hard braking, and he knows to let go of the brake right away. Locking and letting go must be one and the same action! This exercise is also useful because it gives the rider a new technique in his repertoire that can be used to quickly test how much traction is available on a questionable road surface. Consider road surfaces in unfamiliar areas: even if it's a very good road, once the surface is wet, a rider suddenly has no idea whether the road becomes slippery as ice forms or stays reasonably grippy. Around home, with familiar surfaces, this uncertainty is much less common. At least by the time a rider actually tries these braking exercises, he will realize how closely related they are. ∎

OBJECTIVES FOR PRACTICE

Objectives—*supported* objectives—are not only a good aid for getting used to a particular behavior; they also help when one has undertaken to work through particular *exercises* (standard exercises from basic rider training or exercises from other training courses), which would probably never happen without the support of the objectives. Whenever possible, one should do exercises with a group of fellow riders or at least one other rider. People are much more likely to go to an empty parking lot or a vacant sidestreet to give exercises a try when there's someone who will go with them. Each of the following fundamental exercises should be mastered before one moves on to the following exercise.

APPLY THE FRONT BRAKE SEVERAL TIMES BRIEFLY AND FIRMLY TO ACHIEVE A PRONOUNCED DIVE

Short, very hard braking with the front brake is an extremely useful exercise. If done at the beginning of every ride, it's not only a test of one's brakes, but the rider gets a renewed, very concrete idea each time of the corresponding deceleration. The characteristics of the brake will become more and more familiar and expected, even under hard braking, which people don't practice nearly enough. If done in the rain, this practice is also good for getting an idea of how much **grip** is still available in the situation. Usually it's surprising how much **traction** the tires still find. The information gained by performing this exercise also spontaneously increases the rider's confidence about his ability to properly assess the limits of lean angle. A caveat is essential: if one does not have antilock brakes, he must be prepared in advance to instantly let go of the brake if the wheel locks! If one truly wants to approach the point at which the wheel locks in this exercise, it's a good idea to first perform the exercise described in the sidebar "Applying the front brake . . ."

AT A CONSTANT 60 KM/H, SHIFT UP AND DOWN THROUGH THE GEARS: 3 . . . 6 . . . 1 . . . 6 . . . 1 . . . ETC.

This odd abbreviation (3 . . . 6 . . . 1 . . . 6 . . . 1 . . . etc.) is meant to sum up the following exercise: starting at a speed of 50 to 60 km/h, which should be maintained as steadily as possible and which one would usually ride in third gear, the rider shifts up to the highest gear, all the while keeping the motorcycle at the same speed. Then, gear by gear, he shifts all the way down to first, again keeping the bike at the same speed, and then shifts back up to the highest gear, step by step, and so on, several times in a row.

A rider should really try this exercise on every bike with which he wants to become familiar. It's a quick way to internalize a particular bike's individual gear spacing (acquire it as a **program** to get that "gut" feeling), which makes a rider better at using the throttle to achieve more or less the right rpm for the gear when shifting down.

It must be emphasized that this exercise can turn out badly! Some don't even try to match engine speed, or do so only haphazardly. In addition, because the rider knows that when he lets the clutch back out there might be a bit of a jolt, he does so slowly and cautiously, until the rear wheel slows the motor to the right rpm. This isn't "pretty," but it will work well enough most of the time until, someday, the following happens: the rider is approaching an average corner, fairly quickly for his level of experience, perhaps in the rain and perhaps even downhill. He brakes carefully, shifts down, and maybe he's starting to run out of time and is already entering the corner. For this reason, he's even more careful about letting the clutch back out, although he would **very** much welcome some engine braking (*engine drag torque*) at the moment. With this level of caution, he takes even more time to let the clutch back out. The clutch is still not yet engaged, but the rider will soon reach the proper lean angle. Because it's getting urgent, he lets the clutch lever out a little faster at the end of its travel. This leads to just a bit of a jolt, but comes at exactly the worst possible moment: all this time, the tires have been accommodating increasing **lateral forces,** to which suddenly a **longitudinal force** is added. Even though this is only momentary, it's too much, and the rear wheel slides out.

DOWNSHIFT AND BRAKE SIMULTANEOUSLY

The example just described makes clear that it can be very useful to brake and downshift at the same time. There is no reason—except lack of practice—for doing them in sequence. But the brief throttle input with the simultaneous hand braking demands intense concentration at first and should therefore be practiced to the point of mastery. This will make it so that when it is applied in an everyday situation, it's the natural thing to do and doesn't require **conscious thought.**

PRACTICE VERY TIGHT U-TURNS, VERY TIGHT CIRCLES

Tight turns at low speeds have haunted us since our first rider-training classes, but they *can* be improved to the point of perfection.

With the steering at lock, using only the foot brake and the throttle, it takes a long time before one can complete a 180-degree turn or even a complete circle without taking the feet off the pegs. But what's the value of this little feat? Just so that we can turn around on a country road with our feet on the pegs?

Tight turns taken at a walking pace are a very effective way to train **coordination** and also are a good test of the rider's degree of relaxation. Very good riders can also ride *very* slowly. The opposite is also generally true: inexperienced riders with minimal practice not only can't ride especially fast (which is a good thing), but they also can't ride especially slowly. In advanced rider-training courses, the first slow-riding drills are a surprisingly good indicator of how later exercises will turn out.

Even for an experienced rider, it's a good idea to practice, once in a while as a refresher, extremely slow riding and especially slow U-turns and circles. In addition, there's hardly a better measure of how well one is riding at a particular time. However, the least bit of tension is enough to make the exercise turn out badly.

HOLD THE SHIFT LEVER UNTIL THE CLUTCH IS BACK OUT

CLUTCH AND SHIFT ALMOST SIMULTANEOUSLY

LIGHTLY PRE-LOAD THE SHIFTER

These three objectives aren't actually intended as particular exercises. Certainly, one should try out these recommendations for the first time in a safe place, but they can then just be added to one's everyday riding repertoire. As reminders, they speak for themselves. They were explained in greater detail on page 143, where they were used as examples of the use of supported objectives as a training method.

GENERAL PRACTICE

LEAN, LEAN, LEAN

Finally, there are just a few recommendations that aren't actually objectives like those described above. Instead, they are *general* suggestions related to developing certain behaviors to have *at the ready*. They are important for critical situations or emergencies and thus can't really be practiced, at least not under realistic circumstances. However, one can familiarize himself with them through mental training, even while riding. In this sense, they actually are objectives, because the rider can undertake them for a little while (using stickers as reminders) every time the opportunity presents itself, to at least mentally practice how to handle a certain situation.

Just to avoid confusion, it is important to clarify that any mention of "laying the bike over" is about increasing the lean angle, not about laying it down. In every corner that requires more lean, one has the opportunity to pretend, for example, that the corner tightens unexpectedly and he's now going too fast; or that something is obstructing the planned line; or that there's a puddle, a patch of oil, or a bit of gravel that he has to avoid by riding farther to the inside of the corner.

These are situations in which, aside from other measures such as *standing the bike up and braking* or *braking in a corner,* the rider should also have at his disposal further *leanability,* that is, the ability to increase the lean angle. However, this is at his disposal and readily available for immediate use only if he has perfectly mastered the instant increase of the lean—and this is something that one actually can practice! Even though one is only imagining the "surprises" in the corners, he can still carry out—in reality—the necessary reaction to them, that is, instantly increasing the lean angle by means of an clear steering impulse. The steering impulse comes about by means of a sudden but light push with the inside hand and subsequent continued pressure, to maintain the increased lean. (Compare the objective "Push with the inside hand," p. 157). The first few times, this requires some conscious attention, but it really is only a very gentle suggestion of a cautious push—it's surprising how big

the effect is! Gradually, the implementation of the steering impulse (which had been there all along, but only vaguely) becomes automated, after which the proper modulation is also no longer a problem.

The box "He who rides in fear of the lean is living dangerously" (p. 114) contains a detailed explanation of why leaning can be so useful.

ALWAYS BE AWARE OF AN ESCAPE ROUTE

There is hardly a situation in which one cannot practice identifying an escape route. If, at the beginning of a left-hand turn that suddenly becomes blocked, there's a driveway that goes straight, it doesn't take much training to identify and use this as an escape. However, in less benevolent situations, which are also usually less clear-cut, it's crucially important to exploit at lightning speed the best option that presents itself. It's these situations that require specific mental training. Plenty of examples of this were previously described (see p. 127).

If a rider's imagined escape is an offroad one, he can think through the process in his mind. However, one can hardly practice this in a way that adequately mimics an actual emergency—the practice can only happen at a slightly slowed pace and with only suggested braking before one rides off the road. The actual chain of events (indicated only by key words on the reminder sticker) is described in detail, starting on page 132.

BEWARE THE SYMPTOMS OF FLOW; CONSTANTLY MONITOR FLOW

Flow, the state of extreme well-being that can set in when one is completely absorbed in a task he has mastered, was discussed in detail on p. 107. Flow can be extraordinarily helpful in making long-lasting tasks easier to bear, because once one has forgotten himself in pursuit of the task, everything unrelated is blocked out. It is imperative, however, that the condition remain stable and thus under constant monitoring (regulated flow). Especially in motorcycling, if one experiences flow early in training, he'll have the tendency to take it too far—that is, he will continue to ramp up the intensity without any control. This is *unregulated flow,* which has great inherent danger in risky sports such as motorcycling because it allows one's acceptance of risk to grow unnoticed.

Escape offroad

1. Hard braking!
2. Release the brakes!
3. Simultaneously stand and shift your weight to the back!
4. Cautiously continue to brake!

Keep the clutch in!

"NOW I AM INVISIBLE" AS A WARNING

A sticker with the words "Now I am invisible" should instill the utmost vigilance in the rider for a possible situation that initially may seem to be entirely harmless but is actually dangerous, such as a low sun behind him. If one can see his own long shadow directly in front of him, it is cause for significant alarm because a low sun behind is one of the most treacherous situations that a motorcyclist can encounter (Figure 85). It is treacherous because although one's own vision could hardly be better, thanks to the light from behind, that of the other party to the potential accident, usually an oncoming vehicle or one planning to turn, is absolutely miserable. This dangerous asymmetry in visibility (of which one has no idea unless he has specifically *prepared* himself for it) is further heightened by the tiny silhouette of the motorcyclist, which, as we all know, is all too easily overlooked even in more beneficial light.

This situation occurs too seldom to allow for effective simulation training; its low incidence is the reason why we have to train ourselves to recognize this danger immediately when it does occur. Fortunately, we can still achieve a lot with **mental** training. For example: a car on the opposite side of the street stands ahead to the left waiting to turn, or an oncoming vehicle slows, perhaps to turn in front of or behind us. The training question would be: what would my shadow look like if I were completely invisible to that driver? One should then imagine this shadow as concretely as possible: quite long and stretching out precisely in the direction of the other vehicle in the potential accident. However, one can't just train himself do this without a dedicated and supported objective (for more, see p. 138).

JUMP UP BEFORE THE CRASH, HEAD ABOVE THE OBSTACLE

Finally, it is important to address a behavior that can't be trained in reality at all: standing up—or better yet, jumping up—during a crash with a car. By far the most common type of crash is one into the side of a car. And the less something can actually be prepared for during physical training, the more important mental training becomes, not only at night before falling asleep, when nicely relaxed, but also during riding because at this time

Figure 85. Seeing your own shadow stretching out in front of you is a danger signal: the motorcyclist has outstanding visibility with the sun behind him, but for the car driver, the motorcyclist is as good as invisible.

one can actually feel the motorcycle (from which he is supposed to jump in a crash), and this makes it a little more realistic. More detail, especially about how it's a matter of getting one's head up above the top of the vehicle, is given on page 134.

TRACK ERRORS (ERROR COUNTER)

Finally, just one more reminder: we should not just innocently overlook our riding errors and ascribe them to something (or someone) else. Instead, we should recognize them. This works best when one actually tracks them, either by symbolically tapping a certain bolt on the handlebars as if it were a button or by actually using an error counter (see p. 119).

If one catches himself having gone a long time without noting an error, then it's time to implement a reminder sticker stating the objective "Start noticing errors."

EPILOGUE

The Fascination of Motorcycling

Please don't expect that I will actually be able to describe just why it is that riding a motorcycle is fascinating. After all, it's one of the most complex and most widely divergent *constellation of motives* that I know of. Because it's always an entire constellation, one should never believe anyone who says that he knows *the reason* for the fascination. This is just talk from someone who wants to allow only one single reason, one single motive, to be the valid one, preferably his own.

If there weren't a whole bundle of motives, how else could we explain the multiplicity of extremely different types of motorcycles? They extend from chopper to supersport, from trials bike to highway cruiser, from true enduro to café racer, from streetfighter to supermoto, with many subtypes in between and always with new and surprising categories. And how do we explain the multiplicity of motorcyclists' groups with their completely different and often strange preferences?

The individual motives within this constellation of motives are bound with each other in many ways: some connections are quite direct, while others involve only a very loose association. For one rider, a particular motive might be central, and for the next, it might be some other motive. A third motive, of yet another rider, might not have the slightest meaning for either of the other two riders.

To create a picture of the diversity in which this fascination is rooted, a few randomly selected motives are mentioned below, in no particular order. One can immediately "try them on" to consider how far each might get him to the root of his own fascination. Some of these, in this or that form, are things we frequently hear (which doesn't say anything about their actual meaning); others are unusual or simply bizarre; and still others are actually dominant, even if they may only rarely be mentioned. However, with every one of these motives, if a particular rider puts it forward as *the motive par excellence,* invariably another rider will immediately object, making an observation to the contrary, because no single motive is universal and no single one, by itself, is enough to explain the fascination.

For example, there is always talk about the experience of strength, power, and even a supposed *omnipotence* that the motorcycle imparts. A powerful sound can certainly have such an effect. However, there are motorcyclists who exert disproportionately more power in their jobs or who manage disproportionately more powerful machines in their jobs and who are just as fascinated by riding and by their motorcycles.

Others talk about the *"temporary escapism,"* stepping outside of the coddling overprotection of modern society and escaping from the strict rules of everyday life and all of its social constraints. Thanks to the clothing, certain stereotypes, and group rituals, this has been made especially easy for the motorcyclist. However, there are also motorcyclists who, not only while riding but *always,* live outside of these rules and constraints and who nonetheless are consumed by the fascination.

Then there's the revered *group experience,* the strong feeling of "we," which is more pronounced the more emphatically a group distinguishes itself from others. However, as much as motorcyclists like to show up in packs, there are also motorcyclists, afflicted with the fascination, who are committed loners.

Without doubt, there's a notable *competitive aspect* among motorcyclists, and not just among those who favor sporty riding. However, there are many riders who would, in good faith, protest this notion as true of them, because they haven't yet realized that they instantly ride faster if they spy, even off in the distance, the taillight of another motorcycle. However, there are also riders who don't let another rider influence or affect them in the least, whether up ahead, passing, or joining from behind, yet they are still passionate motorcyclists and their fascination with the activity is not remotely diminished.

Still other riders say that the fascination is the unmatched allure of the unbelievable *acceleration* that can't be achieved by anything else on the road, not even a fast sportscar. However, how do we explain the Formula 1 drivers who are also fascinated by motorcycles, in some cases by rather sedate motorcycles at that?

Then there's having one's entire body surrounded by the billowing wind, which can also be an important motive, because it's a *direct sense of one's speed.* It's at least a mini-motive. However, as with the motive of acceleration, it is formulated too narrowly and puts the idea too much front and center, to say nothing of the fact that, beyond a certain speed, the wind is really not that pleasant anymore. Also, sailing and surfing can give one a similar feeling. In fact, there are riders who do everything they can (with fairings, windshields, adjustable spoilers, etc.) to avoid direct contact with all the wind and who nevertheless, or perhaps precisely because of this, continue to have fun riding their motorcycles and might even be obsessed with it.

Finally, there are all the *kinesthetic experiences* associated with riding, a multifaceted feeling of moving and being moved, which might also be called the "riding dynamic" or the melding together of motorcycle and rider. However, there are also real motorcyclists—and I use the term "real" advisedly—who like to ride but do so without great passion and sometimes even ride a little awkwardly, and among whom the fascination and the obsession and the gleam in their eyes start in the garage: in tinkering with or admiring the bike as well as in the planning and discussion of further improvements.

Very few authors have seriously applied themselves to writing about the fascination of the motorcycle and of riding. Above all others, the following deserve mention: Apel (1984), Hagstotz (1990), Koch (1990), Nowak (1986), Rheinberg (1986), Schulz and others (1990), and Würzberg (1985). Their contributions are best in the places where the authors don't explain, but instead describe, thereby imparting a direct insight into the multiplicity of ways in which motorcycles are experienced.

I could spend a lot more time stirring the huge pot of motives and pulling out individual ones. No motive would go unchallenged, even though they all ring true at some point (just not all the time). In any case, the motive par excellence does not exist. The fascination of motorcycles and riding them can be grasped only when one actually gets on a motorcycle and experiences riding for himself. Then, he can also understand much better why it is, for example, that sport riders and "squids" have no ability to understand the cruising chopper rider, and vice versa, and why each responds to the other with a sense of almost moral outrage and shakes his head in dismay. Everyone considers his own motive (or his own narrow set of motives, to the extent that he even grasps them) as the only possible motive for riding, at least for "true" riding. He doesn't have the slightest conception of the great multi-dimensional constellation of motives that exists beyond his own.

Perhaps the fascination of riding lies precisely in the fact that it's so hard to determine what the fascination really is. Maybe it's because the reasons for our fascination are largely hidden in that deep, wordless part of ourselves.

Glossary

The terminology and concepts included in the glossary appear in boldface type in the text. Boldface is also used in this glossary to point out other related terms or concepts included in the glossary.

The following explanations of these terms and concepts are neither complete nor the most generic definitions; they are intended to help orient the reader to the terms and concepts as they are used in the context of this book.

ABS   ABS (antilock braking system) allows total braking without locking the wheels, something that absolutely must be avoided, especially locking the front wheel. Locking the front wheel leads almost inevitably to a crash. The superiority of a brake system with ABS is especially evident in braking on a surface with areas of differing traction. A secondary benefit of ABS that cannot be underestimated is that a rider who is certain that ABS will protect him from overbraking (to the point of lock) is less timid in his braking and thus more likely to brake strongly enough and with a sufficient increase in pressure. This means that even outside of the control range of ABS, he achieves better braking results.

action program   See **program.**

adaptation, adaption, adapted   Accommodation in the widest possible sense to the dominant circumstances in the environment, which can include both an extremely short-term accommodation by an *individual* as well as an extremely long-term accommodation, such as that which occurs in the adaptive changes of a *species.* Adaptation is one of the most important processes in the emergence and development of life and in its continued existence. The mechanisms of accommodation can have quite varied manifestations (compare the instant adaptation of an organ such as the eye on changing lighting conditions; the slightly longer-term adaptation of an individual when he learns to find a useful escape route; the long-term adaptation of a population such as that which occurs in the transfer of a learned behavior to a succeeding generation; and the

extremely long-term accommodation such as an adaptive change within a species). *Pre-adaptation* (accommodation in advance) exists when, for some reason, a change occurs within a species that represents a (coincidental) accommodation to environmental circumstances that don't even exist at the time of the change. With their extremely high center of mass relative to their footprint, human beings were doubtless pre-adapted to the single-track vehicle.

anticipation   Consideration of the possible events or incidents that might happen, such as a hazard (hazard anticipation; see also **hypothesis construction**).

apex   In cornering, the apex is the point on the chosen line on which that line comes closest to the inside edge of the road. The exact location of the apex is thus determined by the rider. In contrast, the geometric apex of the curve is determined by the design of the road. It is located at the point at which the the change in direction of the overall curve has passed halfway through the tangents on the inside of the curve (Figure 86). Neither concept is used consistently and both are often used in the same sense.

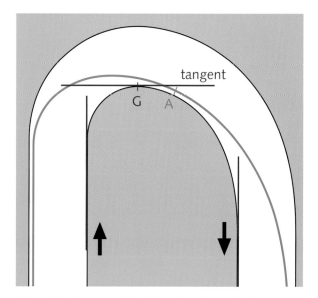

Figure 86. The apex of a rider's line through the corner (A) and the geometric apex (G).

automation, automated, automatic   Courses of action that initially can only be achieved slowly, step-by-step, and under conscious direction (such as a passage on the piano) can, with increasing practice, require less and less **conscious attention** and become increasingly automated. The control and direction of these *automated actions* is taken over by acquired **programs.** Such courses of action can be increasingly automated through training, so that they finally run without any conscious attention at all. Some highly automated actions don't even require a conscious decision to start. All that's needed is a corresponding external stimulus. Some actions are not only initiated by the decision to start but they also require conscious decisions during the process—for example, so that a longer action program is continued or that an alternative program will be selected. Modifications are possible in all automated actions, and in many cases even necessary. These modifications are consciously willed or are likewise automated actions. Modifications occur, for example, to alter the speed of a course of action or to adapt the course of action to respond to external input arising from the course of action itself (feedback-driven courses of action are so-called "sensory-motor programs").

behavior program   see **program.**

body concept   A spatial schematic picture of one's own body that gradually develops through the experience of space. The body concept can be extended beyond the limits of one's actual body, so that, for example, tools can also be incorporated (see **prosthesis**).

braking point   Mainly in racing, but also in certain training exercises, this is the point on the selected line, before a corner, at which the brakes should be applied (beginning of the braking zone). A substantial part of track training is devoted to the precise determination of braking points.

capsize zone   A particular condition that occurs in a single-track vehicle in which the vehicle, because of too little speed, has not yet developed sufficient inherent stability (for more detail, see box The Physics of Riding, 2, p. 46).

cascade of errors   Errors in longer courses of action, such as riding a section of track (or reciting a poem), tend not to occur exclusively in coincidental distribution. It's much more the case—especially when the mastery of the activity is not yet complete or there is a lot of pressure to perform—that individual errors immediately cause another error or several more. In extreme cases, such as when a person is frightened, this can lead to cascades of errors, which ultimately can no longer be managed and lead to a failure in performance (fall, accident, etc.).

conceptual aid   An image or idea that improves an action or makes it easier by calling up a particular feeling. Conceptual aids are often unrelated to the intended action and and may even be factually nonsensical ("imagine that you aren't sitting up on *top* but rather deep *within*."). They can be used in preparation for an activity or while the activity is being carried out.

conditioning   The concept of conditioning was originally used for the connection between *stimulus* and *reflex.* It was later expanded to the connection between stimulus and *response,* and then to *situation* and *response.* According to this, a behavior or action is considered to be *conditioned* if it is a fixed reaction connected to a particular triggering situation (such as when pulling back the hand when one feels sudden pain at the fingertips). Numerous conditioned responses have been genetically transmitted (inborn), such as the fear of snakes, but many are acquired (learned). Just as conditioned responses can be acquired, the *re-conditioning* of responses is possible. An extreme case of this is so-called "brainwashing," which is based on an incomprehensible complex of systematic re-conditioning. In everyday riding situations and in training, this is mainly a matter of individual alterations in conditioned responses. Many riders are unfortunately conditioned, for example, to focus on the vehicle in front of them, whereas a re-conditioning to a focus on the surrounding gaps would be beneficial.

conscious attention   This is required for performance of an action if it has not been sufficiently **automated** to the point that the course of action runs by itself, without constant conscious management.

contact patch   The term for the part of the tires' surface that comes into contact with the road surface. Transfer of all forces occurs by way of the contact patches (**longitudinal forces** under acceleration and braking, **lateral forces** in cornering). Each tire's contact patch can be reduced to a single point, the contact point, and a line can be imagined that connects the two points. In a single-track vehicle going straight, this line runs directly below the center of mass (see also Figures 72 and 73, p. 128).

coordination   The mutually harmonized cooperation among the many individual movements that make up a movement complex, to create an optimally fluid overall movement (**movement plan**). This is not only a purely motor capability. It also involves a complicated *sensory motor* effort, which consists of the following aspects: between the running motor control and the continuous (visual, acoustic, kinesthetic, etc.) perception of the momentary results, there is a constant bidirectional feedback (such as with the visual component of writing: writing without constant visual monitoring is substantially more difficult). Sufficient coordination is not possible when conscious monitoring is involved. Improvements in coordination are possible only through continued training (see also **automation, program,** and **self-optimization**).

cornering, steady state   See **steady state cornering.**

danger anticipation   See **anticipation** and **hypothesis construction.**

data recording   This is a collective term for procedures used to collect all sorts of measured values (rpm, suspension travel, steering inputs, throttle position, deceleration, braking forces, temperatures, etc.), which are recorded on the bike itself or by way of transponders to a fixed station (in the pit, for example).

decreasing radius corner   A dangerous corner that starts out wider but becomes tighter, requiring a decrease in the radius of the selected line and thus an increase in the lean angle. At higher speeds, in some cases, these compensatory measures fail because of the limits of the physical properties involved or, more likely, because of the limits of the rider's capabilities. (In German, such a corner is called a "dog corner," a term with its origins in hunting: a rabbit being pursued can hook very tight corners; a dog following too "hot" on its tail overshoots the rabbit because his initial cornering radius is far too great. The dog has to slow down to correct his course, and the radius of his corner gradually tightens.)

deep relaxation   This can go far beyond the everyday relaxation (such as after a physical exertion or a psychological burden). It is achieved by means of verbal guidance (from a trainer, for example) and brings about a physical and psychological alteration in mood and attitude. The trainee can learn these relaxation techniques so that he gradually becomes able to achieve better relaxation on his own. Mental training can be significantly enhanced through the use of relaxation and deep relaxation techniques.

disposition   For certain behaviors, there are receptivities, which can be more or less definitive, and are called (behavior) dispositions. They prepare the individual to a certain extent for a particular behavior (in contrast to a *trigger,* or catalyst, which demands or requires a particular behavior). In other words, a disposition can make it easy to learn and perform some behaviors. In the opposite direction, however, a disposition can make it almost impossible (compare **learning disposition**).

drift, drifting   A steady sliding out to the side, that occurs in a vehicle as a result of the acting cornering forces. Thanks to the possible **slip angle** of the tires, the cornering forces that are required for this remain available.

electroencephalogram (EEG)   A graphic depiction of brain waves that provides information about the activities in individual regions of the brain. The EEG has been largely replaced by procedures that yield more detailed images, such as functional magnetic resonance imaging (MRI).

escape route   This is a *way out* that allows the rider to get out of a potentially dangerous situation that crops up suddenly. If the escape route requires leaving the roadway, then it's an *escape off pavement,* which is something that can be systematically practiced in training.

evidence experience   A spontaneous insight into a situation, independent of rational or intellectual considerations, with certainty that the insight is correct. The subsequent actions (those that would follow the given situation) can be included in the evidence experience.

fading   This describes the decrease in the braking effect that occurs when the brakes are overtaxed, as occurs, for example, when riding down a mountain. It is often caused by the formation of steam bubbles in old brake fluid. If the brake fluid has been appropriately maintained, fading is a warning that the brakes are overheating and that the destruction of the brakes may be imminent. In any case, the rider must stop immediately and allow the brakes to cool off—but not by pouring water on them.

fearful posture   A body posture and attitude that occurs with a high level of psychological stress associated with a general experience of some threat. It is visibly manifested in the body as physical tension. In general, this posture (rather like cowering) makes it more difficult for a person to get through a difficult situation.

fighting line   See **racing line.**

flow, experience of flow   A condition of heightened feelings of well-being, which sets in when a person is fully absorbed in an activity that he has mastered. In many cases, flow makes it possible for people to withstand long-lasting burdens or stresses. However, it must be monitored. If flow goes unmonitored, it harbors great dangers, especially in risky sports. It has a tendency to "run away," and with the increasing restriction of consciousness, the surroundings and thereby also the dangers, fade ever further into the background.

focus   An important concept in **looking where you want to go.** It is the point at which the gaze is directed and that thus falls into the region of sharpest vision on the retina of the observer. Perceptions in the area surrounding this point, that is, in the periphery of the visual field, generally remain instinctive and subconscious but are nonetheless very important. This is because these peripheral perceptions have a decisive influence on the movement of the eyes and gaze and thus influence what is consciously perceived.

going wide   This describes the relocation of the line toward the outside of a corner during the approach. Going wide makes a larger cornering radius possible— that is, the corner can be successfully taken with a wider arc. One can also undertake a corresponding adjustment at the exit of a corner.

grip   A term used in everyday language to describe the friction (see **static friction**) between the tire and the road surface.

habituation, to habituate   The gradual development of a habit; a deep and fundamental form of "getting used to" something, that makes an action finally become indispensable. Habituation, when it is a matter of behavior, is closely related to **automation** (see also **program**).

hanging off   A special cornering technique used in racing. It is characterized by the movement of the rider's center of mass as far down and to the inside of the turn as possible. The rider's protruding inside knee (knee down), which is used as a "feeler" and can also take on a stabilizing role, is only an external but very conspicuous characteristic (see Figure 70, p. 114).

Contrary to common belief, hanging off does not necessarily make for faster cornering speeds. The reduced lean angle of the motorcycle that is possible when the rider hangs off, however, does mean that there is less wheel camber, which, together with the **slip angle,** allows cornering forces to develop (see **steady state cornering**). Because, during hanging off, the slip angle has to provide a greater proportion of the cornering forces, increased slip angle gives the rider better information about how close he is coming to the limit of traction and thus transmits a greater feeling of security and confidence.

highsider   A term originally used in motorcycle racing. When a bike is sliding to one side, with considerable lean angle, and the wheels suddenly regain traction, the motorcycle stands up abruptly, whereby the rider is thrown up and over the top. This is a highsider. Often the force is so great that the rider is completely disconnected from the motorcycle. The design and composition of the tires has an influence on the sudden re-establishment of traction. A highsider is most frequently unleashed under re-acceleration out of a corner, when the rider, at the moment the bike begins to slide, reflexively gets off the gas. However, it can also happen as lean angles increase in a slide, which allows the contact patches to move to "fresher" (less used) areas of the tires.

hypothesis construction   In the context of this book, this term means preventively taking into account all the possible events that might disrupt one's own planned actions (see **anticipation**).

ideal line   The one line (out of the many possibilities) on which, at a constant speed, the sum of all cornering forces is the smallest. The ideal line may be used in pursuit of the greatest possible speed and the greatest possible safety reserves (contrast the **racing line**).

imitative learning   This is one of the most important forms of learning, especially for actions and behaviors. In imitative learning, an *immediate,* almost simultaneous imitation is far more effective than imitation that is *delayed* or *deferred* until later. This becomes readily evident in the greater training success that is achieved when the trainee follows close behind the trainer, as opposed to following at a certain distance such as occurs in a descent behind a ski instructor or in racing when a top rider "tows" a newer racer through a set of corners. When following the trainer, the trainee notices his performance improvement, gains self-confidence, and can usually retain a substantial proportion of his advancement when he subsequently does the same thing alone. While delayed imitation necessarily includes a phase of rational and willed thinking in between the perception and the trainee's own execution of the activity, in almost simultaneous imitation there is a much more direct path, in the sense of the so-called "mirror reaction."

inherited coordination   Genetically transmitted movement sequences that are specific to species and run relatively inflexibly. The trigger for inherited coordination comes from external stimuli, but the course of the coordination is independent of the triggering stimulus. Inherited coordination is a prime example of an inborn (genetically transmitted) **program** (see also **coordination**).

integration, integrated   The mutual connections and permeation of two systems, which together form a new system as a super-ordinate unit, of which they are the subsystems (for example, tool and user, prosthesis and amputee, cello and cellist, motorcycle and rider, etc.). The newly formed unit has new system characteristics. The *degree* of integration achieved is determined by the degree of mutual penetration of the two subsystems.

interface   The transition (dividing and uniting surface) between two system partners such as the central unit and the peripherals in a data processing system, or even between a computer and its user (man-machine interface, user surface). In the context of this book, it is the interface between man and tool, specifically man and motorcycle, that is germane. The physical and the experiential interface no longer coincide when the tool is used as an *artificial organ.* In this case there is an interface *displacement* into the tool as soon as the tool is incorporated into the physicality of the user as an **integrated** artificial organ or prosthesis; this is what makes possible the high performance that has been achieved in the human use of tools.

Kamm's circle   Also known as the "traction circle." Kamm's circle is a representation of the forces that are exerted by a tire upon the pavement (and vice versa) and the relationships among those forces. On the one hand, there are the **longitudinal forces** that develop under braking and acceleration. On the other hand, there are the **lateral forces** that run perpendicular to the direction of the wheel's travel and which arise when the wheel goes through a curve. These forces are represented as vectors whose lengths indicate the magnitude of the force.

kickback   See **tankslapper.**

lateral acceleration   This occurs when a motorcycle is cornering and is determined by the radius of the curve and the speed of the motorcycle. Lateral acceleration times the overall mass of the vehicle and rider equals the centrifugal force that is exerted on the overall center of mass as cornering force (see **steady state cornering**). The resulting lean angle reflects the magnitude of the effective lateral acceleration.

lateral forces   Forces that affect a vehicle perpendicular to the direction of travel: forces that the wheel has to transmit perpendicular to the direction in which it is moving. Lateral forces arise during cornering and also in straight-line riding on a cambered road or in a crosswind. They are not to be confused with cornering forces, with which the wheel counters the lateral forces that affect it (see also **slip angle**).

lean angle   See **roll angle.**

learning disposition   When a particular course of action or a particular behavior is notably preferred (that is, it is easier to learn and more quickly learned) over other courses of actions or behaviors of a similar degree of difficulty, there is a learning disposition favoring the preferred actions or behaviors (see also **disposition**).

learning intent (training intent)   Although the simple repetition of an action can lead to a gradual improvement in its execution (unintentional, "incidental" learning), without a learning intent the improvement from practice is disproportionately smaller and ultimately stagnates, rendering perfection or even top-level performance unachievable (see also **self-optimization**).

lock   Cessation of rotation in a wheel during braking. A locked wheel has transitioned from **static friction** into sliding or dynamic friction. When this happens, the effectiveness of the brakes is reduced, but more important, the wheel will have only minimal cornering forces available. While it is possible to manage a locked rear wheel when braking in a straight line, a locked front wheel—if not *immediately* released—instantly leads to a crash because of the very minimal gyroscopic stabilization that can still be provided by the rear wheel.

longitudinal, longitudinal forces   Refers to the fore-and-aft axis of the motorcycle (the direction of travel), usually in relation to forward forces that accelerate the motorcycle or backward forces that decelerate the motorcycle. In order for these forward and backward forces to have effect, they must be transmitted through the tires at the **contact patches,** thereby acting as forces tangential to the tire surface (see also **steady state cornering,** and compare **lateral forces**).

longitudinal acceleration   Occurs when the speed is changed and is expressed as the magnitude of the acceleration or deceleration. The longitudinal acceleration, multiplied by the overall mass of the vehicle and rider, equals the amount of **longitudinal force** that acts upon the overall center of mass.

looking where you want to go   This action, which consists mainly of looking sufficiently far ahead, is especially important in sports that take place beyond the speeds for which humans are naturally prepared (such as skiing, riding motorcycles, etc.). An inexperienced person has a tendency, especially in difficult situations, to limit his view to his immediate surroundings, and this detracts from the execution of the **movement plan.** In highly demanding situations, such as emergency braking, even a very good rider may drop his gaze and concentrate only on his immediate surroundings. Learning to keep the proper balance between the near and far views (and points in between) is very difficult because visual preference for the immediate

environment was so important in early human evolution.

loss of skill   Every acquired skill that is not used regularly is subject to degradation. In this respect, even a short training break results in a loss of skill. Loss of skill occurs insidiously and is frequently not noticed by the affected person. The greatest loss of skill can be observed in so-called "returning professionals," who may have been idle for decades. But even after a winter break, a significant loss of skill can be observed. It is more significant with less proficient people than with professionals, although pros, too, experience this.

lowsider   A crash (in a curve) caused by loss of traction, in which the motorcycle slides ahead and the rider behind. Contrast this to the incomparably more dangerous **highsider.**

matrix-patrix relationship   The complicated, often extremely finely interlocked interconnection between two subsystems *of the most diverse sorts,* which builds a new, super-ordinate unit (see **integration**). The relationship may be nearly perfected, or it may be less complete. Patrix and matrix can be represented as profiles, which, in relationship to one another, mesh together like a key and a lock. Inexact fits are manifested as overlaps or gaps in the interlocking of the two systems. Improvements in the degree of interconnection can stem from either of the two system partners. In the context of motorcycling, the interconnection can come from the motorcycle through the accommodation of the different riding positions, the controls (and effort to operate them), and also the character of the suspension and motor; or *it can come from the rider* by means of systematic training.

memory   Beyond our everyday understanding of this word, which is generally focused on the *personal* memory whose contents can be made conscious, spoken about, or at least recognized, in the context of this book, the *procedural* memory is particularly important. The procedural memory stores the **programs** for individual actions and also for entire coordinated courses of action, especially for fast precision movements. The contents of the procedural memory are usually difficult, if not impossible, to bring into conscious consideration, in part because they are not verbally coded.

mental, mentally   Terms used in various contexts and therefore rather imprecise. In this book, they are mostly used in the formulation "mental training," referring to courses of action or behaviors that can't *physically* be performed in training but can be trained only by intensive *imagination* ("training in the mind").

motor   Refers to arbitrary active muscular movements.

movement plan   Every movement complex is preceded by a movement plan that serves as a template, or "instruction," for the action. For particularly difficult actions or for actions that haven't yet been adequately mastered, the movement plan and its execution may be a largely conscious process. The majority of movement plans do not require **conscious attention** and remain on a deep, instinctive level. Training is a matter of improving the movement plan and of improving its execution.

muscle innervation   Nerve stimuli in the form of electric potential that activates a muscle.

objective   1. The firm intent to carry out a particular action, which rests upon a deliberate decision to *undertake* the action. 2. An objective can also be, as mainly used in the context of this book, a matter of the *way in which an action is carried out.* The proper construction of objectives and the gradual internalization of the objective, which can be made easier with systematic *support,* is one of the most important aids in *changing behavior* and deserves the utmost respect in athletic training.

overbraking   Braking in which a wheel's rotation is stopped but the braking process has not yet been completed. Overbraking of the front wheel should especially be avoided (see **lock**). Overbraking can be provoked by means of dynamic overbraking, an application of the front brake that is not only very strong but also very quick, in which the braking pressure increases so rapidly that the wheel is locked before the **weight transfer** (which substantially increases the friction) has occurred. Such rapid increases in pressure are especially likely to occur when the rider brakes out of fright.

panic   An existential experience of threat that arises suddenly, and hinders sensible action, leading to *inadequate behaviors,* including not acting at all (action blockade). However, it is not justifiable to categorize every emergency braking situation, or even every instance of total braking, as panic braking. Similarly, the term "panic crash" should only be used to describe a crash that has come about because of inadequate behavior.

peak acceleration   This is a brief (thus appearing as a peak in diagrams) increase, especially in longitudinal forces, that can cause the tires to exceed the available **static friction,** especially if it occurs simultaneously with high **lateral forces.**

pre-adaptation   See **adaptation.**

procedural memory   See **memory.**

process certainty   This mainly has to do with the experience of the person carrying out an action; it refers to the degree to which the person considers an action **program** to be correct. However, the degree of process certainty is also visible from the outside, for example, visible to a trainer. Process certainty is an important prerequisite for top-level performance and can be trained with special methods.

program   In the broadest sense, a program is a set of instructions for a course of action (action program), here especially in relation to automated action complexes (see **automation**). There is a distinction between genetically transmitted (inborn) and acquired (learned) programs, but even acquired programs contain many inborn program components, just as complete inborn programs often require refinement by means of acquired programs that are layered on top of the original program. Swimming, for example, is an action that nearly all mammals possess (even for those that swim only in emergencies) as an inborn program, but humans must acquire (learn) the program first. However, acquired programs that have been truly and fundamentally mastered, function very similarly to inborn programs. In order to keep them at the highest achieved level, both require a certain amount of "program maintenance" through practice, but they are never completely lost. Anyone who has ever learned to swim will not have "forgotten how," even after decades without swimming. This is also true of bicycle riding. Complex actions, especially fast courses of action with precision movements, would not be possible without automation, which allows the action to be managed in a self-distant (distant from conscious attention) manner by means of acquired programs.

prosthesis, prosthesis-like use   Tools can generally be understood as artificial organs, but they don't truly become prostheses until they have been incorporated into the user's own **body concept.** Once this happens, there is a considerable improvement in the skill and effectiveness of the individual's use of the tool.

pushing   A cornering technique in which the motorcycle takes on a notably greater lean than the rider. With the exception of offroad situations, this technique is justified only in the quick initiation of a swerve at moderate speeds. For this, the rider *pushes* the motorcycle into the lean with a strong motion but does not himself join the motorcycle in the lean. Instead, he pushes the bike away from himself.

racing line, fighting line   A line that is faster and has better passing opportunities than the classic **ideal line.** The racing line is not only shorter than the ideal line (see Figure 40, p. 66) but also allows much later braking, even if harder braking is required. This is the case because this line is slower in the area of the corner **apex** than the ideal line. However, after the slower apex, the racing line allows a substantially earlier acceleration. The application of the racing line and how extremely it is applied depend on the amount of available acceleration reserves. The racing line places very high demands on the rider, places more strain and wear on the motorcycle, and is dangerous if inadequately mastered.

rain-phobia   Most motorcycle riders experience a degree of uneasiness when riding in the rain. In a rider with less experience, this uneasiness is manifested as a tendency to shy away from, or even fear, the rain, which may reach the point of becoming a *phobia of rain,* particularly if the rider experiences an unfortunate event in such conditions (for example, a crash in the rain). Once phobia sets in, the affected person develops an action blockade, and his performance of the activity heavily associated with fear—in this case, riding in the rain—will be extremely imperfect, if he can perform the activity at all. In severe cases, the lifting of the blockade can only be accomplished with therapeutic support.

redundant, redundancy   Superfluous or repetitive parts of a message or a system (such as the brain) or even a course of action, are described as "redundant." With a message, however, redundant parts can enhance comprehensibility or confirm the information in the event of incomplete or inadequate transmission (*con-ducive* redundancy). In systems, redundancies can increase the robustness of the function (as with twin-spark ignition). In courses of action, redundancies can ease the transition from one individual action to the next, or they may even make certain individual actions possible. However, so-called "empty redundancies," which are not only superfluous in certain situations but also can be left out in all circumstances, should be recognized by the trainer and dismantled.

resting tone   The baseline tension that exists in a non-activated muscle, which can be further reduced during sleep or in a state of deep relaxation.

risk composite   The risk composite is a form of the so-called "expectancy-value model" in which the value—in this case the risk—is negative. It shares with other expectancy-value models the idea that the value of action alternatives is weighed against the subjective probability of the desired outcome (or the occurrence of the feared event), whereby the weighing is performed by means of a multiplication of value by probability. The risk composite presumes that in the anticipatory processing of a highly dangerous but rare occurrence, there is a sort of mediation between the probability that the event will occur and the gravity of its consequences, almost like an average. However, this averaging leads to inadequate anticipation, which can magnify the danger.

roll, roll movement   A movement around the **longitudinal** axis of a vehicle, which leads to a change in the lean angle.

roll angle (in aviation: angle of roll)   A concept in automotive technology, referred to in everyday language as "lean angle," usually measured as the departure from vertical of the vehicle's attitude around the longitudinal axis.

self-organization   See **self-optimization.**

self-distant   Mental processes (in particular, **sensory-motor** processes) are distant from the self (self-distant) when they play out without conscious involvment. (See also **conscious attention.**)

self-optimization   Even in the realm of lifeless nature, spontaneous self-organization, and thus self-optimization, can be observed as a process (such as in the formation of a whirlpool). In these cases, there is always a goal to reach a higher level of organization in the form of a describable higher order, along with a progressive elevation of efficiency, however that is defined. Biological evolution, in the broadest terms, follows the same principle, but with entirely different mechanisms. The same self-optimization can also be observed in the learning of complicated courses of action, which means simply that the **programs** that control the actions continue to improve themselves independently through continued use and without any outside influences. (Improvements can also occur that lead in detrimental directions; see also the dead end, p. 36). Since courses of action, just as with all other processes of self-optimization, are clearly progressive, comparable to a melody, the individual members of the body of the action do not stand in isolation, without relationships with each other. Instead, they have mutual influences on each other, accommodate each other, and thus become more fluid. In this way the program gains efficiency, and the sensory-motor effort decreases. Last but not least, the program becomes more stable and less easily disrupted because the soundness of the overall program has increased. (See **learning intent.**)

sensory-motor, sensory   This term refers to a course of events (such as an action **program**) when sensory and **motor** processes are intertwined and exist in a tight "back-and-forth" relationship. For example, when coming to a stop at a planned point, the braking force that has been created by the motor process is constantly compared and weighed by sensory input against the momentary speed and position of the vehicle relative to the planned stopping point, and the amount of braking force is correspondingly adjusted. Most processes that are designated motor processes should actually be understood as sensory-motor processes.

sensory   This term refers to the processing of the perceptions of the five senses (sight, hearing, touch, smell, and taste).

shimmy   Speed wobble. See **tankslapper.**

slide   See **drift, drifting.**

sliding or dynamic friction   See **static friction.**

slip angle   The angle between the direction of travel and the rotation plane of the wheel, dependent on the necessary cornering force, which the wheel can only develop with slip angle. (See also **steady state cornering.**)

stabilizing throttle   This describes the increase in power (usually only minimal) necessary to prevent a further increase in the lean angle when cornering. This continued increase in lean can occur after initiating the corner, as the lean is still increasing, or during so-called **"steady state cornering,"** as a result of the slowing of the motorcycle caused by the substantial increase in rolling resistance in a corner.

standing up   This is a tendency of the motorcycle to straighten up vertically out of a lean if the rider brakes in a corner. It comes about because, when the bike is leaned over, the **contact patches** of the tires move in the direction toward the inside of the corner (Figure 87) and thus away from the steering axis (*L*). If braking is applied to the front wheel, for example, a lever effect is created, over which the braking force on the wheel creates a torque (the so-called "braking-steering moment"), which moves the front wheel around the longitudinal axis toward the inside of the turn. This causes the radius of the curve to shrink, and the resulting increase in centrifugal force causes the motorcycle to stand up. Depending on suspension and tire design and on lean angle and deceleration, the standing up can be considerable, especially since there are also gyroscopic forces that come into play and have similar effects. The standing-up effect makes it difficult to maintain the planned line through a corner and can scare less-experienced riders.

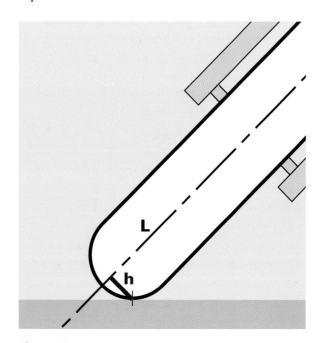

Figure 87

The opposite of standing up can also occur. If the rider tries to compensate by suddenly letting go of the front brake later in the corner, the standing-up effect is no longer present, resulting in the opposite effect: an increase of the **lean angle.** This effect is initially very surprising to a less-experienced rider, even though it directly results from his own action.

static friction   If, when one body is in physical contact with another body (for example, by resting upon it), a force is exerted on one body that tries to slide it against the other body, up to a certain force it is static friction that keeps the two bodies from sliding against each other. As the exerted force is increased, one body begins to slide, and the sliding force between the two bodies is then defined by dynamic friction (sliding friction), which is lower than than static friction. A rolling wheel also demonstrates static friction, or, for that matter, dynamic friction. That becomes evident when one looks at a single particle of the wheel's contact area. For the short moment in which this particle moves along the **contact patch** from front to rear, it is in stationary contact with the pavement. (See also **Kamm's circle.**)

steady state cornering   This is a concept from physics. Cornering has achieved a steady state when all exerted and resulting forces are in balance and constant; thus, cornering is not steady state at the initiation or ending of a corner or while correcting the line. The resulting forces exerted include the centrifugal force that tries to stand the motorcycle up as well as the gravity that works against it; the necessary forward propulsion and the opposing rolling resistance, which increases considerably when the bike is leaned; and the tendency of the motorcycle to turn in, against which the rider's stabilization on the handlebars is directed.

steering input   The **steering moment** that the rider exerts on the handlebars before the start of a corner to initiate the required amount of lean. This movement of the handlebars, of which the rider generally has no conscious awareness, is in the opposite direction of the planned corner. Thus, it is sometimes called "countersteering."

steering moment   In physics, the term "moment" means torque. In this context it usually refers to the torque on the steering head that results from forces applied by one's hands on the handlebar grips to initiate or maintain a particular steering angle. The word "maintain" is used here because the motorcycle itself also creates a steering moment, such as the positive steering moment (i.e., one causing tighter cornering) which begins to develop with the slightest deviation from riding straight ahead (it is this self-correcting effect that makes it possible to ride with no hands). At steeper lean angles, the positive steering moment generated by the motorcycle gradually decreases, and can actually become a negative steering moment.

tangential forces   See **longitudinal forces.**

tankslapper (also called "kickback")   A fast oscillating movement of the handlebars that starts suddenly and, in extreme cases, can range from lock to lock. Kickback occurs especially at high speeds, when the front wheel is unloaded, and is triggered when the wheel is set down (or once again bears weight) at an angle. Thus, it is often observed under acceleration, especially when cornering forces are still present at the exit of a corner, and even more so if the road goes uphill. It should not be confused with the relatively harmless shimmy *(wobble mode),* which occurs at about 35 to 50 mph and has a somewhat smaller frequency (about four to eight oscillations per second), occurs more softly, and can be brought under control by a firm grasp on the handlebars. It should also not be confused with the dangerous weave mode associated with *inadequate suspensions.* Weave occurs at higher speeds, at about one to two oscillations per second, when the inherent frequency of the steering system (front wheel with fork and handlebars, etc.) and the frequency of the rest of the motorcycle achieve a resonance that continues to build.

tire contact patch   See **contact patch.**

tone   See **resting tone.**

traction   The condition that exists when a connection (either sticking or sliding) exists between two bodies (such as between tires and road surface), over which forces are transmitted. (See also **static friction.**)

trance   A condition of more or less strongly reduced environmental coherence, that is, minimal involvement in the surrounding situation, accompanied by a lack of readiness for self-critique and increased suggestibility. Precursers of trance can arise during a state of **flow.**

turn-in point   The turn-in point is located at the beginning of a corner (the end of straight-line riding).

With a motorcycle, there are also steering movements that bring about the lean (but are not performed consciously) that occur *before* the actual turn-in point. It is perfectly acceptable for the turn-in point to lie *within* the braking zone. A rider with less experience usually stops braking at the turn-in point (and doesn't look into the curve until then either; compare **looking where you want to go**). The turn-in point might also be called the "release point" or "breakaway point" because the selected line moves away from the outside edge of the road at this point. However, the term "turn-in point" is preferable because, in certain cases, this point is not located on the edge of the road.

vagotonal economy   A deep resting state close to sleep. Instead of control by the sympathetic nervous system, which is dominant in the wakeful state, the parasympathetic system has taken over control by means of the vagus, which is the counterpart to the sympathicus nerve (see also **resting tone**).

weight transfer   This occurs under braking and acceleration and depends on wheelbase and the height of the overall center of mass. Weight transfer between the wheels of a motorcycle is thus more pronounced than weight transfer between the axles of a car.

References

Aicher, Otl (1984): Kritik am Auto. Schwierige Verteidigung des Autos gegen seine Anbeter [*Critique of the Automobile. The Difficult Defense of the Automobile Against Its Devotees*]. München

Alsberg, Paul (1922): Das Menschheitsrätsel. Versuch einer prinzipiellen Lösung [*The Puzzle of Humanity. An Attempt at a Fundamental Solution*]. Dresden

Apel, Friedemar, and Horst *Baumann* (1984): A Roaring Life oder Die Lust am Motorrad [*A Roaring Life or The Joy of the Motorcycle*]. Berlin

Bammé, Arno, et al. (1983): Maschinen-Menschen, Mensch-Maschinen. Grundrisse einer sozialen Beziehung [*Machine-Humans, Human-Machines. Outlines of a Social Relationship*]. Reinbek

Burckhardt, Manfred (1985): Reaktionszeiten bei Notbremsungen [*Reaction Times in Emergency Braking*]. TÜV Rheinland. Köln

Calvin, William H. (1993): Die Symphonie des Denkens. Wie aus Neuronen Bewußtsein entsteht [*The Symphony of Thinking. How Consciousness Arises From Neurons*]. München

Code, Keith (1982): A Twist of the Wrist. Code Break. Los Angeles

Code, Keith (1993): A Twist of the Wrist II. Code Break. Los Angeles

Csikszentmihalyi, Mihaly (1993): Das flow-Erlebnis. Jenseits von Angst und Langeweile: im Tun aufgehen [*The Flow Experience. Beyond Fear and Boredom: Absorbed by the Activity*]. Stuttgart

Csikszentmihalyi, Mihaly (1996): Flow. Das Geheimnis des Glücks. 5. Aufl. [*Flow. The Secret to Happiness, 5th Ed.*]. Stuttgart

Damm, Johannes, and Gerold *Lingnau* (1980): Eine Klasse besser. Schnell und sicher auf dem Motorrad [*A Class Above. Speed and Safety on the Motorcycle*]. Stuttgart

v. Ditfurth, Hoimar (1992): Ein Renegat rechnet ab. In: Das Erbe des Neandertalers [*An Apostate Settles an Account. In: The Inheritance of the Neanderthal Man*]. Köln

Eberspächer, Hans (1990): Mentale Trainingsformen in der Praxis. Ein Handbuch für Trainer und Sportler [*Forms of Mental Training in Practice. A Handbook for Trainers and Athletes*]. Oberhaching

Eberspächer, Hans (1991): Psychological Consideration on Brake Use Patterns of Motorcyclists. Safety Environment, Future: Proceedings of the 1991 International Motorcycle Conference, edited by Institut für Zweiradsicherheit. Forschungshefte Zweiradsicherheit, Nr. 7 [*Research Journal on Two-Wheeler Safety, No. 7*]. Bochum

Eberspächer, Hans (2002): Realistische Selbsteinschätzung. In: Perfekt fahren mit MOTORRAD [*Realistic Self-Assessment. In: Ride Perfectly with MOTORRAD*]. Stuttgart, p. 114ff.

Eibl-Eibesfeldt, Irenäus (1984): Der vorprogrammierte Mensch. Das Ererbte als bestimmender Faktor im menschlichen Verhalten. 5. Aufl. [*The Pre-Programmed Human. Genetic Inheritance as a Crucial Factor in Human Behavior, 5th Ed.*]. München

v. Frankenberg, Richard (1958): Schachspiel ohne Bedenkzeit. Ein Versuch, auf die Frage zu antworten: Was ist Motorsport? [*Chess Without Time to Think. An Attempt to Answer the Question, What is Motorsports?*]. Stuttgart

Gallese, Vittorio, and A. Goldman (1998): Mirror Neurons and the Simulation Theory of Mind-Reading. Trends in Cognitive Science 2:493–501

Gazzaniga, Michael S. (1985): The Social Brain. Discovering the Networks of the Mind. New York

Gehlen, Arnold (1975): Die Seele im technischen Zeitalter. Sozialpsychologische Probleme in der industriellen Gesellschaft [*The Soul in the Technical Age. Social Psychological Problems in Industrial Society*]. Hamburg

Gehlen, Arnold (1978): Der Mensch. Seine Natur und seine Stellung in der Welt. 12. Aufl. [*The Human Being. His Nature and his Position in the World, 12th Ed.*]. Wiesbaden

Gustafsson, Lars (1979): Die Tennisspieler. Erzählung [*The Tennis Players. A Short Story*]. München

Hagstotz, Werner (1990): Zur Typologie von Motorradfahrern. In: Motorradfahren. Faszination und Restriktion [*Motives of Motorcycling. In: Motorcycling. Fascination and Limitation*]. Forschungshefte Zweiradsicherheit, Nr. 6 [*Research Journal on Two-wheeler Safety, No 6*]. Edited by Hubert Koch. Bochum

Hampden-Turner, Charles (1983): Modelle des Menschen. 2. Aufl. [*Models of the Human, 2nd Ed.*]. Weinheim

Hass, Hans (1970): Energon. Das verborgene Gemeinsame [*Energon. The Hidden Community*]. Wien

Hass, Hans, and Horst **Lange-Prollius**(1978): Die Schöpfung geht weiter. Station Mensch im Strom des Lebens [*Creation Continues. The Human Being as a Stopover in the Flow of Life*]. Stuttgart

Hass, Hans (1987): Das verborgene Gemeinsame. Energon-Theorie I und II. Naturphilosophische Schriften, Bd. 2 und 3 [*The Hidden Community. Energon Theory I and II. Writings on the Philosophy of Nature, Vol. 2 and 3*]. München

Hass, Hans (1994): Die Hyperzeller. Das neue Menschenbild der Evolution [*Hypercells. The New Human Picture of Evolution*]. Hamburg

v. Hayek, F.A. (1983): Die überschätzte Vernunft. In: Evolution und Menschenbild [*The Overestimation of Reason. In: Evolution and the Human Image*]. Edited by Rupert Riedel and F. Kreuzer. Hamburg

v. Hebenstreit, Benedikt (1993): Sehen im Straßenverkehr. Serie indirekte Verkehrsbildung an weiterführenden Schulen [*Vision in Traffic. A Series for Indirect Traffic Education in Advanced Schools*]. München

Herrigel, Eugen (1979): Zen in der Kunst des Bogenschießens. 19. Aufl. [*Zen in the Art of Archery, 19th Ed.*]. Weilheim

Kaminski, Gerhard (Editor) (1986): Ordnung und Variabilität im Alltagsgeschehen [*Order and Variability in Everyday Occurrences*]. Göttingen

Kapp, Ernst (1978): Grundlinien einer Philosophie der Technik. Neudruck der 1. Aufl. 1877 [*The Fundamentals of a Philosophy of Technology. New printing of the first edition published in 1877*]. Düsseldorf

Keiter, F. (1938): Rasse und Kultur. 2 Bde. [*Race and Culture. Vol. 2*]. Stuttgart

Klebelsberg, Dieter (1982): Verkehrspsychologie [*Psychology of Traffic*]. Berlin, Heidelberg, New York

Koch, Hubert (1990): Die Lust am Motorrad. Fahrermotive und Erlebnisformen gestern und heute. In: Motorradfahren. Faszination und Restriktion [*Motives of Motorcycling. In: Motorcycling. Fascination and Limitation*]. Forschungshefte Zweiradsicherheit, Nr. 6 [*Research Journal on Two-Wheeler Safety, No. 6*]. Edited by Hubert Koch. Bochum

Kraft, Georg (1948): Der Urmensch als Schöpfer. Die geistige Welt des Eiszeitmenschen. 2. Aufl. [*The Ancient Human as Creator. The Spiritual World of the People of the Ice Age, 2nd Ed.*]. Tübingen

Krahnstöver, Felix, and Harry **Niemann** (1988): Trial. Akrobatik auf zwei Rädern [*Trials. Acrobatics on Two Wheels*]. Stuttgart

Krech, David, and Richard S. **Crutchfield** (1982): Elements of Psychology, 4th Ed. Vol. 2: Perception. New York

Lorenz, Konrad (1966): Psychologie und Stammesgeschichte. In: Über tierisches und menschliches Verhalten. Gesammelte Abhandlungen, Bd. 2 [*Psychology and Species History. In: On Animal and Human Behavior. Collected Proceedings, Vol. 2*]. München

Lorenz, Konrad (1984a): Vergleichende Verhaltensforschung. Grundlagen der Ethologie. 2. Aufl. [*Comparative Behavioral Research. Fundamentals of Ethology, 2nd Ed.*]. München

Lorenz, Konrad (1984b): Vom Weltbild des Verhaltensforschers. 13. Aufl. [*On the Worldview of a Behavioral Researcher, 13th Ed.*]. München

Lorenz, Konrad (1985): Die Rückseite des Spiegels. Versuch einer Naturgeschichte menschlichen Erkennens. 8. Aufl. [*The Other Side of the Mirror. Attempt at a Natural History of Human Cognition, 8th Ed.*]. München

Niemann, Harry (1999): Der Kniff mit dem Knie. Sportlich und sicher Motorradfahren. Aus der Praxis der Profis. 3. Aufl. [*The Trick with the Knee. Safe Sport Riding. How the Pros Do It, 3rd Ed.*]. Stuttgart

Nowak, Horst (1986): Die Lust am Motorradfahren. Vortrag anläßlich des Festaktes „Hundert Jahre Motorrad", München 1985. Tagungsbericht der VDI-Ges. Fahrzeugtechnik [*The Joy of Motorcycling. Lecture on the Occasion of the "100 Years of the Motorcycle" Celebration in Munich in 1985. Conference Report*]. Düsseldorf

Osche, Günter (1982): Die Sonderstellung des Menschen in biologischer Sicht: Biologische und kulturelle Evolution. In: Evolution. Bedingungen, Resultate, Konsequenzen, 2. Aufl. [*The Special Position of Human Beings in a Biological Sense: Biological and Cultural Evolution. In: Evolution. Conditions, Results, Consequences, 2nd Ed.*]. Edited by Rolf Siewing, Stuttgart, New York, p. 379ff.

Penick, Harvey, and Bud *Shrake* (1999): Harvey Penick's Little Red Book. Lessons and Teachings from a Lifetime in Golf. New York

Petermann, Franz, and Dieter *Vaitl* (Hrsg.) (1994): Handbuch der Entspannungsverfahren. Bd. 2: Anwendungen [*Handbook of Relaxation Techniques. Vol. 2: Application*]. Weinheim; see Vol. 1 under Vaitl and Petermann (!)

Porter, Kay, and Judy *Foster* (1987): Mentales Training. Der moderne Weg zur sportlichen Leistung [*Mental Training. The Modern Way to Athletic Performance*]. München, Wien, Zürich

Restak, Richard M. (1981): Geist, Gehirn und Psyche. Psychobiologie: Die letzte Herausforderung [*Mind, Brain, and Psyche. Psychobiology: The Final Challenge*]. Frankfurt

Rheinberg, Falko, U. *Dirksen,* and E. *Nagels* (1986): Motivationsanalysen zu verschieden riskantem Motorradfahren. In: Zeitschrift für Verkehrssicherheit, Jg. 32 [*Analyses of Motivations in Motorcycle Riding at Different Levels of Risk. In: Journal of Traffic Safety, Year 32*].

Rheinberg, Falko (1991): Flow-Experience when Motorcycling: A Study of a Special Human Condition. Safety Environment, Future: Proceedings of the 1991 International Motorcycle Conference, Edited by Institut für Zweiradsicherheit. Forschungshefte Zweiradsicherheit, Nr. 7 [*Research Journal on Two-Wheeler Safety, No. 7*]. Bochum

Rheinberg, Falko (1996): Flow-Erleben, Freude am riskanten Sport und andere „unvernünftige" Motivationen. In: Motivation, Volition und Handlung [*Flow Experience, the Enjoyment of Risky Sports and Other "Unreasonable" Motivations. In: Motivation, Volition, and Action*]. Edited by Kuhl and Heckhausen. Enzyklopädie der Psychologie, Bd. C/IV/4, Göttingen

Rosch, M. (1985): Verhalten im sozialen Kontext. Soziale Förderung und Unterdrückung von Verhalten. In: Theorien der Sozialpsychologie, Bd. 2: Gruppen- und Lerntheorien [*Behavior in the Cocial Context. Social Demands and Suppression of Behaviors. In: Theories of Social Psychology, Vol. 2: Group and Learning Theories*]. Edited by D. Frey and M. Irle. Bern

Sack, Manfred (1987): Mit dem Ingenieur durchs Ziel. Der Sport und seine gestalteten Werkzeuge [*Crossing the Finish Line with the Engineer. Sport and Its Designed Tools*]. In: in rotis, edited by Hans Hermann Wetcke. München, p. 48ff.

Schulz, Ulrich, H. *Kerwien,* and H. *Koch* (1990): Motive des Motorradfahrens. In: Motorradfahren. Faszination und Restriktion [*Motives of Motorcycling. In: Motorcycling. Fascination and Limitation*]. Forschungshefte Zweiradsicherheit, Nr. 6 [*Research Journal on Two-Wheeler Safety, No. 6*]. Edited by Hubert Koch. Bochum

Spiegel, Bernt (1953): Enthemmung durch Geschwindigkeit [*Dis-Inhibition Through Speed*]. Schweizerische Automobil-Revue, Nr. 29

Spiegel, Bernt (1967): Der Nischenbegriff in Ökologie und Sozialpsychologie [*The Concept of the Niche in Ecology and Social Psychology*]. GFM-Mitteilungen, 13. Jg., 3/1967

Spiegel, Bernt (1989): Was hat der Mesokosmos-Begriff auf einer Motorradtagung zu suchen? Eröffnungsvortrag auf der 3. VDI-Motorradtagung in Darmstadt [*What is the Concept of the Mesocosm Doing at a Motorcycle Conference? Keynote speech at the 3rd VDI motorcycle conference in Darmstadt*]. VDI-Berichte No. 779

Spiegel, Bernt (2000): Über das Bremsen aus der Sicht des Verhaltensforschers. XX. Internationales F-Symposium. Fortschritt-Berichte VDI [*Braking from the Viewpoint of the Behavioral Researcher. 20th International F-Symposium*]. Reihe 12, Nr. 440. Düsseldorf

Spiegel, Bernt (2004): Analyse eines exemplarischen schweren Alleinunfalls anhand eines zufällig aufgenommenen Video-Spots. 5. Internationale Motorradkonferenz, München. Forschungshefte Zweiradsicherheit Nr. 11 [*Analysis of a Classic Serious Single-Vehicle Accident Based on a Coincidentally Recorded Video. 5th International Motorcycle Conference in Munich. Research Journal on Two-Wheeler Safety, No. 11*]. Essen

Spiegel, Bernt (2006): Motorradtraining—alle Tage! [*Motorcycle Training—Every Day!*]. Stuttgart.

Stoffregen, Jürgen (2006): Motorradtechnik. Grundlagen und Konzepte von Motor, Antrieb und Fahrwerk. 4. Aufl. [*Motorcycle Technology. Fundamentals and Concepts of Motor, Drivetrain, and Chassis, 4th Ed.*]. Braunschweig, Wiesbaden

Syer, John, and Christopher **Connolly** (1997): Sporting Body Sporting Mind: An Athlete's Guide to Mental Training, 3rd Ed. Oxford.

Vaitl, Dieter, and Franz **Petermann** (Hrsg.) (1993): Handbuch der Entspannungsverfahren. Bd. 1: Grundlagen und Methoden [*Handbook of Relaxation Techniques. Vol. 1: Fundamentals and Methods*]. Weinheim; see Vol. 2 under Petermann and Vaitl (!)

Vollmer, Gerhard (1985, 1986): Was können wir wissen? Bd. 1: Die Natur der Erkenntnis. Bd. 2: Die Erkenntnis der Natur [*What Can We Know? Vol. 1: The Nature of Cognition. Vol. 2: The Cognition of Nature*]. Stuttgart

Vollmer, Gerhard (1986): Wissenschaft mit Steinzeitgehirnen? [*Science with Stone Age Brains?*] Mannheimer Forum 86/87, edited by Hoimar v. Ditfurth. Mannheim

Weidele, Alois (1994): Untersuchungen zum Bremsverhalten von Motorrädern unter besonderer Berücksichtigung der ABS-geregelten Kurvenbremsung. Fortschr.-Ber. VDI-Reihe 12, Nr. 210 [*Investigations of the Braking Behaviors of Motorcycles with Special Attention to ABS-regulated Braking in Corners. Progress Reports. VDI Series 12, No. 210*]. Düsseldorf

Würzberg, Gerd (1985): Rocker, Hexen, Kamikazen. Geschichten aus dem Motorradalltag [*Rockers, Witches, Kamikazes. Everyday Motorcycle Stories*]. Reinbek

Zimmer, Dieter E. (1979): Unsere erste Natur. Die biologischen Ursprünge menschlichen Verhaltens [*Our First Nature. The Biological Origins of Human Behavior*]. München

Index

A

abdominal muscles
  looseness of as goal 169
**ABS (antilock braking system), definition
  of 164**
**acceleration 24, 61–63, 96, 98–99, 102,
  127, 162**
  and braking 65
  and speed 61
  early, for exiting corners 153–154, 169
  early, in racing 63
  lateral 66, 96, 101
  longitudinal 66, 101
accessory, aftermarket 20
accident(s) 23
  and speed 23
  See Also crash(es)
  evading 131
action
  spontaneous 54
  stutter 52
  undesirable, overcoming 142
action blockades 52
  self-observation and self-awareness as 74
action complex 54
**action program(s) 30, 34, 40, 42–43, 45,
  67, 153, 157**
  and coaster experiment 68
  automated 80
    disruption of 80
  automation of
    and muscle innervations 126
    See automation of action program(s)
  closed and open
    ball toss as example of 69
  development and refinement of 40
  for motorcycling 32
  for offroad escape(s) 132
    stages of 132
  in mental training 122
  input and output 34
  learned vs. inborn
    swimming, as example of 30
  mental training of 126, 128
  use of hands in cornering 157

adaptation 28, 32–33, 40, 84
  after break from motorcycling 84
  appropriate
    positioning of motorcycle controls as
      example of 104
  definition of 30, 132, 164
  genetic 30
  gradual
    operation of clutch as example of 42
  gradual accustomization 42
  man as master of 26–28
  mutual man-machine 41
  of subsystems 42
  See Also pre-adaptation
  species', to environmental conditions 27
    spider as example of 29
  to disturbances 43
  to standing-up tendency 157
Adenauer Forst 67
Aicher, Otl 45, 84
Alps, hairpin corners in 47
Alsberg, Paul 89
angular momentum 48
anticipation, definition of 164
Apel, Friedemar 163
apex of curve 69, 98
  definition of 98, 164
  late 153
archery
  role of subconscious in 76
Aresti, J.L. 140
Arlberg method 75
artificial organs
  advantages of 89–90
  and integrated artificial organs 90
  and use as communal organs 89
  disadvantages of 90
  function fulfillment vs. function control
    90
  use of as prostheses 88
Ascari, Alberto 83
attitude 124
Autobahn 130
automated, automatic, definition of 165
**automation 31, 36, 68, 76–77, 80–81, 106,
  112, 117, 122, 126, 132, 134, 140**
  and emergency situations 133

  and undesirable behaviors 142
  definition of 165
  degrees of 107
  disruption of
    learning to ride bicycle as example
      of 80–81
  in opening the throttle 153
  of action program(s)
    difficulty in achieving 143
  of proper head and neck position 156
  of steering impulse 160
  or looking far ahead 150
  subconscious level of 106
  use of reminder stickers for 141

B

back-up 130
balancing
  and contact patches 38
  and human evolution 34–35
  and steering 37, 40
  drinking of coffee as example of 44
  of broomstick as example 37–38
  of shovel as example of 38
ball-of-foot
  position of
    objections to 155
    personal objectives and use of 154,
      156
Bammé, Arno 89
Barichello, Rubens 84
behavior
  adaptation of 73
  and degree of habituation 76
  animal
    and "play face" 52, 146
  automated 76
    and concrete training objectives
      144
    See automation
  change in 26
    brought about by practice 117
  changing, setting objectives and 139
  erroneous (bad habits) 52, 117
  human 22, 151
  inborn 50–51, 76, 151
    and human evolution 151
  intelligent vs. dumb 21
  program(s) 85
    See under program(s)

Osche, Günter 89

over relaxation, danger of 124

overbraking 150
  definition of 170
  dynamic 158

P

panic, definition 170

parable of the centipede 56

parasympathetic system and vagotonal
    economy 125

passing 119

peak acceleration, definition of 170

Penick, Harvey 137

penny-farthing 39

perceived image 152
  and mental image 73

perception
  and external dangers 112
  and figure-ground reversible images 132
  and hypothesis construction 111
  and sensization 129
  psychology of 73
  sensory 94
    and channel capacity 53
  sensory, and communication 105
  spatial 105
  subjective, and objective reality 123
  tactile 94
  visual 94

Petermann 127

phantom limb 91

photography, use of in teaching lean angle
    116

physical interface
  See interface physical

physics 148–149
  of motorcycling 33
  of riding 37, 45–46

plasticity, human 28
  See Also adaptation

play face 146

Porter, Kay 122

posture, fearful
  See fearful posture

posture, riding 154–157

power slide 98

practice exercise(s) 158–159
  for training of basic skills 158
  general, for critical situations and
      emergencies 160–161

pre-adaptation 35, 113

precession movement 47

pre-load method of shifting 142–143

procedural memory 78, 106

process certainty 29
  definition of 170

program 28, 73
  acquired 30
    riding of bicycle as example of 31
  acquired (learned) 33, 57, 76
    bird flight as example of 29
    in humans vs. animals 29
  acquired (learned) vs. inborn 31
  acquired (learning) and shifting gears
      143
  action
    See action program
  adaptation of 33
  and gear spacing 159
  and language acquisition 29
  automated 51, 117
  automation of 31
  behavior 85
  behavior managing 30
    genetically transmitted 35
  closed 30
  complete 31
  definition of 170
  fixed 40
  improving 117
  inborn 28–29, 31–32, 34, 43, 50, 76
    balancing on bike as example of 43
  input-output scheme 80
  learned 31
  linear, simple 28
    spider spinning web as example of 28
  maintenance of 31
  mixed 29
  open 28
  redevelopment 34
  rigidity of 28
  self-optimization of 31
  sensory-motor 34
  superimposition of new over old 117

proper line
  See ideal line

prosthesis 88, 90, 92
  as model of integration
    pointer as example of 91
  classic craftsman's tools as 92
  derfinition of 170
  instrument as 92

psychology 148

psychology of perception 73

psychotraining 122

pushing (away) 157
  definition of 171

R

racing 60, 98
  crashes or disqualifications 103
  dis-integration 94
  in wet conditions, and tire abrasion
      149
  maintaining closeness in 144
  tactical decisions in 117
  use of conceptual aids in 138

racing line 64–66, 153
  definition of 171
  difficulty with 67

rain 98
  and experience of risk 147–148
    English riders 147
  and reduced tire abrasion 149
  and reduced visibility 149
  and rules for riding in slippery
      conditions 147, 150
  and sudden slipperiness 150
  posture 148
  riding curves in 148
  riding well in 148

rain-phobia, definition of 171

raised beam study 79

rational
  analysis 49
  knowledge 26
  thought 43
    importance of 74

razor scooter 48

reaction time 22

reading the road, looking where you
    want to go 151

reasoning, flawed 23

redundancy
  benefits of 52
  definition of 171
  drawbacks of 52

relaxation 124, 159
  and degree of integration 125
  and use of conceptual training aids
      136
  and vagotonal economy 127
  as aide to slipping in 127
  chains 124
  conceptual aids for 138
  deep, exercise for 125
  exercises for 125, 127, 138
  methods of 146
  self-observation of 125
  states of and electroencephalograms
      (EEGs) 125
  techniques for 54, 126
  training 124

About the Author

Bernt Spiegel began doing man-machine-interface work in the early 1950s, primarily in the automotive field. He taught psychology from 1951 to 1961 at the Universities of Mannheim and Saarbrücken, and was director of the Institute of Industrial and Social Psychology at the University of Göttingen (Göttingen, Germany) from 1962 to 1969. Since then, his work has been centered at the Spiegel Institut, a research organization he founded in 1949 to pursue market psychology and anthropotechnology.

His research, commissioned mostly by the automobile industry (for example, Porsche), focused primarily on the multifaceted psychological challenges and problems that come into play when operating an automobile. This research eventually extended to automotive electronic systems and peoples' ability to use them effectively as well as accept them. In this context he advanced the concept of tool use as parallel to "artificial limbs."

Spiegel's later intensive involvement with the motorcycle was, in contrast to his professional activities, a hobby and personal "love affair," although it greatly benefited from his previous work in the automobile industry.

Dr. Spiegel is experienced not only in recreational motorcycling but also in motorcycle racing. He has intimate knowledge of the Nürburgring Nordschleife, one of the most demanding racetracks in the world, where he passed on his insights and expertise as senior instructor for *MOTORRAD* perfection training sessions. (*MOTORRAD* is the major European motorcycle magazine.)

The U.S. magazine *Cycle* once wrote about his performance as a trainer, "Bernt Spiegel, a professor from the university, who rode a beautiful Bimota . . . swiftly and with an ethereal smoothness, was to give a speech on the philosophy of riding, of the *unity of rider and machine*." This unity is what the book you hold in your hands is all about.

Books and Videos to Develop Your Riding Skills, from Whitehorse Press

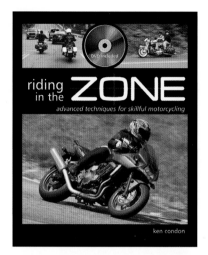

Riding in the Zone: Advanced Techniques for Skillful Motorcycling

Ken Condon

Veteran motorcycle riding instructor and writer Ken Condon offers valuable insight into perfecting each rider's own personal riding style for maximum enjoyment and satisfaction. In a clear, highly visual style with detailed diagrams and extensive full-color photos and illustrations, Condon identifies the many factors that help you enter "the zone." He shows you how the ability to ride "in the zone" goes hand in hand with mastering basic motorcycling skills and achieving mental and emotional control. Sftbd. book and DVD, 8 × 10 in., 144 pp., color illus.

ZONE $29.95   978-1-884313-76-9

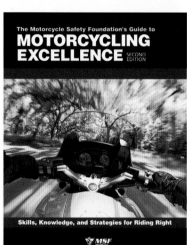

Motorcycling Excellence, Second Edition

Motorcycle Safety Foundation

Founded in 1973, the Motorcycle Safety Foundation (MSF) is recognized internationally for its rider-training curriculum, which has been used worldwide by thousands of trainers in teaching more than three million motorcyclists the skills necessary to stay safe and have fun on the road. This book is the essence of what the MSF has learned about teaching students of all ages and experience levels. It is the definitive reference for the sport—a perfect refresher for anyone who has ever taken an MSF course, and an eye-opener for those who haven't. Sftbd., 8-1/4 × 10-1/2 in., 192 pp., color illus.

MCX2 $24.95   978-1-884313-47-9

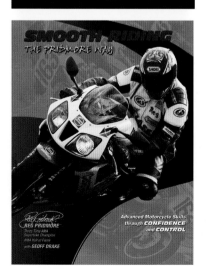

Smooth Riding the Pridmore Way

Reg Pridmore and Geoff Drake

Former AMA racing champion Reg Pridmore, known worldwide for his popular CLASS Motorcycle Schools, brings his decades of experience on the track, street, and classroom to the readers of this classic riding skills book.

A long-time proponent of the value of smoothness, control, and body-steering, Pridmore's insightful text explains how the techniques that helped him win championships can help everyday motorcyclists and budding racers become better, safer riders. Pridmore shows how to focus on control in cornering, braking, and acceleration. There are also chapters devoted to riding psychology, throttle management, shifting, and body positioning, as well as tips on bike setup and accident avoidance. Sftbd., 8-1/4 × 10-1/2 in., 160 pp., color illus.

SRPW $24.95   978-1-884313-46-2

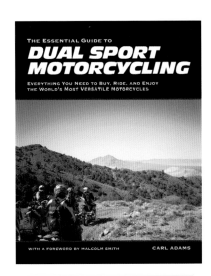

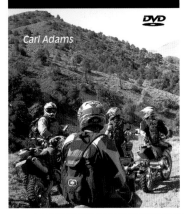

The Essential Guide to Dual Sport Motorcycling

Carl Adams

The author shares wisdom gained in 45 years of riding off-road and teaching dual sport riding. Written to help adventuresome motorcyclists buy, ride, and enjoy dual sport motorcycles, the book is organized into four sections covering motorcycle selection, setup, riding skills, and specialized activities such as exploring remote areas, organized rides, and touring. Several chapters include exercises designed to improve riding technique and impart new skills. Riders at all levels will gain a broader perspective of the dual sport experience, from which they can begin their journey to new motorcycle adventures. Sftbd., 8-1/4 × 10-1/2 in., 192 pp., color illus.

EGDS $24.95   978-1-884313-71-4

Dirt Riding Skills for Dual Sport and Adventure Riders (DVD)

Carl Adams

Scripted, directed, and narrated by Carl Adams, this video teaches critical skills necessary for safe off-road travel and may be used alone or as a perfect companion to the book above. Riding skills are presented in a series of simple exercises which are meant to be ridden. They build in a logical sequence to show increasingly difficult techniques. Each technique is explained in simple, but complete detail, demonstrated by expert riders in spectacular locations, with many close-ups and slow motion sequences. The DVD package includes a printed Field Guide that may be taken on training rides as a reference for all the exercises. DVD video, NTSC, 67 minutes.

DRSD $29.95   978-1-884313-87-5

Stayin' Safe: The Art and Science of Riding Really Well

Lawrence Grodsky

Larry Grodsky devoted his life to motorcycle safety. Through the riding courses he taught and his "Stayin' Safe" columns in *Rider* magazine, he helped thousands of motorcyclists improve their skills and their ability to ride really well. This collection of Grodsky's columns reveals his ability to illuminate complex and sometimes highly technical subjects with an entertaining and personal style, spiced with his trademark wry wit and keen observations of human behavior. Readers will be rewarded by the beautifully written stories of a great motorcycle riding instructor who has left his mark on a generation of grateful riders. Hdbd., 6-1/4 × 9-1/4 in., 352 pp., b/w illus.

GROD $24.95   978-1-884313-72-1